CAROL L. RUSSELL, ED.D.

Sandwiched!

Tales, Tips, and Tools to Balance Life in the Sandwich Generation

iUniverse, Inc.
New York   Bloomington

Sandwiched!
Tales, Tips, and Tools to Balance Life in the Sandwich Generation

iUniverse books may be ordered through booksellers or by contacting:

iUniverse
1663 Liberty Drive
Bloomington, IN 47403
www.iuniverse.com
1-800-Authors (1-800-288-4677)

ISBN: 978-1-4401-5482-9 (pbk)
ISBN: 978-1-4401-5483-6 (ebk)

Printed in the United States of America

iUniverse rev. date: 8/17/2009

This labor of love is dedicated to
my loving, supportive, and unbelievably wonderful family: Fletcher, Cassie, Mikelle, and Tally, without whom I could not survive "my sandwich,"
and
my dear parents, Armin and Gladys Deye, who have
taught me unconditional love, perseverance, determination, seeing the positives, and knowing that
I can make a difference.

Our family with Grandma—puppies, too! Top row: Cassie with her puppy, Cooper; Mikelle; Fletch with Tally's puppy, Cally; Middle: me (Carol), in the middle of my lovely family; Bottom row: Tally and Grandma

Contents

Preface

If you are in the Sandwich Generation, you know it! No explanations or definitions are needed for you – you already know that the "Sandwich Generation" refers to the increasing numbers of middle-aged people who care for both their children and elderly parents, while attempting to manage stress, jobs, and finances. For those of you who have chosen this book because you are interested family members or professionals, please know that the formatting—with short sections in each chapter—is intentional for two reasons:

- The first is for ease of reading for those *in* the Sandwich Generation, who may think, "I don't have time to read about something that I am so busy doing that I can hardly *breathe*!" It's often easier to read a short segment at a time or go directly to the chapters that deal with the issues in which you are currently involved.

- The second is self-serving. Most days I think, "I don't have time to write about something I am so busy doing that I can hardly *breathe*!"

My personal and professional hats have merged and prepared me for my own "sandwich." As an associate professor of early childhood/elementary teacher education, with my doctorate in special education and a master's degree in human development and family studies, I have worked with family issues in the field of early childhood for over thirty years. I have blended my roles in the past, using my knowledge and experience of special education and early childhood to advocate for our daughter who has special needs. Now, I merge my personal and professional hats once more to bring together my knowledge, skills, and experience to confidently work with systems, team and collaborate, organize, communicate, work with assistive technology, and steadfastly advocate for my mom.

Reflection is also an essential part of this process. I am grateful for this project, which has given me the opportunity to reflect upon, on a larger scale, my own "sandwich" and the Sandwich Generation, in general. I take my computer everywhere these days. For example, as I write this, my husband, daughter, and I are sitting in the office of a wheelchair-lift company, waiting for a repair of the new van lift we had installed last week for our youngest daughter, Tally, after she was stuck in the van for forty-five minutes the other day. Our lives are "sandwiched" on a daily basis, as we scramble to meet the needs of my mom and our daughter, who has special needs.

Another day I had my laptop open at my hair salon, waiting for my turn at "fewer grays." After years of coloring my own hair, I now enjoy pampering myself by getting professional haircuts, coloring, and highlights—at age fifty-five, this is the first year of my life that I have done this, and I believe this is significant. Being in the Sandwich Generation, I have learned that I must find little things that help me to keep my sense of self! Getting my hair done professionally is one of those things.

ORGANIZATION

Although there are short subsections in the text, they are organized in chapters. There is some overlap as the topics are integrated, and reference may be given to another section or chapter for ease of locating full information on specific topics and resources. Resources can be found at the end of each chapter and in the appendixes.

LARGER FONT

Most of us in the baby-boomer generation need glasses, particularly when reading. It seems as if printed material in our daily lives is getting smaller and smaller. (Have you looked at the back of pain-relief medication lately? So much information is crunched on the back of the bottle, one needs a magnifying glass to read it!) I have had this book printed it a larger-than-standard font for easier reading.

REAL NAMES

Names of some individuals mentioned in this book have been changed, unless I received permission to use the original names. Frankly, I see our family as an open book; we have no secrets. With the permission of my husband and children, I have written about our challenges and experiences. I believe that others can learn from our mistakes, our successes, and our problems, as well as our solving of problems. That is my purpose in writing this book.

I especially want to thank …

My dear parents, Armin and Gladys Deye, who have taught me unconditional love, perseverance, determination, seeing the positives, and knowing that I can make a difference; my loving, supportive and *unbelievably wonderful* family, without whom I could not survive! The support, strength, and unconditional love of my husband, Fletcher, could not be surpassed. There are not many sons-in-law who would do what he has done for my parents and particularly for my mom. He and my mom have a special bond (they also share an astrological sign—Pisces), and I think she truly understood his years as an at-home-dad.

I cherish our children beyond measure! Our three lovely daughters have matured into the most delightful young ladies. I am more than proud of each of them—their spirit, ambition, and accomplishments. They are treasured gifts to the world, and I tell them this often. They have supported our "sandwich" and were the mayo and mustard holding it together, in addition to the pickles, tomatoes, onions, or relish to bring spice, joy, and diversity to our sandwich experience.

- Our ambitious Cassie, while pursuing her own professional goals, spent over two years of her life assisting several days each week in direct care for Grandma and Tally. Her friendship, intelligence, and supportive encouragement give me focus and strength.

- Our creative Mikelle, while working on her art degree and professional goals, also helped with direct care for Grandma and Tally over the years. Her friendship, humor, laughter, support, and creativity help keep me sane.

- Our precious, positive Tally has taught me so much. She supports our care for Grandma, delights in Grandma's inner and outer beauty, and enjoys making her laugh. She assists with companion hours for Grandma. Our lives, with many years of caring for, assisting, and advocating for Tally, essentially prepared us for our sandwich. More recently, Tally's sharing of the evening ritual of feeding the fish in the pond at sunset with Grandma has been a source of enjoyment for both of them and an inspiration for the front and back cover of this book.

"Our dear, sweet daughters: Mikelle, Cassie, and Tally"

Thanks to Patty, our dear nighttime provider and friend for over three years now, without whose support, dependability, care, and skill we could not have managed our sandwich.

Thanks also to all the other providers, therapists, nurses, and doctors through the years.

"Patty, our wonderful nighttime provider for over
three years. We couldn't do this without her!"

Thanks to my father-in-law, Tom, who has directly observed and at times was a part of our sandwich. His perspective has been very interesting. Although he has not fully understood why we have done this, his support, honesty, and input have been helpful.

"Fletch's amazing dad and our family"

Thanks to my siblings, who, overall, have taught me the importance of respect, trust, individuality, and diversity and with whom I have practiced patience and unconditional love. I do not understand my oldest brother, but in spite of everything and behavior to the contrary, I believe he still loves my mom. Thanks to my oldest sister, Dottie, who assists monthly with loving care and emotional support, as well as financial assistance. She truly shared our belief that our parents did not need to live their last years—or die—in a nursing home or hospital. Her presence and strength during the last days and hours before Papa's death meant more than words. Her support and the support of her family have meant a great deal. Her husband and her dear children and grandchildren have been very supportive and source of great joy for Mother with their visits. Thanks to my middle sister, Kathy, who has had several struggles in life and who has supported my family and me through many of our life challenges. She and her sons greatly helped with our parents' move. Her financial assistance and support for Mother, when she could, has been helpful. Her traveling for visits and calls have meant much to Mother. Thanks to my brother, Don, who is closest to me in age and well bonded as siblings as we were growing up. As a physician, he greatly assists with the medical issues and consults with Mother's physician to manage the best medical care. Our numerous calls about "med-mixes and non-mixes" have helped keep my mom healthy. His financial assistance has also made it possible to continue the care for my mom in her home. His visits mean a great deal to her.

A recent family reunion where Mother was delighted to be
with four of her children. Surrounding Mother, from left
to right are: Don, Kathy, Dottie, and Carol (me).

Introduction

Sandwiched! openly shares our journey as baby boomers in the Sandwich Generation, while offering our unique solutions and arrangements. We feel that others in a similar time of life and living situation also are trying to cope with various feelings, emotions, skills, and attitudes. In an attempt to balance life—and actually live life, rather than frantically surviving it—we, as a family, have learned many things in our voyage that we wish to share.

I have combined my personal and professional roles in the past, using my knowledge and experience of special education and early childhood to advocate for our daughter who has special needs. Now, I merge my hats once more to bring together my knowledge, skills, and experience to confidently work with systems and assistive technology, and to team and collaborate, organize, communicate, and persistently advocate for my mom. Reflection is essential; it is at the core of this project and a major source of personal release. I appreciate the opportunity to share my sandwich and hope it will assist others in the Sandwich Generation.

Consider these statistics regarding the Sandwich Generation:

- Many of baby boomers are, in varying degrees and capacities, taking care of parents and children. According to the New York Academy of Medicine, "Some 42 million American women make up the Sandwich Generation—meaning they are 'sandwiched' by the needs of their own children and their aging relatives. At a time when women are having children later and their parents are living longer, an increasing number of women find themselves caring for both kids and parents at the same time."[1]

- According to the statistics and research reports found on the National Family Caregivers Association Web site under "Who Are Family Caregivers?" there are an estimated fifty million family caregivers here in America providing "free" caregiving services, conservatively estimated to be worth $306 billion a year. "That is almost twice as much as is actually spent on homecare and nursing home services combined ($158 billion). Over 30 percent of family caregivers caring for seniors are themselves aged 65 or over; another 15 percent are between the ages of 45 and 54."[2]

- The article "Caregivers Cope with Stress, Mixed Emotions about Aging Parents" discusses the range of emotions, stating, "A USA TODAY/ABC News/Gallup poll of 500 boomers with living parents found that 31 percent of them are providing financial or personal care assistance to a parent. Slightly less than half of those providing help say it has caused them some stress or a great deal of stress, shows the poll, conducted May 24–June 3, 2007."[3]

- According to researchers at Georgetown University, "More than fifty million people, provide care for a chronically

---

1   New York Academy of Medicine, 2008, http://www.nyam.org/news/
2   http://www.nfcacares.org/who_are_family_caregivers/
3   Sharon Jayson, "Caregivers Cope with Stress, Mixed Emotions about Aging Parents," *USA Today*, June 26, 2007.

ill, disabled or aged family member or friend during any given year. The typical family caregiver is a forty-six-year-old woman, caring for her widowed mother who does not live with her. She is married and employed. Approximately 60 percent of family caregivers are women." There will be an increase of the need for family caregivers. "People over sixty-five are expected to increase at a 2.3 percent rate, but the number of family members available to care for them will only increase at a 0.8 percent rate."[4]

- In August 2008, the Census Bureau projected that the population, aged eighty-five and older, will more than triple by 2050, to nineteen million.[5]
- The U.S. Department of Health and Human Services states that more than fifty million people provide care for a chronically ill, disabled, or aged family member or friend during any given year.[6]

Many today can relate to the term "Sandwich Generation"—those of us in our middle years who attempt to balance our lives (and our sanity) with caring for our children as well as for our aging parents, while keeping a full-time job, stabilizing our marriage, and having little time to manage our own "hot flashes of life"!

My husband and I have learned so much in the process within our "sandwich." Between the care of our youngest daughter—who has special needs, lives at home, and is a

4   Mack, et al., 2001, http://www.thefamilycaregiver.org/who_are_family_caregivers/care_giving_statstics.cfm
5   http://www.census.gov/Press-Release/www/releases/archives/income_wealth/012528.html
6   Informal Caregiving: Compassion in Action. Washington DC: 1998, and National Family Caregivers Association, Random Sample Survey of Family Caregivers, Summer 2000, Unpublished.

college sophomore—and both of my parents (although only my mother now needs twenty-four-hour care), our plates are full. We have three lovely, supportive daughters and some very helpful extended family members.

This book was created, both in content and design, for the reader in the Sandwich Generation—short subsections in each chapter are provided, as Sandwich Generation readers often do not have much time to read; even five- to fifteen-minute reads are sometimes a luxury. Within Sandwiched! you'll find strategies, options, charts, problem-solvers, mistakes, environmental adaptations, emotional adaptations, relationship preservers, and blunders. Topics can be quickly accessed, with tools and references easy to find. The life stories, positive and negative experiences, and illustrative photos openly offer the reality of our "sandwich". An optimistic attitude, commitment, and communication have been key to our balance. It can turn a "sandwich" from meatloaf on white into prime rib on fresh whole wheat!

Each chapter ends with:

- What We've Learned (a summary that relates to each topic)

- Quotes (some I've made up; some from other sources)

- Tips and Tools (a host of resources)

WHAT WE'VE LEARNED

- No family secrets! These can only hurt. My family and I have worked hard to be transparent with our lives and the entire process of our sandwich.

- You can't make everyone happy. Someone will find fault or

think you have a hidden agenda, no matter how honest or transparent you try to be with your actions.

- It's okay to blend hats. My professional and personal hats have merged and prepared me for my sandwich. Bring together your resources, knowledge, skills, and experience to confidently work with systems, team and collaborate, organize, communicate, advocate, and reflect. It will support your sandwich.

QUOTE

"Asking for help is a sign of strength!"
—Author unknown

You cannot do it alone, and if you try to, you may not survive. I believe we are on this earth, together, because we need each other and no one should face challenges alone. Some are too proud to ask for help. I see it as a strength!

TIPS

Check out the following Web site: http://thefamilycaregiver.org/who_are_family_caregivers/care_giving_statstics.cfm

It offers many statistics gathered by the National Family Caregivers Association. The caregiving statistic on this site is organized from various resources into the following categories:

Caregiving Population
Economics of Caregiving
Impact of Caregiving
Caregiving and Work
Caregiving and Health Care

Caregiving and Self-Awareness
State-by-State Statistics

Mack, Katherine and Thompson, Lee with Robert Friedland. (2001). Data Profiles, Family Caregivers of Older Persons: Adult Children. The Center on an Aging Society, Georgetown University, page 2, May 2001.

In 2006, the National Association of Social Workers and the New York Academy of Medicine's Social Work Leadership Institute commissioned a survey to better understand the challenges faced by sandwich generation women. In 2007 they conducted a qualitative, online journaling project, exploring the thoughts and feelings of women in the Sandwich Generation. See:

Not Ready for Prime Time: The Needs of Sandwich Generation Women,

A National Survey of Social Workers and A Window into the Lives of Sandwich Generation Women, An On-line Journaling Project

socialworkleadership.org/nsw/news/press/Sandwich-GenerationStudy- http://www.helpstartshere.org/Default.aspx?PageID=1342

Chapter 1

WHERE TO START? OUR SANDWICH BEGINS

According to Family Caregiver Alliance, the number of "unpaid family caregivers" will reach 37 million by 2050, increasing by 85 percent from the year 2000.

It's hard to know where to begin. My husband and I feel that our journey is and has been one to share, as many others of a similar age also are facing the Sandwich Generation with various feelings, skills, and attitudes. Feelings are often bottled up; our parents are our history, our source of life—and sometimes our source of guilt, fear, anxiety, and love. (Ways to cope with or expand those feelings are discussed more fully in chapter three.) This chapter offers the timeline, facts, planning, and process of our "developing sandwich."

OUR JOURNEY IN BRIEF

When my dad was still alive, our sandwich began when we moved my mom and dad from Minnesota to Kansas, into an addition that was built twelve feet from our front door. Two of our three daughters were living at home at the time. Relationships changed, along with physical and emotional adjustments, which required constant communication, challenges, and problem solving. We saved our reflections on the process, and we developed charts and strategies that have made this process work. We have learned from our mistakes and perfected our techniques. A positive attitude and commitment to making it work has been the key. We are blessed to have a wonderful family who supports this endeavor.

Our youngest daughter, Tally, was born with spina bifida, hydrocephalus, and Arnold-Chiari Malformation. She uses a wheelchair and has several other significant medical issues. We built an accessible home in the country when Tally was eleven and her sisters, Mikelle and Cassie, were thirteen and sixteen, respectively.

My parents lived in Winona, Minnesota, where my father retired from over sixty years in the ministry. When my mom was eighty-seven and my dad ninety, they found they needed more support to live in their own home. They tried some assisted-living arrangements, but they didn't want to live in a nursing home or die in a hospital. They decided to move back home and hire support—they needed twenty-four-hour care. I think they thought they wouldn't live long. One year of nursing and supportive care, however, rang up a bill of approximately $244,000! At that rate, they would quickly run out of money.

My family and I have lived in Emporia, Kansas, for twelve years. I teach at Emporia State University in early childhood/elementary teacher education. My husband, Fletcher, teaches part-time in visual arts and is a remarkable Renaissance man who can do and fix just about anything. He suggested we use some of our land to build a small guesthouse for my parents, next door to us in the country. It was a long, carefully planned process, but we did it. With the help of my siblings, we were able to get both of my parents safely to Kansas. They lived with us as we finished the building of their little wheelchair-accessible home. We had lowered their annual twenty-four-hour-a-day care cost to less than $60,000 a year, a savings of $184,000 from their former arrangement in Minnesota, although still very costly.

Because our daughter Tally uses a wheelchair, we were already specialists regarding accessibility and design. My parents lived in their little home for six months before my dad passed away. We were able to grant his wish of his not dying in a nursing home or hospital. My mother, my sister, and I were by his side.

At age ninety, although Mother grieved for the loss of her husband, it was as though my mom had a new identity. We still learn so much from her. We consider our arrangement as unique. Mother's little home is twelve feet across the deck from our house. We have arranged for twenty-four-hour care, previously using agencies and now privately hired providers, including a wonderful nighttime provider. My daughters also help me with Mother's care, as does my sister, with her monthly visits. It's quite a coordinated effort, but we are blessed to have Mother with us.

TIMELINE OF OUR JOURNEY

- Summer 2002. Parents moved from their larger home to a townhouse in the city where my father had been a minister for over sixty years.

- 2003. Mother fell, was hospitalized, and was in rehabilitation for six months.

- August 2003. Parents tried assisted living in hometown for one month.

- August 2003. After a family meeting, moved parents to assisted living, located near oldest son for one month.

- September 2003. While living near oldest son, Mother almost died from taking Vioxx. Assisted-living program was not aware of how sick she was. Apparently, medical records stating she had trouble when taking Vioxx in the past were not transferred or read. She had acute renal failure and was dehydrated, among various other health problems. Issues with my siblings intensified. Meanwhile my mom was hospitalized, and thought she was dying. No one from assisted-living nor my brother or his wife would take my dad to see my mom, even though my older brother and his wife had moved our parents to their town, saying they would take care of them. Mother thought she was going to die without seeing her husband of sixty-plus years one last time. After calls from other siblings, transportation was finally arranged for my dad to visit my mom in the hospital. Fortunately, she survived and was able to return to the assisted living.

- Sibling conflict continued. Things did not work out for various reasons, and my brother said, "Come get them— the sooner, the better."

- October 2003. Moved parents back to their townhouse with the help of my sisters and my husband. We had arranged twenty-four-hour care with an agency in their town. My parents did not think they would live much longer, so the expense was something they chose to do. They lived in their townhouse with full-time care for about one year and ten months. The expense was great, approximately $244,000/year.

- February 2005. The person authorized with power of attorney (POA) for my parents contacted us to let us know they were running out of money.

- March/April 2005. Made tentative house-addition plans to present at the family meeting. Met with contractors for many hours to plan as accessibly as possible, as my dad was using a wheelchair full time, and my mom was using a walker and wheelchair.

- May 2005. Family meeting took place with all siblings (except my oldest brother, who chose not to join us), POA, and attorney to help make decisions. The options were sending them to a nursing home or to Kansas—with the plan of building a structure next to our home. I can still hear the attorney's words to my dad: "Well, I guess you're moving to Kansas!"

- August 2005. With gracious help from family members, my parents moved to Kansas. My sisters, my younger brother, and some of their children moved our parents' belongings in a truck. My two sisters flew with them from Minnesota to Kansas, and my nephew drove the truck down to Kansas. My parents were able to sleep in their beds one night in Minnesota, and by the time they arrived in Kansas, their beds were assembled to sleep in that night. Various friends and family assisted the unloading of the truck into our garage, as the structure (we call it the cottage) was not yet complete. My parents stayed in a bedroom in our basement (we have a wheelchair lift to help them up and down) for two weeks until their cottage construction was complete. Deck building continued with the help of extended family, so our homes were connected with decking around three sides of each of our places.

The cottage comes down the driveway in two parts.

The cottage is lifted by crane over our house! We were holding our breath.

Grandson Jon drove the moving truck—a ten-hour drive. What a wonderful grandson!

Mikelle and the "unloading team." Family members and friends volunteered their time to unload. This all occurred while my parents were still in transit via plane and car.

Unloading the moving truck's contents into our garage. No room for cars!

They made it! After the moving van with all of my parents'
belongings was unloaded into our garage and my parents' beds
were unloaded in a basement bedroom, they finally arrived,
safe and sound, thanks to my sisters and brother-in-law.

The move into our house, where they lived for two weeks
while waiting for their cottage to be finished.

Fletch, Cassie, niece Nicki, and her dad, Al, help
with the decking between the houses.

Papa and Mother check out the progress on the
deck-building between the houses.

The moving crew, checking out their not-quite-finished
cottage. It was another two weeks before completion.

The cottage with completed deck.

Both of our places, with decks all around. Pretty close neighbors!

- Fall 2005. This was a gift! It was a most beautiful fall in Kansas, with warm fall days all the way through November. My parents were able to be out on the decks, enjoying the sun, guinea fowl, horse, lamb, and various other birds and wildlife in the country. We enjoyed a large, wonderful family Thanksgiving and Christmas together, with family and extended family coming and going.

This was during Tally's senior year in high school, so she was busy, and we kept busy being a part of this important year of her life. We had struggled to get and keep therapies and special education services for her throughout her elementary and secondary educational years. Our advocacy and challenges with her school continued. We also transported Tally to doctor appointments in both Kansas City and St. Paul. Mikelle, our middle daughter, was still living at home and attending college at this time and had to share her basement apartment with Grandpa and Grandma for two weeks—not her favorite time. Cassie, our oldest daughter, was living in an apartment in town and just starting her master's degree program in psychology (coincidentally, in the same building where I taught on campus).

At this time, my father had diabetes and was on a sliding scale of insulin. With sporadic blood sugar levels, stroke-like symptoms, heart issues, and falls, we were in the emergency room with my mom's or my dad's medical needs almost every other week. My mother had been on large amounts of pain medication while in Minnesota. She had been taking up to eight Darvocet and four methadone per day! We were trying to wean her off the Darvocet and lower the methadone amount. Between both my parents' needs, we were often at the doctor and had several hospitalizations and numerous ambulance trips to the emergency room. We were getting to know many of the emergency medical technicians (EMTs), and they were appreciative that our ramps allowed them to easily get into my parents' place with every visit.

Fun on the deck with great-grandchildren.

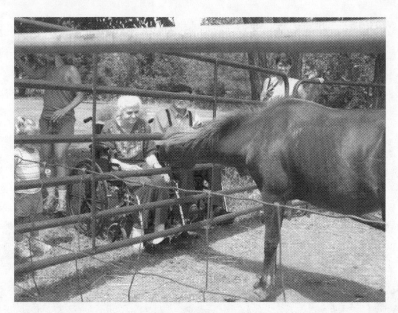

Grandma feeding Tally's horse, Midnight.

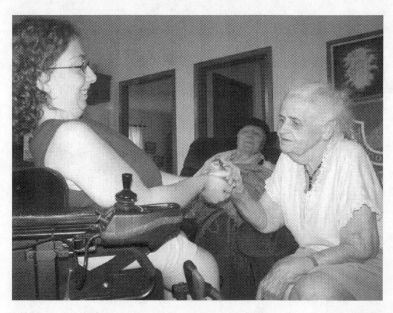

Tally brings a baby guinea over to share with Grandma and Grandpa.

Grandma loves the baby guinea! She told us stories about when she was little and her job was to take care of the baby chicks on their farm.

Grandma shares the baby guinea with Grandpa.
She doesn't want to let go of it.

Grandpa and Grandma were able to make it to Mikelle's art-show opening.

We had a beautiful fall 2005. My mom and dad were able to
spend much time on the decks their first fall in Kansas.

Grandpa and Grandma with the girls at Christmas 2005. Our girls give Grandpa and Grandma a Beta fish (on table) for Christmas. Grandpa is focused on "Flippy," the new Beta. Grandma is looking at cute as ever.

- January 2006. My dad was failing. He was hallucinating and was quite unstable, but still knew us. We discussed hospice. They day we signed my dad on for hospice, we had another emergency room visit. The doctor was quite rude and seemed to justify his rudeness with the fact that my dad was on hospice now, and there was nothing he (the doctor) would do. He went on to explain hospice to me as though I were a child. The hospice nurse was there with us and was also appalled by this doctor.

It was that trip home from the hospital emergency room that was the last drive my dad had in his car—a 1999 Cadillac DeVille, his "baby."

He had not spoken more than a word or two in several days. I still remember; it was early evening. As we got outside of the city and on a paved country road, my dad stated, loudly and clearly, "Nice car ride!" I about fell out of my seat! I think of him every time I pass that part of the road.

The hospice nurse said he probably had about two weeks left with us, and those who wanted to see him should come. All of my siblings came to see him, but not at the same time. Sibling differences and issues continued.

- January 26, 2006. Papa died, lying next to his dear wife, with my oldest sister and me on either side of them. We sang songs, said prayers, and said good-bye. My sister Dottie recalls:

"Papa passed away at home, with Mother lying next to him on one side, and I sitting on the other, reading his prayers, singing favorite songs, and saying the German Prayer that he had mailed to each one of his children, at an earlier time, when he thought he was near death.

"When he stopped breathing, shortly after 7:30 AM, I called to the hospice helper to phone Carol, next door. His pulse was gone, and his color, which was slightly yellow, turned chalky white, and the tips of his ears and toes started to mottle. Mama kissed him many times, and in the middle of tears said, 'Oh, honey, I don't want you to go!'

"Then something happened that I'd never seen before. When the door slammed, the helper yelled, 'Carol's here!' Papa gasped and resumed breathing, while Carol climbed on the bed, next to his ear, and assured him of her love and that she would take care of Mother, and told him that it was all right to go."

This greatly impacted me! It was as though my father waited to see me once more before he left this Earth. This, I will never forget.

We were able to help my mom make selections of the stone design for my dad's grave. We put their wedding photo, along with a recent photo, on the stone. This is the front, with their wedding date and symbol in the middle.

The back of the stone has a brief family tree, with my parents' names at the bottom of the tree, their five children around the tree, and their parents on either side of them. It is very special.

- March 2006. My mother turned ninety years old! Great party and celebrations! She was healing from the loss of my dad, and seemed to be finding herself. Her health was better, and she was even happy again. We all chipped in to give her a laptop computer! She started attending church on Saturday nights and Bible class on Wednesdays. She attended our daughters' orchestra concerts, art shows, and graduations. Now, she has dinner at our house most nights and has twenty-four-hour care.

Mother's ninetieth birthday

- May 2006. Tally graduated from high school, and Cassie finished her master's in psychology. We had two graduations, and Mother was delighted to be a part of these milestones in her granddaughters' lives.

- August 2007. "A Fall in the Fall." My mom managed to get up quietly in the night and fell before it was discovered she was up. With the fall, she broke her arm and badly bruised other areas and was treated in the hospital for a few days. We had to put in a bottom railing on her bed to assure that she wouldn't get up again in the night. I later learned that you couldn't do this in a hospital or nursing home, as it is considered "restraining." My mom, however, did not see it this way—it was the only way we could assure her safety. She has a doorbell-type button that she rings for help in the night. It took her some time and wrist surgery to recuperate from this fall.

- December 2007. Mother started on Medicaid. I had written the family at least a year prior to this time to let them know that Mother soon would be out of money, and we would be applying for Medicaid. A note also went out to family, letting them know how much money and time we were committing to her care and needs each month. We requested monthly assistance for her.

- April 2008. I was nominated to run for second vice president of the faculty. After much discussion with Fletch and sleeping on the possibility, I agreed to run—and I was elected! With this four-year commitment, little did I know what was in store for me.

- May 2008. Mikelle graduated with her degree in art. Grandma was able to celebrate yet another graduation in my daughters' lives. Before my folks moved here, I had resigned myself to the thought that my parents were not going to be able to be there for any of our daughters' graduations. And now, we have been blessed that my mom has been part of graduation celebrations for each of our daughters.

- August 2008. Cassie and Mikelle moved away from the area. Previously, they lived a few miles from our home, were very supportive and wonderful direct caregivers for both Grandma and Tally. At this point, however, Cassie moved to Colorado to work on her doctorate in educational psychology, and Mikelle moved to Lawrence, Kansas, where she'd gotten a job. This was—and continues to be—an adjustment for me; it left a hole in my soul and gap in my life. I miss them, even as I celebrate their accomplishments, ambition, and moving on. E-mail and calls help, but it's not the same as seeing their sweet faces. Mikelle is a little over an hour away, so we can pop up to see her now and then. Cassie is ten hours away; too far for a weekend jaunt. In addition, Tally moved part-time into an apartment, which was a celebration of her move toward increased independence. We assist her directly with care and transportation, as well as arrange care for her and assistance with classes. Coordinating our schedule with hers is a constant puzzle.

Also in August, more than two years of advocacy produced results! My mom's had a stressful experience at a nonaccessible business two years prior to this. We contacted the business, went to the community's Human Relations Commission, and ultimately, filed an Americans with Disabilities Act (ADA) complaint. The issue was finally resolved. We went to the business location and saw the lift that had been installed, and she even rode up and down it. It was beautiful! This was really the first time I had ever seen my mom advocate and stand up for something (even in a seated position). We took pictures to remember the event and her advocacy to make a better, more accessible community for others.

- September 27, 2008. My brother's wedding. With the help of a wonderful couple (a provider and her husband), we were able to take both my mom and Tally to my brother's wedding, which took place on a boat on the Mississippi River. It was quite something—not just the wedding, but also the fact that we made it there and back in one piece!

- September/October 2008. On the Monday morning after our late-night return from my brother's wedding, I was notified that the first vice president of the faculty had re-signed. That put me fast-forward a year. I thought, This is all I need—an even a faster life! Actually, it meant one less year to serve. I thought I was handling it in stride until I re-alized that my one eye was twitching sporadically (I started squinting so that no one would notice); I had a muscle strain in my back; and my former ulcer discomfort seemed to have revived. My body was telling me that I needed stress management, but I didn't have time to de-stress!

- November/December 2008. Planning for holidays, and I have my deadline to finish the writing of this book. My old-est brother came to visit my mom for the first time in over three years. I was so glad for her to be able to see him again. My mom is doing pretty well, and we are looking forward to our fourth holiday season with her in Kansas—and to our older daughters coming home for the holidays.

Planning for the Move, and the
Sandwich Develops

- The Plan—How It Came to Be, How It Was Revised

As we learned that my folks were running out of money, we brainstormed several possibilities. When we came up with the plan to build a cottage and to have my parents live next to us, for whatever reason, there appeared to be an apprehensive and suspicious response from some of my siblings. Fletcher and I could offer the land and make the plans, but we could not pay the entire bill.

- Response to Our Plan and Its Outcome

"All about money?" Although there appeared to be suspicion from several of my siblings, a visit from my cousin, who is older and wiser than I, reinforced our efforts. He did say something interesting and thought-filled: "When it comes down to it, it's all about the money!" The reality of this struck me. Our sole purpose in providing a home for my parents had nothing to do with money. The only concern about money was if there was enough to set them up in their own safe, comfortable place for their last days, months, and years of life. I could not quit my job to stay home to care for them full time, but I could do some of the care; I could hire, coordinate, and supervise the care; I could pay some of their bills and coordinate their financial situation; and I could file papers for support (Medicaid, grants, and other support in the area). (Specifics on financial issues are covered in chapter nine.) The philosophy and perspective of "the money" (or lack of it), however, is an important issue from the get-go and should be fully discussed well in advance, within the planning.

Money can be a touchy subject, but all the money in the world cannot buy happiness, trust, or respect. In general, I do think money is sometimes used to take care of guilt within families and relationships, (such as guilt gifts, when we don't have the time to be with someone). Many of us have done this; I did it when I had to work full time and spend less time with my children. These gifts may truly be from the heart, but guilt may drive us to spend a little more or may take the place of the time we don't have.

When your elderly parent has little money to even buy toilet paper or paper towels, large gifts that he or she may not need or use seem senseless. Sometimes, the family needs specific practical suggestions. I send out a list before every birthday and holidays.

"What's the catch?" This was another unspoken (sometime spoken) response. It was as though people thought we built the cottage for my parents in order to receive some reward. Well, we did get one—we got to see my parents (now, my mother) every day!

"Who would do this?" or "You've got a good deal, getting a cottage next door after they're gone." I'm not sure that some of my siblings will ever get over these thoughts, but I do think that with each year, as they learn of the daily issues, coordination of care, direct caregiving, and covering of bills that we do, most of them assign more value to what we do. I send updates and photos periodically to keep family aware of what is happening with Mother and us. E-mail helps tremendously. Still, no one—except, perhaps, my oldest sister, who gives care monthly—really understands the daily responsibility and the hours we have taken on in our "sandwich."

- Family Meetings—Everyone on the Same Page? Not Always.

Our family members were not all on the same page from the start. Even getting all family members in the same room was not possible, which was most unfortunate. We tried some problem-solving strategies and communication tools, but it is difficult to implement some of these tools when you are involved with care. It helps to have a third unbiased party or mediator. In the end, the way this worked for us was having a designated power of attorney hired through my parents' bank, in addition to their legal attorney at the meeting.

I would suggest creating an agenda for family meetings, and share information—I found an article titled "15 Ways to Take Care of Your Elderly Parents" by Sarah Baldauf in *U.S. News & World Report* (November 2, 2007) that was one of the most organized and comprehensive resources I've read. (See: http://health.usnews.com/articles/health/2007/11/02/15-things-you-can-do-to-keep-mom-and-dad-at-home.html.) Below is a summary of the article, along with suggestions that we have tried. It's a great place to start the discussion for your family meeting.

The article "15 Ways to Take Care of Your Elderly Parents" is divided into four sections:

- Preparing the Home
- Safeguarding Their Health and Safety
- Protecting Their Finances
- Keeping Them Socially Connected

The section on preparing the home includes suggestions, such as hiring a professional, who can be neutral, to help from the beginning. It suggests contacting the National Association of Professional Geriatric Care Managers for various needs, from finding a companion service, to locating a mediator to assist with family differences about options, to discussing finances. (See www.caremanager.org) This is particularly helpful, as family members are so emotionally involved that it is difficult to be objective. Other helpful resources are also provided in this section.

One thing to remember, particularly if finances are an issue, is that these services are not free. If it helps in the long run, however, then it is worth it. I remember that one of my sisters suggested hiring a financial advisor. This would have been a great suggestion, if Mother or we could have afforded it. She did not even have enough money to even pay her utilities, so we could not justify hiring a financial advisor. Hiring an advisor may be more logical if it's done from the onset of planning.

The article also suggests using technology for organization and safety. Products such as QuietCare, which is a motion sensor, can help monitor an elder family member. QuietCare calls designated family members, other close individuals, or emergency services immediately when there is anything out of the ordinary or of concern. (See www.quietcaresystems.com/index_fl.htm.) Information on the product's Web site reads:

> "QuietCare functions as a 24-hour-a-day, seven-day-a-week early detection and early warning system that lets caregivers and family members know that a loved one is safe. It recognizes emerging problems before they become emergencies. The system utilizes small, unobtrusive, strategically placed wireless sensors to monitor the senior in [his or her] own home. It is virtually invisible. No video camera or audio intrudes on the seniors' lives."

Another suggested idea is to use webcams to have "virtual" family meals. What a great idea, whether you live five or five hundred miles away! (Refer to chapter eight for more ideas on the ways assistive technology can assist with your sandwich.)

"Remove booby traps" is the article's next suggestion. Resources include certified aging-in-place specialists from the National Association of Home Builders, who can serve as consultants to make things safe and accessible; the Home Safety Council, which can suggest anti-scald devices for sinks and showers (e.g., H2O Stop) or setting water heaters to 120 degrees or lower. Additionally, carbon monoxide detectors are needed, as older people are more susceptible to even low concentrations. Strobe lights or vibrating smoke detectors can help alert the elderly of a fire when the sound of traditional smoke detectors isn't enough. Grab bars by the toilet and shower are essential. (Moen's SecureMount is a reliable brand. See Moen's Home Improvement News and Information Center: www.homeimprovementtime.com/idea_file/bath_shower_safety_377.asp.)

Nothing can replace visits for connecting with your loved one, as well as checking to see if he or she is safe, mentally sound, and in the best living arrangement. The Baldauf article refers to The Caregiver's Survival Handbook by Alexis Abramson (2004, Berkley Publishing Group), which suggests caregivers should "keep an eye out for subtle changes: Are the plants watered? Is unopened mail piling up? Do they have bruises, suggesting they may have fallen? Enlist your family and your parents' trusted neighbors to check in."

Finally, Baldauf states, "To help maintain your parents' independence and health, you'll very likely need to pay for a few services. The national average for a home health-care aide to assist with hygiene and medication, say, is $19 per hour … and adult day care averages $61 per day, according to a MetLife Mature Market Institute analysis." Medicare will not pay if the need is based on a chronic condition. For example, when my mom fell and broke her wrist, she was eligible for home health support for showers, nursing care, and therapies but not regular hours of care. We did contact the local Area Agency on Aging to do an assessment of need for care, and Mother was allotted a certain number of hours a day for care through Home and Community Based Services (HCBS) under Medicare. (More information on HCBS and services and qualifications for eligibility are addressed in chapter six.)

Baldauf's "Safeguarding Their Health and Safety" discusses the importance of regular exercise and cites the American College of Sports Medicine and the American Heart Association's "A Workout Plan for Seniors." (See http://health.usnews.com/articles/health/2007/10/30/a-workout-plan-for-seniors.html.) She also offers the following suggestions:

- "Work with the pharmacy." According to Baldauf, the pharmacist may be the only one who sees the full picture regarding your loved one's medications. Ask your pharmacist about side effects, interactions of medications, and over-the-counter medications. Baldauf also states that many pharmacies can repackage medications taken together in a bubble pack, arranged in a calendar to assist taking medication at appropriate times.

Our daughter has her medications delivered monthly this way. I am fortunate that our nighttime provider is certified to dispense medications, and she orders and arranges Mother's medications every two weeks. This is a tremendous support!

- "Get help behind the wheel." Baldauf describes this as "one of the messiest challenges."

This was a particularly difficult one for us and one that ended very tragically. My dad was from the era when a man's car was his "castle" (next to his home). We tried to get him to stop driving, but sadly, he had a major accident when he was driving in a heavy rain and hit a woman, critically injuring her. The woman lived but had a very lengthy hospitalization and lifelong injuries. Still, my dad wanted to continue driving—he said he would rather die than stop driving. Even when we moved him to Kansas, six months before he passed away, he wanted us to take him to get a Kansas driver's license. (Needless to say, we did not.) My mom got her first license when she was in her sixties. She did pretty well but had several accidents. Fortunately, once my parents hired providers to assist them, the providers would drive them wherever they needed to go.

Baldauf shares: "AAA and AARP offer classes for 'mature operators' that can yield car insurance discounts. AAA also has started CarFit, a program that invites seniors to bring their vehicles in for ergonomic adjustment; staff may recommend gadgets like mirror add-ons or tools to help arthritic wrists turn a key with less pain."

She comments that older parents may experience depression, stubbornness, and resistance to suggestions to "hang up the keys," but the reality of delayed reaction time and cognitive abilities, along with less range of motion, makes for hazardous and unsafe driving. This must be addressed. She suggests, "If met with resistance, enlist authorities, like the parent's doctor or the DMV—flunking a vision or driving test won't get a license renewed."

I urge you to address this, not only for your parents' safety but for others' safety as well. It could end disastrously, as it did for my dad. He carried the guilt with him until the day he died. We, as family members, also lived with the guilt for not stopping his driving before this unfortunate accident. Guilt is nothing, compared to the pain, anguish, and lifelong injuries that the woman my dad hit had to endure.

• Complete needed documents. Baldauf emphasizes that all adults need a health-care power of attorney and should complete paperwork to make this legal. A health-care power of attorney helps make health-care decisions, when and if the person is not able to do so. Another important document is a living will, which specifically describes one's wishes regarding such things as resuscitation or being tube fed to keep one alive. Go to www.caringinfo.org for a free form specific to your state. Attorneys may charge about $320 or more to create a living will. You can find some forms on-line from approximately $39 to $79 at sites such as Legal Zoom (www.legalzoom.com/legalzip/living_wills/lw_procedure.html). This site does not use attorney services; it helps you act as your own attorney, going through the same questions an attorney might ask. You then give the answers and the site will send your submitted answers in a legal document.

Janet Luhrs, founder of Simple Living (www.simpleliving.com) suggests the following additional steps:

• Make copies of your document and give them to relatives and friends.

• Be very clear with the person to whom you have given durable power of attorney. This should be someone who knows you well and who is competent and capable. Make sure he or she knows exactly what you want done.

- Make a little card to put in your wallet with names and phone numbers of your contacts.

- File your will with the U.S. Living Will Registry. There is no charge to file. This is an organization that is funded by health-care providers, so they can check to see if you are registered in the event of an accident. You can find them at www.uslivingwillregistry.com.

   In the third section titled "Protecting Their Finances," Baldauf says, "Senior citizens are particularly vulnerable to financial distress once they're living on a fixed income and experiencing some cognitive decline." This section includes suggestions, such as:

- "Discuss the money." Baldauf notes that the generation from the World War II era is more likely to not want to share information on finances. This can be a touchy subject. We certainly found this to be true with my dad. Even when we had meetings with the family and their legal attorney, he would whisper to the attorney how much money he thought he and my mom had. Baldauf suggests starting this discussion with the approach that you're looking for advice for yourself, such as discussing whether you should get long-term care insurance and then asking your parents if they did that.

- Durable power of attorney and a backup person: Baldauf suggests that an additional person be a check-and-balance for the person named durable power of attorney. It is recommended that a statement be included naming a second person who would look over the bank statement every month and over all finances every year. I wish I had this; I have no one to do this, other than my husband. He does look at the figures frequently to make sure they're correct. (I hate doing finances. I tell Mother that I love her so much that I do something that I hate.)

- Locate additional funds. Some programs can assist, such as programs to reduce utility costs or reduce prescription costs. Some authorities suggest getting a reverse mortgage or moving into a condo or senior housing. My parents moved into a smaller townhouse from a larger house with land. The irony was that the townhouse cost about the same as the larger home they sold. It was, however, more manageable. We were blessed to have also found that the national church organization for which my dad had been a minister for more than sixty years had a grant for older ministers and their spouses. As with many programs, you must take the time to search, apply, and sometimes interview to access benefits. (See National Council on Aging, Benefits Checkup: http://benefitscheckup.org/.)

- Protect against scams. Baldauf discusses the telephone solicitation vulnerability of older people and how they can be tricked into sharing Social Security numbers and other confidential information. She notes that "residents of all states can put a reversible 'security freeze'—different from a fraud alert—on their credit report, which should block identity thieves from obtaining new lines of credit."

In the section "Keeping Them Socially Connected," Baldauf discusses how older people may become isolated and are at risk for depression. Suggestions are offered to help seniors be more connected with others, including:

Get them involved. Connecting with others and helping others is a good way to get uninvolved with oneself. I have found this to also be true when working with children who have special needs. Individuals, young or old, who are often dependent on others and are constantly being helped by others need to be the helper whenever possible. Helping others gives us purpose and value. Seniors have much to offer with their history, wisdom, and experiences. Baldauf explains: "Research has linked participation in Experience Corps to boosts in cognitive and physical abilities and metabolism and to having a broader social network. Other organizations, like Senior Corps, arrange a variety of volunteer programs that include helping kids get immunized, counseling new business owners and teen parents, building houses, and more."

Meal sharing. According to Baldauf, cooking meals can get increasingly difficult for seniors, and they may lose interest in eating. Senior centers can offer food and socialization. Also Meals on Wheels or similar programs can be helpful. As mentioned earlier, one family was considering virtual meals. With the use of Web cams, families could talk during dinner times or other scheduled virtual visits.

"Keep them mobile" is Baldauf's last suggestion. If a senior no longer drives, the loss of independence can be devastating. My parents purchased scooters and were able to ride them around the bike paths near their townhouse while still in Minnesota. Once we moved them to Kansas, my mom was able to drive her scooter safely on our land, on visits to the horse, and around the deck for the first two years she was here. She delighted in the independence, and because she was in the country, there was not much she could run into.

I hope the above information will give you a place to start and a direction for family-meeting agendas. It's better if everyone adds to the agenda, but someone needs to be the organizer and facilitator. One tool to assist with the problem-solving is to remember "SODAS," which is described below.

SODAS

State the problem.

Sometimes everyone's agreeing on just what the real problem might be is a key to the solution. There are often different perspectives on the problem. Saying it out loud or putting it in writing clarifies what needs to be done or the possible solutions.

Options.

Come up with at least three possible solutions. Additional solutions should be recorded, but starting with three options makes this more manageable.

Disadvantages and

Advantages.

List the disadvantages and advantages of each of your options.

Solution.

Choose which option seems best to try, and write a plan of action to solve the problem—what you will do, when, how, and how will you know if it worked or if you need to try another option.

One More Step: Follow through with the plan, assess success, and return to other options if needed.

* Important to this process is everyone's input and participation. All ideas must be considered, and no single person should be "calling the shots" or naming all the options. Some situations may require a mediator or facilitator of this process.

Communication is essential, including verbal, nonverbal, and written word. Teaching in higher education in the field of early childhood special education, I use the following lists and tools in all my classes. Personally, I try to practice using these in my daily communications, and with family, this has to do with giving and receiving feedback (which is often negative). This can be done with respect and grace. It can also preserve family relationships. If we put off sharing feedback, the conflicts can grow and become less manageable. Good communication and teaming includes giving and receiving feedback.

The following guide is adapted from Getting to Yes: Negotiating Agreement without Giving In by Roger Fisher and William Ury.[7]

(See: http://www.colorado.edu/conflict/peace/example/ fish7513.htm for a book summary.)

How to Give Feedback

Get Ready:

- Face the person.
- Keep a straight posture.
- Keep a serious facial expression.
- Keep eye contact.

If on the phone or via e-mail, be aware of your tone of voice or choice of words; perhaps having your notes in front of you will prepare you to include all you want to say and prompt responsible and respectable choice of words.

The Conversation

- Ask if you can have a moment.
- First say something positive about the person or situation.

---

[7]   Roger Fisher and William Ury. *Getting to Yes: Negotiating Agreement without Giving In*, New York: Penguin Books, 1983.

- Tell how you feel and/or what you think the person did wrong.
- Check for understanding; repeat if he or she did not understand.
- Thank the person for listening.
- Change the topic.
- Be sure the person understands that you are concerned about him or her.

If on the phone or via e-mail, again, be aware of your tone of voice, choice of words, and use your notes, perhaps checking off what you have covered or underlining what you want to emphasize. If you need words or cues to prompt responsible and respectable choice of words, do it! Tactfulness is important.

Accepting Feedback

Get Ready:

- Face the person.
- Keep a straight posture.
- Keep a neutral facial expression.
- Keep eye contact.
- Stay near the person; don't move away.

If receiving feedback on the phone or via e-mail, you may not be prepared, and it might catch you off guard. Be aware of your tone of voice and choice of words; perhaps you could grab paper and pen to make some notes that might quickly prepare you to include all you want to say and prompt responsible and respectable choice of words.

THE CONVERSATION

- Keep a normal tone of voice.
- Listen closely (verbally and nonverbally).
- If you do not understand, ask for clarification.
- If you agree, apologize, say that you understand and ask for suggestions.
- If you don't agree, say that you understand what the person is saying, and ask permission to tell your side with the facts; or thank the person for his or her concern and say you will think about it. This step may depend on whether this person is an authority figure or on the importance of the feedback.
- Remember to stay calm. If you are upset, count to ten before saying anything.
- Do not interrupt when the other person is speaking.

Again, if receiving feedback on the phone or via e-mail, you will probably not be prepared, and it might take you by surprise. If reading e-mail or a letter, one can "over-read" or read into the message something that may not have been the intent. Still, be aware of your tone of voice, choice of words, and use paper and pen to make notes, perhaps checking off how you want to respond or emphasize. If you need to think about what is being said, or if you are angry or upset about the message, you might want to pause, call back, or have someone else read the message or your reply. I *always* have Fletch read or listen to my message if I am concerned about getting everything said and keeping the tone positive, yet direct. Again, tactfulness is important!

The above tools are also included in chapter six, along with some additional examples and illustrations. I do believe our own perspective on this situation and our family meetings was due to our general response to life's happenings. We have control over some things; some we don't. Our response and perspective when Tally was born with spina bifida influenced how we faced other things in our lives. It was *very* difficult—it still is, some days—but it makes us stronger. We have been problem-solvers; it's almost a way of life each day.

So, in getting started, we asked ourselves, "Are we the Spam in the Sandwich Generation, or can we be creative and efficient with our choices and be the prime rib?"

MORE DETAILS OF THE PLAN

We learned that planning ahead for the moving process was so important. You will find more of this in chapter five on organization, but to give you a picture of the need for planning ahead from the start, I have included the following itinerary example for the transition, as well as menus during the process:

Folks' Moving Itinerary
Fri. July 29
- Cass takes Fletch to J's in KC.

Sat. July 30
- J & Fletch get moving truck & head north.
- D & K drive up in ?? vehicle (or J drives his car & Fletch drives the truck).

Sun. July 31
- Moving crew to Winona.

- Pack the truck, all but the folks' beds, chairs, toilet seat lift.
- Belongings& meds & supplies packed for 2 1/2 weeks (I added 1/2 due to dr. appt. on 8/15).

Mon. Aug. 1

- K leaves early with Cadillac for KC.
- Pack beds & chairs in truck, Fletch & ? leave with truck ASAP.
    - Folks' farewell to Winona.
- Papa, Mama, J?& D leave for LaCrosse in K's van. Stay at friend's until flight.

Midwest:

Flight #1094 August 1 with wheelchair assistance and Best Care Club

1:05 Lv LaCrosse, WI

2:02 Arr. Milwaukee

Two-hour layover with resting place at Best Care Club

Flight #404

Lv. Milwaukee 4:04

Arr. Kansas City 5:50

- Dinner at S & S's
- Drive on to Emporia arriving at bedtime.

Hopefully, the truck would be in Emporia in time to get the beds in & ready in Cassie's room for bedtime. Otherwise, we'll set them up in another bed.

- K & J to Emporia Aug. 1 or 2 (would be helpful if K could be there for meeting with agency on Tues. at 10:00 AM).
- K, D, & Carol will help with care Aug. 1 evening, night & Aug. 2 AM.

Aug. 2
Caregiving agency here to do evaluation at 10:00 AM.
D & K will help orient caregiving agency, providers & Carol
with care needs.

- Deck-building can start.

Aug. 3
- Delivered lunches start for folks.
- Pastor T will visit at 11:00 AM.

As important as planning can be, flexibility is even more important. As it turned out, since my parents' cottage was not yet complete, my husband, Fletch, ended up staying in Kansas to consult with the builders.

We also kept a marker board out in the living room with current tasks to do, such as: assisting my parents with various things, helping with building on the deck between the houses, moving needed items from the garage to their temporary bedroom in our basement, etc. This helped organize and allowed for everyone to know how they could assist.

Another part of the planning was food and a menu for all the people who were coming and going in those first days after the move. Although basic, I have included the menu for the fifteen to twenty people who were coming and going. This planning ahead made for more focus on what we needed to get done, while making sure everyone had "fuel" to do it! I have reduced five days of menus into one sample day, seen below.

Day 1
Breakfast—please help yourselves!

- Sticky buns
- Bagels & cream cheese
- Oatmeal (in crock)
- Raisins, honey, brown sugar
- Variety of little cereals
- Juices, milk, coffee, tea

Lunch—please help yourselves!

- Buns, meat, cheeses
- Chips
- Mixed fruit
- Brownies, cookies

Supper

- Lasagna
- Garlic bread
- Salad
- Angel-food cake, strawberries/blueberries

I will conclude this chapter by referring readers back to "15 Ways to Take Care of Your Elderly Parents"—the article in *U.S. News & World Report*. This is a very helpful resource when getting started, no matter what level of involvement you might have in this process. I wish I'd had this resource back when we got started. I would have shared it will all of my family members.

WHAT WE LEARNED

- Time in the Sandwich Generation takes on a different meaning. Spontaneity does not exist.

- Time is the greatest gift of all.

- Choices are important at any age, but they must be appropriate and safe choices.

- We'll all be in our parents' position, if we're lucky enough to life that long. How do we want life to be for ourselves, as we get older?

- For some, it is all about the money, getting their share of any inheritance, or avoidance of contributing financial support if needed when there is no inheritance.

QUOTE

"There is no recipe approach for the Sandwich Generation; it's what works best for your family, while assuring the respect and dignity of those who have given us life."
　　　　　　　　　　　—Author unknown

TIPS AND TOOLS

A Time to Talk: How to Discuss Care Options with Elderly Parents

http://www.roanoke.com/extra/wb/173492

This site includes warning signs indicating when it's time to start talking about options, encouraging adult children to initiate this discussion while elderly parents are cognizant and able to talk about long-term care options.

The following information and Web sites are sources for planning ahead:

See "15 Ways to Take Care of Your Elderly Parents" (*U.S. News & World Report*)

http://health.usnews.com/articles/health/2007/11/02/15-things-you-can-do-to-keep-mom-and-dad-at-home.html

Elder Care—First Steps
Beginning Your Journey through Elder Care
http://www.aging-parents-and-elder-care.com/Pages/Elder_Care_First_Steps.html

Elder Care Checklists
(http://www.aging-parents-and-elder-care.com/Pages/Elder_Care_Checklists.html)
This wonderful source provides well-designed checklists; very helpful for new caregivers or when conditions are changing. This includes excellent Web sites with the best checklists, including:
 Elder Care—First Steps
 Seniors and Driving Checklist
 Getting Started—What kind of help does your loved one need?
 Home Alone—Are They Okay?
 Home Safety Checklist
 Care Interpreter Living Arrangements—What is recommended for your loved one?
 Prescription Drug Reference Checklist
 Alzheimer's Living Facility Checklist
 Assisted Living Facility Checklist
 Nursing Home Checklist

AARP offers an excellent comprehensive resource, with checklists, tips, and talking points. It is probably not too early to

look at the list for yourself and talk with your children. This resource is very well organized, and the content includes:
Planning Ahead:

- Starting a Dialogue
- Involving Others
- Thinking Ahead
- Assessing the Situation
- Long-Distance Issues
- Work and Caregiving
- Community Services
- Organizing Document

Providing Care at Home:

- Care at Home
- Managing the Stress
- Hands-on Care
- Engaging Activities
- Choosing In-Home Care
- Hiring Home-Care Help
- Talk to Health Pros
- Health History

Preparing Your Home:

- Is Your Home Safe?
- Home Repairs
- Preventing Falls
- Helpful Gadgets
- Lighting Your Home

Housing Options:

- Knowing Your Options
- Comparing Facilities
- Assisted Living
- Nursing Homes
- Nursing Home System
- Nursing Home Costs
- An Advocate to Help

Legal and Insurance:

- Legal Issues
- Public Benefits
- Insurance
- Medicare Basics

End of Life:

- The Conversation
- Facts about Hospice
- Providing Comfort
- Managing Symptoms
- Dealing with Pain
- Advance Directives
- Spirituality

Source: http://assets.aarp.org/external_sites/caregiving/planAhead/index.html

I found a great article titled "Top 10 Secrets That Aging Parents Keep—and What to Do about It" by Leonard J. Hansen at http://www.agingcare.com/Featured-Stories/133477/

Top-10-Secrets-That-Aging-Parents-Keep-and-What-To-Do-About-It.htm.

The "secrets" they may not tell you include issues with:

- Falls

- Pain

- Dizziness

- Money shortages

- Frivolous purchasing

- Financial abuse

- Elder abuse

- Auto accidents or driving infractions

- Alcohol or drug abuse

- Gambling

The article also covers ways of dealing with these secrets. It is well work checking it out.

Chapter 2

PHILOSOPHY AND ATTITUDE

COMMITMENT WITH A CAPITAL "C"

Fletch and I have long had a strong commitment to family. Before we were married, Fletch's mom was very ill. He took a semester off from college in his senior year to go home and work a night shift so he could be at home with his mom during the day. I observed him with my nieces and nephews and knew he would be a wonderful dad. When we first were married and soon off to graduate school, we were committed to waiting to have children until we had more time to focus on them (if we were blessed to have them). We observed many fellow graduate students with children who had to squeeze in time for their children amid the toil and perils of graduate work. We also decided that once we had children, whoever was making more money would continue to work, while the other would stay home with our children. We were delighted to have our first baby, Cassendra Monique (Cassie), after we had moved to South Dakota, where I had my first university teaching position. Fletch had various part-time jobs and was an at-home dad. We welcomed Mikelle Eve into our lives two and a half years later. Fletch continued to be the primary caregiver. I had a flexible schedule and was also able to enroll both Cassie and Mikelle in our university preschool program, where I was coordinator. We *loved* being parents and delighted in every milestone.

Two years later, we became stronger and more committed parents—our parenting was tested when our youngest, Tally Love, was born. She faced many challenges, with spina bifida, hydrocephalus, Arnold-Chiari Malformation, using a wheelchair, and various other significant medical issues. She had three surgeries in the first week of her life and has had a total of twelve over the years. Medical issues were major, hospital visits frequent, and doctor visits a way of life. We struggled with the school district and special education. We forged through several due processes, mediations, and complaints over the years, advocating for inclusion and support services for Tally. We became stronger parents and committed our lives to special-needs awareness, advocacy, and inclusion. Because much of this content was related to my profession—teaching at universities in the field of early childhood special education—I was able to wear both my personal and professional "hats." We presented information at conferences, sometimes including the whole family on various issues of inclusion, sibling issues, accessibility, advocacy, and parent rights.

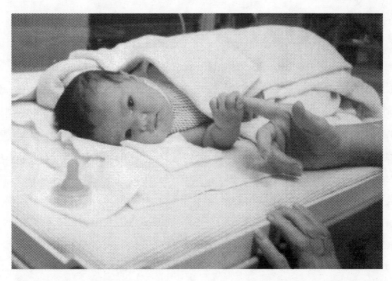

Newborn Tally holding Grandma's finger while in NICU.
Little did I know that eighteen years later, I would be, literally,
in the middle of this loving sandwich on a daily basis.

Mother and Tally in the field of clover by our house the
first spring (2006) after Mother moved here.

We moved to Kansas in 1996 for a better university teaching position for me, improved special education for Tally, less snow, and being closer to some family. Within three years, we built an accessible home in the country when Tally was eleven, Mikelle was thirteen, and Cassie was sixteen. This move was a huge step toward freedom, accessibility, and independence for Tally. After living in Kansas for nine years and after having built an accessible environment for Tally, assisting my parents with their situation was a natural challenge and one that we already had experience with, of sorts. Although the systems and issues are a bit different for a younger person with special needs than for our aging parents, there are many similarities in caring for them. Accessibility, problem-solving, thinking "outside the box," inclusion of people with and without special needs – both young and old, offering choices, and need for flexibility are very similar.

We have always tried to face challenges by viewing the glass as half full and seeing the positive. Challenges are frustrating but also are opportunities for learning. We have taught our children to surround themselves with positive people. We have learned from our mistakes, and we are the first to admit we have made them. We try to creatively solve problems, and we have taught our children that every problem can be solved in one way or another. No doesn't always mean no; there is always a way. It is not a matter of "if" but "how" something might be done. Our response to life's happenings has formed our philosophy. We learned to recognize that which we had control over and that which we didn't; what we could change and what we couldn't. We couldn't change that fact that Tally has spina bifida, but we could make a difference in her world to make a more accessible, accepting environment. We couldn't change the fact that our parents were getting older, running out of money, and were more dependent, but we could make their world safe, caring, and grant their wish to not die in a hospital or nursing home.

We have been sincere in our efforts. More aspects of our philosophy are detailed below. This may explain our commitment—why and how we do what we do.

COMMITMENT—YOU CANNOT DO IT ALONE!

In order to make our plan work, we had to believe in the process and be committed to the purpose. We could not do it alone; we needed to have others also committed to the cause.

At times, you may feel like you're alone, but I believe we are all here to help each other, and God gave us others to make the seemingly impossible, possible. Asking for help is a sign of strength. When someone asks if he or she can help, say yes!

The National Family Caregivers Association offers a wonderful brochure titled "Share the Caring." This short pamphlet presents suggestions for creating an action plan for a caregiver who may need support or for a friend or family member who would like to help. It offers a checklist for this plan, "Help I Need" and "Help I Can Offer." The section on "Help I Need" includes items such as a night out with friends; dinners prepared; a weekend away; someone to ask how I am; pick up prescriptions and other health-care items; and help with paying the bills. Under "Help I Can Offer" are suggestions that coincide with the "Help I Need" column, such as dinner and movies on me; a meal prepared a certain number of times a week; a weekly phone call; run errands; or a check for a certain amount of dollars. There is also a section at the bottom of the page to personalize where help might be needed or offered. You can locate this helpful brochure through the National Family Caregivers Association's Web site, or go to www.thefamilycaregiver.org/pdfs/326503_SharetheCaring_broch.pdf.

COMMITMENT! NO SNOW DAYS!

The alarm went off, and I found my fingers pushing the snooze more than once. Wednesdays are my 7:00 AM to 8:00 PM days this semester. We had freezing rain last night, and it snowed all night. My thoughts of a snow day were racing and pleasant but seemed impossible, particularly because the university at which my husband and I both work and where Tally attends *never* closes. As I turned the TV on (muted, so it wouldn't wake up Tally or the dog), and after watching for several minutes, the multiple closings did include the university. Yippee! My mind started making lists of all the things I could do to catch up with my work and home. I soon realized that the catch to my commitment is that I *never* catch up. Most of us don't catch up with everything we want to do, but I'm talking about catching up with essentials, like laundry, dishes, or cleaning.

The phone rang; it was my mom's provider saying she didn't think she could make it today. So much for my "snow day."

One of the agencies working for my mom, we called "the fair weather agency".

Some time after signing on with this agency I learned that the owner/coordinator told her employees that they did not have to come in when there was bad weather or on holidays. Another important question to add to the provider or agency interview list is "Do you take snow days?" This is particularly important if you are coordinating from afar. You have to have some kind of backup plan if providers can't make it. Unfortunately, you may find this out after the fact.

The capital "C" in commitment means that you are always on call; you must always have a cell phone or some way you can be reached; you don't really have any respite, and you're always on guard. Many people cannot understand or pledge to this kind of commitment—the kind with a capital "C."

This is different from making a commitment to be a parent. There is planned parenthood and methods to assist us with our timing of having children when we're ready to commit (although this doesn't always work out). As children, however, we did not pledge to take care of our parents. There is no ceremonial baptism or wedding that commits us to the overwhelming yet rewarding task of taking care of our aging parents. It's just in your heart, and if you do this, you know that it's right.

THE BOX: THINKING INSIDE, OUTSIDE, AND AROUND THE BOX

Commitment also means constant problem-solving about many issues—how to pay the bills when there is no money; advocating to make change; deciding which problem to tackle first; transportation (to appointments, keeping the vans running, who has the accessible vehicle on which end of campus and where it is needed for Tally, especially on rainy days); what is needed to be done and who, where, and when will someone do it. It is truly difficult for some to think "outside of the box," as "the box" is familiar, comfortable, and safe. I would refer back to the SODAS problem-solving tool (discussed in chapter one) and thinking beyond traditional solutions. Plowing new pathways and making them accessible is a constant process. Fletch is my out-of-the-box thinker who keeps me grounded and creative, yet productive and some-what sane.

No Doesn't Always Mean No—but You Have to Work for It

We have learned that no does not always mean no. It does take some work and educating ourselves (e.g., calls about the American's with Disabilities Act (ADA) or Individuals with Disabilities Education Act (IDEA) requirements or even filing a complaint, mediating, or due process). It is worth the confrontation and conflict, particularly if it is a priority for equal access or quality of life for your loved one. I do believe that much of it is about attitude. If you approach the conflict or disagreement with a smile, grace, and a positive attitude, you get a lot more done, and people may want to work with you. Also, if you're going to complain, do it to someone who can make a difference. It doesn't help to complain to a person who cannot make the change. It also helps to surround yourself with positive people who can help support your advocacy efforts. Advocacy and protection agencies in each state can be helpful. (Check the advocacy organizations and resources at the end of this book.)

Inclusion—at Any Age

When you travel with two wheelchair-accessible vans, accessibility as well as inclusion of individuals with and without special need – young or old, make a difference, and it takes a bit more planning, time, and seeking out accessible entrances. I think people were hesitant to invite us to some locations or gatherings because of accessibility issues with Tally. I think this is even more evident now, with both Mother and Tally.

We do have to be selective with my mom, as her energy and health are definitely issues, but when she is in good health, we try to get her out beyond the deck and home. My mom joins us at art shows and going out to eat; she attends church every Saturday, Bible class on Wednesdays, and the Senior Center for lunch on foot clinic days. Tally, of course, goes everywhere, and we advocate for accessibility wherever we go.

Inclusion starts with physically accessible environments. Once you "get in the door," you may then have additional physical barriers, particularly in the bathroom. The following are some areas you might want to address in order to fully include your loved one, who may use a wheelchair or walker or have other equipment.

At family gatherings, let the family know how to set up the environment. This includes having enough space to move, ramps into the house, and sitting with the family at the table (rather than having the person off by himself, using a tray). In special education we talk about what we can change in the environment, rather than changing the person. Because two of our family members use wheelchairs, when we are in other locations I try to educate others about integration of placement of people who use wheelchairs. When at home, my mother and Tally sit together almost every evening for supper. At family gatherings I feel they need to be integrated with others, not always sitting together in the "wheelchair section". Several times, on both sides of our family, my mom and daughter were "grouped" at the same table, away from the rest of the family. At one family gathering, our entire family was blatantly seated back in the kitchen at Christmas dinner, separate from the rest of the family gathering. It was very frustrating, and I did not react positively to that kind of segregation. I don't think one side of the family ever understood how insulting that Christmas dinner incident was. However, when noted, change has occurred with seating arrangements at most family gatherings. It comes down to awareness. Someone has to speak out and advocate for change to occur.

Consider accessible locations when planning family vacations, reunions, etc. We learned to request "fully ADA" to go beyond just getting in the front door. Keep accessibility in mind, even when making reservations at restaurants.

Restaurants:

- ask about accessible entrances; space to get in and around
- check for enough room, even with chairs pulled out from the table
- in most settings, the person in a wheelchair usually has to sit at the end of the table, due to space needed
- consider seating inclusively; think about with whom the person will be seated, what kind of assistance he or she may need, etc.

Restrooms: Accessibility is often lacking in some restaurant restrooms, particularly the older ones.

You cannot always take someone's word that there is accessibility. I would be rich if I had a dollar for every time someone assured me of a facility's accessibility, and we found problems once we got there. You must check it out yourself.

Our latest situation was a wedding, where we traveled a great distance with both my mom and daughter in two separate vehicles. I had e-mailed the coordinator of the location of the wedding and reception well ahead of time to check on the arrangements and was assured that they would make the needed accommodations. The wedding location was fine, but the reception was held on a second floor—with no elevators!

We ended up carrying Mother and Tally up a steep flight of stairs, with the help of friends and family. What was most frustrating was the response I had from the staff when I asked, "So how are we going to solve this?" The reply was, "We can bring some food down to them." I said, "But the party's upstairs!" We then carried them upstairs. Of course, the staff wouldn't help, as they could be liable if there had been an accident. After getting Mother and Tally settled, the mother bear in me came out, and I went back down and told the staff that *if* there was an emergency or fire, they had better be there to help us get my mother and daughter out! The frustrating part was they could have easily set up the dance downstairs, with the food upstairs and taken food down for them. There were several solutions, but the accommodations were not given a second thought. I did follow up with a letter and considered filing a complaint, but later reconsidered—my life did not allow for that amount of energy.

You can find some great resources for making environments more accessible, safety checklists for environments for the elderly, and ADA checklists at the end of this chapter under "Tips."

PERSON-FIRST PHILOSOPHY

Person-first philosophy is something in which I strongly believe, teach in all my college classes, and try to promote and live on a daily basis. The following is a handout I use in classes and share with others:

PERSON FIRST

When you see someone in a wheelchair, what do you honestly see first: the wheelchair, the physical disability, or the person? Do you find yourself still using phrases like "wheelchair bound," "confined to a wheelchair," "handicapped," or even "blind as a bat" or "crippled"? If so, you may need to review and make a conscious effort to use person-first philosophy and language.

WHAT IS PERSON-FIRST?

Person-first is a philosophy of seeing the person first, the disability second. This does not deny the disability; it simply views the person first. The person is *not* the disability (e.g., don't refer to the person as "the disabled" or "the handicapped"); rather, the person *has* a disability.

Person First means:

- Referring to the person first and then the disability
- Emphasizing abilities, not disabilities or limitations
- Not labeling people as part of a disability group, such as "the disabled" (rather, say "people with disabilities")
- Not patronizing or giving excessive praise or attention to a person with a disability
- Giving the person with a disability a choice and independence; letting the person do or speak for himself/herself as much as possible and as his or her ability permits
- A disability is a functional limitation that interferes with the person's ability to walk, hear, talk, learn, etc. We no longer use the term "handicap" or "handicapped." Use the word handicap to describe a situation or barrier that society and the environment imposes by not making environments accessible (for example, not making curb cuts, not placing

Braille signage in needed locations, not building ramps or elevators for accessibility for people who need it).

Here are some examples of person-first and non-person-first language:

Say …	Instead of …
Child with a disability	Disabled or handicapped child
Person who is deaf or hard of hearing	Deaf and dumb
Person with mental retardation	Retarded
Person who uses a wheelchair or wheelchair-bound	Confined to a wheelchair
Child who has a congenital disability	Birth defect
Person of short stature	Dwarf or midget
Has paraplegia/quadriplegia	Paraplegic/quadriplegic
Accessible parking	Handicapped parking
Accessible bathroom	Handicapped bathroom

- How would you introduce someone (e.g., John Doe, who doesn't have a disability)? You would most likely introduce him by giving his name, where he lives, what he does or what he is interested in, such as that he likes to swim, ride horses, eat Mexican food, and cook.

- Why say it differently for a person who has a disability? We all have many characteristics that make us who we are, mental as well as physical, and not many of us want to be identified only by our ability, for example, to play tennis, or how much we love onion rings, or the freckles or mole on our face.

- People with disabilities are like everyone else; they just happen to have a disability and may need some accommodations.

- Person-first philosophy and language is a matter of respect for a person with special needs—respect for who he or she is: a person first. Attitudes are reflected in what we do and say. An attitude of respect is reflected in person-first philosophy and practice.

Person First has been around for a long time. In 1990, Federal Laws reworded special education and civil rights laws—IDEA (Individuals with Disabilities Education Act) and ADA (Americans with Disabilities Act)—in person-first language. For several years, special-education journals have required that person-first language be used in articles, and some text publishers require it. If you do a Google search of person-first language, you'll find 25,300,000 sites listed. Still, many people are struggling with its use, and some even ignore the use of Person First. I encourage you to "think before you speak" and choose words that demonstrate your respect for seeing the person first!

My daughter Tally also promotes Person First. She's experienced many situations where people see her chair first or define or identify her by her chair. She shares an example of how she heard one of the assistant principals at her school calling and calling the name of another young lady in her school, someone who also uses a wheelchair. The frustrated principal finally came up to Tally and asked, "Why didn't you answer me when I called you?" She replied, "Well, you weren't calling my name." He apologized and was probably embarrassed that he'd mistaken one person who used a wheelchair for another. I doubt, however, that this short incident impacted him the same way it did Tally. Tally was frustrated and offended that her assistant principal saw her chair, rather than looking at her as a person. (The other student looked markedly different from Tally—different color and length of hair and very different build.) On the positive side, Tally also shares experiences of how friends or teachers treat her with respect and see her before her wheelchair. An example of this was when she recently got her hair cut, darkened, and straightened. It really gave her a new look. One of her teachers saw her, stared, did a double-take, and then told her he wasn't sure if was her. He said he felt badly that he had to look at her chair to be sure it was her. These are refreshing occurrences that give me hope.

CHOICES, CHOICES, AND MORE CHOICES

The following is an excerpt from an e-mail I sent my sister, as we were deciding where to go for dinner with my mom when they came to visit:

"Mother/Grandma thinks Applebee's would be nice. What do you think? Choices are important for her. One of my professors and friend used to say, 'It's all about options and freedoms.' How true this is! I have worked both personally and professionally on appropriate choices. Toddlers need choices, but they need to be developmentally appropriate: choosing what to wear from two or three options; which toys to play with; options of choosing some of the menu items, etc. Some are not appropriate choices, such as whether or not to go to bed. However, whether to brush teeth first or get p.j.'s on first is an appropriate choice, as is which book to have read before bedtime. Life is *full* of choices. When we start taking them away, having little to no control over any part of our lives, that is tragic. I have also read that good care and choices equals fewer meds.

If there is one thing I've really learned about, being in the Sandwich Generation, it is how *very* important choices are. I have taught this for years but it becomes more prominent to me each day. Therefore, one of the chapters of this book is called 'Choices, Choices and More Choices.'"

I have a friend who took care of her dad for seven years, before he died at age eighty-seven, while at the same time assisting her son who has autism become more independent. She remembers well the double duty and felt that having a child with special needs really prepared her family to care for her dad. I agreed with her that the assistance and guidance for our children who have additional needs prepare us for elder care. Maybe we are just used to being more flexible, adapting, and solving problems. Maybe we're used to the pace and not rushing as well. We certainly know how to advocate!

FLEXIBILITY—THE KEY!

PRAYER

I grew up praying. Because my dad was a minister, we were brought up to believe that prayer was the answer to all worries and woes. Prayer occurred throughout the day; from the time we got up until the time we fell asleep. Besides going to all church functions (even funerals of people I didn't know—when I was a young child, and my mom didn't have anyone to stay with me, she'd take me along), we had daily devotions. By the time I was ten years old, I had probably been to more church functions than most people attend in a lifetime. Although many churches do great things and support people in very positive ways, I have observed the hypocrisies and politics of the church. I currently have a difficult time being a part of the organized church, in general, but I do pray, have faith, and consider myself to be very spiritual.

I had a particularly difficult faith-time after Tally was born. I questioned God and why he or she would allow such a horrible condition to afflict a sweet, innocent newborn baby. As my daughter went through three surgeries in her first week of life and spent the first month of her life in the NICU, I prayed numerous times each day for her to know a life beyond the IVs, tubes, injections, and surgeries. At the age of twenty-one, she is now thriving, attending college, and has an apartment of her own. This is not without great effort, but I believe prayer helped give us the tools, strength, and knowledge to support her. I also pray each morning for my own health and strength to get up and face the challenges of the day. I pray for Fletch, my children, and their loves. I pray for the health of my mom and Fletch's dad and for them to feel less pain today. I pray for my extended family and thank God for another beautiful day. I love nature and see our Creator in everything around us.

WHAT WE'VE LEARNED

- It's all about attitudes! Flexibility and communication are the keys to most successful experiences. Choices (appropriate and safe ones) are essential for a sense of self-worth and dignity. Respite and a sense of humor can help keep you sane.

  Also:

- Commitment needs to be with a capital "C." In order to make this work, we had to believe in the process and committed to the purpose.

- The box: thinking inside, outside and around the box

- No doesn't always mean no—but you have to work for it.

- Inclusion is important—at any age.

- Choices, choices, and more choices: choices + good care = fewer meds

QUOTE

"Congress cannot change attitudes with a stroke of a pen."

—Author unknown

I ran across this quote years ago. It refers to the civil laws, such as the Rehabilitation Act of 1973, the Americans with Disabilities Act of 1990, and other civil rights laws. We can have laws that require accommodations, ramps, curb cuts, elevators, and lifts for equal access. These things (although sometimes a challenge to get implemented) are easy to see and fairly easy and clear to implement. Attitudes, however, cannot be changed via the law. This calls for more awareness, education, flexibility, and sensitivity.

"It's all about options and freedoms"
—John Wheeler

TIPS AND TOOLS

Elder Care Checklists
http://www.aging-parents-and-elder-care.com/Pages/Elder_
Care_Checklists.html

This *wonderful* source provides well-designed checklists—very helpful for new caregivers or when conditions are changing. This includes *excellent* Web sites with the best checklists, including:

Elder Care—First Steps

Seniors and Driving Checklist

Getting Started—What kind of help does your loved one need?

Home Alone—Are They Okay?

Home Safety Checklist

Care Interpreter Living Arrangements—What is recommended for your loved one?

Prescription Drug Reference Checklist

Alzheimer's Living Facility Checklist

Assisted Living Facility Checklist

Nursing Home Checklist

Chapter 3

A Day in the Life of the Sandwich

This chapter includes journaling of some days and weeks. Reading some of it makes me tired. Reviewing it makes me wonder how we make it work on some days and weeks. Described below are a few days and week in the life of our sandwich. The first entry was while on my sabbatical from university teaching.

7:30 Call regarding an extended family member having problems
8:15 Another call about family member
8:30 Started e-mail response regarding family member
9:00 Helped daughter who uses wheelchair with morning routine, eating breakfast in between
9:30 Call to sibling regarding family member and update on Mother; continued assisting daughter with AM routine while on phone (needed earphones)
10:00 Started organizing Mother's tax information to take to the taxperson tomorrow
11:00 Ran over to Mother's while home-health nurse visited

12:00 Call from another sibling about extended family member's problems; lunch—gulped a Slim-Fast

1:00 Shower; assisted daughter with medical needs

2:00 In mail received packet from the Dept. of Justice about a complaint sent 7½ months ago, requesting permission for mediation

2:30 Called consultant about mediation; daughter upset with me while I was on the phone, as she didn't feel well, and I wasn't giving the attention she needed

3:00 Continued organizing tax papers

3:45 Call from older daughter coming back from spring break, checking to see if I still wanted to go out for my birthday drink from her (my birthday was Dec. 26; this was March 20, and we finally had a time to do this).

4:00 Back to tax papers for my mom

4:30 Over to my mom's to orient a new home provider

5:00 Back to tax papers; assisted daughter with medical needs

6:00 A bite to eat; took dinner over to my mom

6:30 Dressed to go out with my daughters for my overdue birthday drink. Usually, my mom comes over for dinner and the evening, but this night I had a provider for the evening.

7:15 This was a treat. My middle daughter picked me up for an evening with her and her older sister. Although it was a needed respite, we spent much of the time discussing Grandma's health, my youngest daughter's needs, and the situation regarding the extended family member having serious problems. It was nice to sit down and talk with my two young-adult daughters—a rare delight! My husband stayed home with our youngest daughter, and was available to the new provider covering care for my mom.

Midnight. My middle daughter took me home; I talked with

my husband about our day and headed for bed, as I needed to meet the taxperson in early AM.

* ANOTHER DAY

Just one of many but so fresh in my memory:

- A combined trip to get our and Grandma's groceries and meds; go by my office to pick up mail for class; take Tally to get swimsuit before the weekend to take a vacation w/ our family—first in *years*!
- Going shopping for swimsuit for Tal
- Cassie, our oldest daughter, stayed with Grandma.
- The van we were planning to take for our vacation had transmission problems.
- Mikelle, our middle daughter, drove back to our house to get Tally's manual chair after driving me by my office in town to pick up mail for class I'm teaching on-line.
- Fletch drove back to drop off Tally's power wheelchair, made appointment to get van in for repairs; then left in Nissan to get groceries and meds for Grandma and groceries for us…

* ONE OF THOSE WEEKS—JUNE 22, 2007

This week was crazy, so I thought I'd include it in this section, as well:

- Appointment with deputy sheriff. It was discovered that one of my mom's caregivers had stolen money from another caregiver and had stolen from my mom.

- ADA mediation meeting regarding nonaccessibility of a business in town
- Dr. appointment for my mom
- Dentist appointment for my mom
- Foot appointment for my mom
- Getting ready for vacation!
  - Arranged care coverage for Mother while we will be gone
  - Arranged care for horse/sheep
  - Packing: two wheelchairs, supplies, etc.
  - Finding accessible location for stay at Resort Condominiums International (RCI) Timeshare
  - Support from sisters: RCI & care for Mother during day while we will be gone
  - Kept night care, so my sister will have energy during the day and won't get sick
  - Taking the puppy, collecting everything for her
- Working on three Web classes, taking my laptop so I can "teach" while on the road and vacation
- My immediate family agreeing to not "push buttons," *respect*, take a breath—to enjoy our rare vacation time together

SOMEWHAT NORMAL—IT DOESN'T EXIST

What is normal? Normal in itself does not exist. Normal is an average of many differences. Normal is different for each of us.

"Normal is what those of us who are family caregivers want more than anything else. We want to be like other families that take walking and talking and eating and toileting and swallowing and thinking for granted. We want our loved ones to be well. No, normal isn't boring at all, except perhaps to those who have never experienced the outside-the-norm situation of caregiving."[8]

Typical does not really work either. Perhaps "usual" or "ordinary" best describes what we usually do on a regular or daily basis. An ordinary day in the life of the "sandwiched" is not the ordinary for most people. There is nothing mundane about it! Some days are spent taking care of one mini-crisis after another. Some days have major crises, such as:

- Emergency room visits almost every week (for some time)
- Providers not showing up or quitting
- Depleting funds
- Agency problems
- Provider theft

FRIDAYS—CRUNCH DAYS, TRULY SANDWICHED DAYS

My schedule was set to have Fridays as meetings, writing, and catch-up days. Almost every Friday was literally filled with appointments for my mom or my daughter. We would have at least two or three meetings with Social Rehabilitation Services, doctors, case managers, home health, mediation advocacy—*all* directly related to the care and advocacy of our situation. Since much of this has to occur during business

---

[8]   ___ Mintz, 2002. Love, Honor & Value: A Family Caregiver Speaks Out about the Chices & Challenges of Caregiving. Herndon, VAL Capital Books, Inc., p. 33

hours during the week, it would land on Friday. So my weekends would be filled with catching up from the previous week
and trying to prepare for the next. This included helping my
daughter get organized, assisting with homework, if needed,
or trying to hire and train someone else to assist. There were
certain classes for which some of us were able to assist more
than others.

I soon learned to not feel guilty about having time to get
my work done. So I would schedule care for my mom for the
weekend and would visit from time to time. This way, I did
much of my work, particularly on-line classes, during the
weekend. Weekday evenings are when I would schedule my
shift with her. That way, we could have dinner together, and
I could still get some work done on my computer, do laundry,
and assist Tally while Mother watched TV after dinner.

MONDAYS—WHAT'S NEXT?

During the fall semester 2008, Mondays seemed to bring
mini-crises. Several occurred as I was going out the door on
a Monday morning, including:

- First vice president of faculty senate stepped down,
  making me first vice president rather than second, and
  fast-forwarding my life a year
- Night provider had family emergency—needed three
  nights off
- My shoulder/neck pain—had to see my doctor and
  arrange physical therapy
- My mother's erratic behavior—was it a urinary track
  infection? Her meds? Arranged doctor appointment
- Provider for my daughter decided to quit, giving us

two days notice to arrange supports for her in class and at her apartment.

What will next Monday bring? I was feeling "the curse" of Mondays almost to the point that my mind told me that my mom would die on a Monday. Weird, huh? It certainly gave me opportunities to start my problem-solving early in the week!

RESPITE

I do not practice what I preach on this topic. I'm sure you've heard that you have to take care of the caregiver or that you cannot take care of someone else unless you take care of yourself. Respite should not be running to Wal-Mart and spending a half-hour looking for sales while you wait for your mom's prescription to be completed—but sometimes, it is.

Respite can also bring with it some guilt. Then you can get back in the "resentment/guilt yo-yo." (See chapter three for a description.) My view of respite has changed over the years. We knew respite was important and were encouraged to take our respite time from the time when Tally was a baby. Encouragement for respite is in all the brochures and family development literature and came out of the mouths of numerous counselors. We rarely allowed ourselves respite when Tally was younger. This was partially due to our not having confidence that Tally was well taken care of when we were gone. We had a few quite frightening examples of providers who did not know what to do; some even neglected her or put her in a dangerous situation. One example stands out in my mind. We were at a family reunion. My family of origin organized a reunion every other year when our children were younger. One of my nephews had his girlfriend along. She asked if Cassie, Mikelle, and Tally would like to go to another area of the resort. The location we thought they were going to was the main lobby, which was level, and it seemed like a safe, fun idea. Tally was three years old at the time and had her first wheelchair. This girlfriend had worked in nursing homes and with people who used wheelchairs, and she appeared trustworthy. Yet she took Tally to another area of the resort, up to the top floor, which had a very steep ramp. The ramp was actually built right over the steps, so the incline was extremely steep and unsafe. She asked Tally if she needed help going down! The child was only three! Predictably, there was an accident, which I discovered when the girl carried my baby in to me. Tally appeared almost unconscious. She had gone down the ramp, ran into her sister (which was bad for her sister, but it did break Tally's fall), and Tally ran into the wall! She could have been killed! It took us a long time to trust anyone else with her care.

We have always taken our children everywhere. We love going places and doing things with them. We felt they were only young for a short time, and we wanted to be with them to enjoy their childhoods. We camped, traveled, often went to conferences (even presenting together on various topics related to special needs and accessibility) and family reunions, and went to Tally's doctor appointments together. I even found a way for them to be a part of my dissertation on inclusive creative movement, "I Can Move." We tried to support our older two daughters by doing research on siblings of children with special needs, and by starting Don Meyer's Sibshops locally and in the state of Kansas. It's a great program, with wonderful information. (If you are interested, please see Don Meyer's information at http://www.siblingsupport.org.)

Cassie, Mikelle, and I wrote an article together called "We're Special, Too!" We did many things as a family. Fletch and I were not a couple who had nights out when our children were young. Rarely did we have a date night. For several years, our night out was the annual winter college party.

This changed last year—for the first time since Cassie was born twenty-six years ago. Tally started having one overnight a week at her apartment with her sister on Thursday nights. After a month of Fletch and me having dinner with my mom without Tally on Thursday nights, Fletch said, "Why don't we get someone to take care of your mom on Thursdays?" So that's what we did. We couldn't arrange it every week, but most weeks, Thursday was date night. My mom's providers encouraged us to do that, and it has worked well. We choose to go out to eat, bring something in, or cook something special. There is often a bottle of champagne in there somewhere. We often sit down by the pond and watch the sun set. We talk and talk and talk. Much of the conversation includes our sandwich. We do a lot of problem-solving during this time.

So, now I believe in respite and promote it where I can. It took a few years, but the value is immeasurable!

What We Learned

"Somewhat normal" doesn't exist, so there is no reason to strive for it. How dull might normal be?

Quote

"Normal isn't boring at all, except perhaps to those who have never experienced the outside-the-norm situation of caregiving."

—S. Mintz

TIPS AND TOOLS

Respite: See chapter eleven.

RESOURCES ON RESPITE

- Take care of the caregiver:
ABC News: "Coping with Stress While Caring for Elders"
abcnews.go.com/Health/ElderCare/Story?id=3316565&page=1

- See "Ideas to De-stress Your Day"
http://www.ebc.state.ok.us/NR/rdonlyres/7FA2C7BB-1164-42F0-9469-5AC471A6D68B/0/destress.pdf

- "Adult children caring for elderly parents 'need more help in coping with stress'"
http://www.jrf.org.uk/node/366

RESOURCES ON SUPPORT

"Help I Need; Help I Can Offer"; National Family Caregivers Association's (NFCA) brochure www.thefamilycaregiver.org/pdfs/326503_SharetheCaring_broch.pdf

NFCA Web site: www.thefamilycaregiver.org

Russell, C. L. (1997). "We're Here Too: Brothers and sister of children with special needs." *Disability Solutions*, Sept./Oct.

Russell, C. L. (2008). "How Are Your Person-First Skills? A Self-Assessment
Tool." *Teaching Exceptional Children,* May 2008.

Sibshops information
http://www.siblingsupport.org/

Chapter 4

RANGE OF EMOTIONS: THE GOOD AND NOT-SO-GOOD FEELINGS OF BEING IN "THE SANDWICH"

THE EMOTIONAL INVESTMENT

A study from the National Family Caregivers Association[9] offers statistics not only on the financial expenses related to caregiving but also the emotional ones. Results of this study indicate that half of those caring for an older loved one spend an average of 10 percent of their yearly income on caregiving expenses. (More details of the financial findings of this study are discussed in chapter nine.)

Other key findings of the National Family Caregivers Association study that impact the emotional aspects of family caregivers include:

- 34 percent of respondents used some of their savings to cover this cost.

---

[9] National Family Caregivers Association. Winter, 2008. New Study Reveals the High Financial Cost of Caring for an Older Loved One, *Take Care: Self-Care for the Family Caregiver.*

- 23 percent of respondents said they cut back on their own health-care spending.

- 53 percent of respondents did not work; 37 percent quit their jobs or reduced work hours.

- Respondents spent an average of 35.4 hours of caregiving per week; 19 percent caregiving for more than three years; 32 percent for more than five years.

- Respondents made the following sacrifices: leisure activities, vacations, saving less or not at all, using their savings, cutting back on basics (clothing utilities, transportation, groceries) and personal medical or dental expenses.

- Respondents reported heightened stress or anxiety (65 percent); difficulty sleeping (49 percent); increased financial worries (43 percent); depression or hopelessness (37 percent); new or increased health problems (26 percent).

- Time was listed at the most significant sacrifice, although most considered caregiving as a labor of love and did it willingly.

These numbers represent significant emotional and physical investments of time and energy, in addition to the financial investment. The feelings associated with investments can be both positive and negative at the same time, which I call a natural yo-yo of emotions.

RESENTMENT/GUILT—IT'S A NATURAL YO-YO OF EMOTIONS

Many of is face being part of the Sandwich Generation with various feelings, skills, and attitudes. The feelings are often bottled up; our parents are our history, our source of life, sometimes our source of guilt, fear, anxiety, and love. Contrasting feelings and a yo-yo of emotions can occur. This is a natural and somewhat normal roller coaster of emotions for a non-normal situation. We don't have control over some of the changes that occur, and we must deal with the emotions that accompany this change. "Regardless of whether the changes come swiftly or slowly, they play havoc with our emotions, and we are forced to deal with what I have come to think of as the bridge between anger and acceptance."[10] This chapter will express these feelings and ways to cope with or expand those feelings.

Immediate feelings and emotions related to our sandwich that come to mind include both good and not-so-good feelings. When Tally was born with spina bifida and several other serious medical complications, life thrust us into a swirl of emotions and challenges. We had no control over the situation. We learned about various normal categories of feelings and emotions and supports that we should seek when we were on overload. We tried to educate ourselves, look at the positives, advocate, and stay true to our feelings and convictions. We tried to create some sense of normalcy as a family. (Chapter three has more discussion and definitions of normalcy.)

Suzanne Mintz states,
"It isn't an easy thing to do, recreate normalcy when you've been hit by what feels like the equivalent of an atomic blast, and yet that is what is expected of us, and indeed what we always strive to do. But I have come to realize that for my family and other caregiving families, normalcy is very different than it is for families

---

[10]   ___ Mintz, 2002. Love, Honor & Value: A Family Caregiver Speaks Out about the Chices & Challenges of Caregiving. Herndon, VAL Capital Books, Inc., p. 34

that don't have to deal with disability, with the almost perverse attention to the basic acts of life that come with it, and the myriad arrangements we must make to do ordinary things."[11]

When Tally was born, we did seek support and tried to find supports for our children as well. We knew the risks and tried to prevent more challenges when we could and prepare and deal with the challenges we had no control over. This problem-solving and version of normalcy assisted us when facing our sandwich.

When we proposed to have my parents move down to Kansas from Minnesota and into the cottage next to us, this was a choice that we had some control over. Although was a *huge* commitment, we had control over the main plan, and we could set the parameters and coordinate and integrate the plan into our daily lives as best we could. Many feelings surrounded this time—and intensify as we continue our sandwiched lives, including both good and not-so-good feelings. I have tried to summarize these below:

THE NOT-SO-GOOD FEELINGS OF BEING IN THE SANDWICH

GUILT

Our parents were there for us, but are we there for them? Society seems to have made some options to assuage our guilt over not being there for our parents: nursing homes, assisted living, agencies for care in the home. Although these are often justified services, they also assist us in dealing with our guilt.

---

[11]   ___Mintz. 2008. Mintz, S. Finding Normalcy in a Caregiving Life. *Take Care: Self-Care for the Family Caregiver.* National Family Caregivers Association Newsletter, Winter, 2008, p. 2.

Then there are guilt gifts. When we don't have the time or do not make the time to be with our aging parents, we buy them things. Some of us do this with our children as well. I've done it. Besides my enjoyment in buying fun and educational toys (part of my early childhood passion), I would buy gifts while at a conference, or spend a little more on Christmas gifts when I was feeling bad about spending too much time away from my dear children. It was a temporary fix, as time was the greatest gift I could give them. I believe the same goes for our aging parents.

RESENTMENT

As much as you want to deny it, it's there. There is a disruption of life, no matter what level of involvement you have in caring for your parents. If you are in the Sandwich Generation, there is resentment and guilt that you are taking away time from your own family when you are caring for your aging parents. If you contribute monetary support, you may think of what you could have done for your own family or yourself with that money. If there are siblings who are not doing their part or contributing with time, money, or resources, there may be resentment there as well. Once you have made a commitment to a level of care or coordinating care, there may be resentment for making the commitment. When I missed some of my children's activities because I spent the evening in the emergency room with one of my parents, there was resentment—and then there was guilt for feeling the resentment. I also resented not having any other family members close enough to take on more of the responsibility. I resented others' spontaneity, when I had made a commitment to evening care for my mom. We had to work, coordinate, and plan ahead to take any kind of family trip, even a day trip. Once you admit and allow the resentment, it feels better—but then the guilt may follow. It can be a cycle or natural yo-yo of emotions.

FEAR AND ANXIETY

Fear can permeate your life, if you let it. There is much to fear. I fear the present, and I fear the future. I can generally let go of the past, but there are times when I fear for our sanity in having made this decision. In the morning, I pray to make it through the day as the sequence and responsibility of the day rushes through my brain. I fear how I will cope if a if a provider calls and can't make it and I have to teach a class, attend a meeting, or give a final; I fear that a provider could take advantage of my mom or our daughter (e.g., steal from or neglect—which has happened); I fear that we may not have enough money to make it through the month; I fear I have taken on too much; and I fear that stress and anxiety may get the best of me. Most of all, I fear that something may happen to Fletch or me, and one of us could not possibly handle our sandwich alone. One of the greatest fears that parents of children with special needs have is what will happen to the child when the parents are gone. I have tears in my eyes just putting this on paper. Planning ahead, arranging a "safety net" when things go wrong, and basic problem-solving when you have no safety net can battle some fear. Documenting and journaling your feelings can be a release. Again, professional help can assist with handling the fear and putting a plan into place for those nightmares.

I also fear for the well-being of other elders if they do not have the support like we have given my parents. I fear that our country will not focus on the needed programs to keep older folks in their homes, if they wish, or to give them choices and dignity during the last years, months, and days of life. I fear that society has made it okay to basically dump our aging parents in nursing homes or hospitals for someone else to handle the hard times. I fear the "Me Generation" may not take the time or prioritize supports for the older population, even though there will be many more of us in the future.

There is always anxiety. We worry about our parents' or children's health, the quality of medical professionals and providers, getting the needed services, our immediate family needs, finances (discussed in chapter nine), and general anxiety about balancing life. This worry and anxiety can take over our entire being. Stress relief is critical but often is not utilized until we are beyond the level that affects our health. (See chapter eleven for resources and tips for respite and relaxation—a must!)

ANGER AND FRUSTRATION

"Anger is an emotion we have been taught to try to hide, but these days I think of it as a very healthy emotion, one that reminds us that we are very much alive and that we burn with the fire of desire for the good things of life"[12] You will feel anger and frustration with the system (Medicaid, Medicare, insurance companies, agencies); with family members who don't understand the importance, effort, time, and energy that it takes to be in and undertake the responsibilities of the sandwich; with a few providers who prove to be less than trustworthy (stealing money, meds, and trust itself); or the general misunderstanding and lack of awareness or support that exists related to caring for our aging population. We have

---

[12] ___Mintz. 2008. Finding Normalcy in a Caregiving Life. *Take Care: Self-Care for the Family Caregiver.* National Family Caregivers Association Newsletter, Winter, 2008, p. 12.

found that putting this anger and frustration into advocacy and awareness efforts helps. Journaling can help. Some anger and frustration flows out my fingers, through my computer, and onto this page. This project helps me get the feelings out and may help someone else with the feelings within his or her own sandwich.

CONFUSION/AMBIVALENCE

There will be mixed feelings and uncertainty about what you're doing and conflicting feelings about whatever level of involvement you may have. Other family members may also be confused as to why you would choose to be a caregiver for your parents.

TRUST/BROKEN TRUST

Trust could be placed under the good and the not-so-good categories. I believe that, by nature, I can be naive, gullible, and trusting. I have become a bit wiser (although Fletch may not agree). I tend to believe in and trust people, which is not always my best asset. I have learned to ask myself, "Can I really trust anyone?" My answer some days is, "Very few," but when you find those few, hang on to them. No one is perfect. You look at the important aspects and look past some others. We have used providers who have stolen money and medications—and who knows what else? Others have left during their shift, quit doing tasks (leaving them for others to do), and even have had my mom or my daughter sign papers when we were not present. Each situation where a provider has lost our trust has made it that much more difficult to trust the next provider. Happily, there are those providers, medical professionals, and therapists, who have earned our trust. Their work and professionalism results in our loved ones thriving, learning new skills, or getting the help they need. Trust is essential, but once it is broken, it is difficult to earn it back. Trust makes collaboration work, and collaboration is crucial when caring for loved ones.

FEELINGS ASSOCIATED WITH CHANGE OF ROLES

Our parents are our history and our source of life. They have been there for us our entire lives. It is natural for us to care for our children and their basic needs—changing diapers, feeding, bathing, dressing, transporting, and meeting various other physical and emotional needs. It feels different—sometimes uncomfortable and even strange—for some of us to assist our parents with these same daily living needs.

I feel it is important to set your own guidelines for levels of care with which you are comfortable. Personally, I had trouble helping my dad with some of these self-care tasks and procedures. With my mom, it was much easier. As a result, I would have the hired provider assist my dad. Now, with only my mom, I do more direct care than I did when my dad was living and care required meeting both of their needs. At first, I felt guilt about this; then I allowed myself to be honest and respect my own feelings.

Roles will change—this cannot be overemphasized! It is essential to understand the role change and how this affects the parent/child relationship, as well as parent/grandchild, mother-in-law/daughter-in-law, sibling or whatever other relationship your situation might present. There may not be time to work on any unresolved issues in relationships of the past, as the situation is usually in crisis mode by the time the family realizes or is willing to intervene. As the need for care increases, family members should consider the level of care that they are able to provide; the type of professional involvement that is needed; the family's history and patterns when resolving issues; how the parents dealt with the care of their own parents and grandparents; sibling relations; and siblings and one's own feelings regarding parents' decisions about their future.

I believe that our parents must have ownership in decisions and be a part of discussions. This is also a matter of respect. It also is a matter of change of roles.

Depression/Sadness

Watching your loved one, who once cared for you and once had energy and ambition in life, fail and become dependent on others for daily living activities and even bodily functions can be difficult, sad, and depressing. Seeing one of your parents lose the other is also very sad. You may have lost a parent, but he or she has lost a partner in life. My mom and dad were married for sixty-four years. My mom misses my dad every day. I can't imagine living life without Fletch. Sensitivity to this loss is important. Old pictures, videos, and stories are important to encourage and help with this process for both you and your surviving parent. Again, professional help may be needed if depression and sadness permeate your life and interfere with your daily functioning.

These not-so-good feelings are natural and should be acknowledged. The danger is when one of these feelings takes over your life and perseverates. If you are stuck in one of these feelings or times, seek help. Know that sometimes you need support to validate your feelings and to move on, to see the positives, and to see and feel the good.

THE GOOD FEELINGS OF BEING IN THE SANDWICH

HONOR

I do not think I could honor and respect my parents more than I have in this process. It has been an honor to care for them. That does not deny the daily hard work, time, and effort it takes to plan and coordinate. It is simply an honor that not everyone has in life. This particularly hits me when I talk with people who have lost their parents before they had a chance to be a part of their lives in their "golden years." This was true for Fletch, as he lost his mom when he was twenty-three years old. She never got to see him marry, see her grandchildren, or enjoy a long life with her love, Fletch's dad. I think this may drive some of the commitment he has for caring for my parents. We will do the same for his dad, in terms of promoting the choices he has, if and when the time comes that he needs our help. Fletch's dad turned ninety-one this month and still lives alone in his own home.

RESPECT

What we do and the choices we make stem from respect for the human condition, respect for our parents and our children, and respect for life itself. Our decisions for Tally, from the day she was born, were based on our respect and value for life and quality of life. After supporting her through three surgeries during her first week of life and nine in her first year, we were further committed to supporting and advocating for her out of our love and respect. The work we did with sibling groups (Sibshops—workshops for siblings of children who have special needs, developed by Don Meyer) resulted from our respect for the feelings and issues with which Cassie and Mikelle were dealing. Children are suddenly thrown into a host of feelings and issues when a sibling with special needs arrives in the family. Now, our efforts to give my mom (and as we did for my dad) a safe, comfortable place and space of her own are based on respect. This all sounds wonderful and admirable, but it does not come without a price, physically and emotionally.

PRIDE/JOY

I feel true pride and joy when I see my mom at our dinner table most nights. I felt joy, seeing my parents sit on the deck, eating their popcorn on a beautiful fall day or taking my mom down to our pond to feed the fish with Tally on spring, summer, and fall evenings. I felt pride when my mom got involved in advocacy efforts for accessibility in the community. I felt pride when our two older daughters were willing to contribute hours, days, and years of their lives to assist with caregiving for their grandma and sister. I feel pride when I see my sweet Fletch do all that he does for my mom, Tally, and me on a daily basis. I feel joy seeing Tally and Mother share precious time together at the supper table and in the evenings, sharing the day's happenings. This would never have happened if my mom had been in another setting. I will *never* regret what we have done for my parents, particularly for my mom. With no regrets, I feel pride, joy, and love.

LOVE

Love is at the core of what we do. I learned love—unconditional love—from my parents. Love is how I continue to do what I do. Love motivates me to get up in the morning, face each day as positively as I can, and do the best I can do.

This discussion of the range of emotions in this chapter illustrates the mixed bag of feelings that goes with being in "the sandwich." The emotional yo-yo is inescapable, no matter how much you are or are not involved with the care of your aging parent.

Sharon Jayson, in a 2007 *USA Today* article, wrote that dealing with a range of emotions is common when caring for an aging parent:

"Ambivalence is common—even a good relationship doesn't prevent mixed feelings. There's often some anger and resentment as unresolved family issues resurface. And there's plenty of guilt."[13] Jayson also reported that "A *USA Today*/ABC News/Gallup poll of five hundred boomers with living parents found that 31 percent of them are providing financial or personal care assistance to a parent. Slightly less than half of those providing help say it has caused them some stress or a great deal of stress, show the poll, conducted May 24–June 3, 2007."[14]

Roberta Satow, a sociology professor at Brooklyn College, was quoted in Jayson's article: "No matter how much you love your parents, it's going to disrupt your life." Jayson also notes that one woman who is currently caring for her eighty-four-year-old mother-in-law, overseeing her eighty-six-year-old mother, and caregiving her grandchildren relieves her stress with one or two gambling trips a year, traveling with her husband, or overindulging on food. She states, "You deal with a lot of ups and downs. You get frustrated. You want to be able to help your parents, but you don't want your own health to go downhill."[15] According to Jayson, caregivers may feel they are not doing enough; they may sacrifice their jobs, family members, even spouses or children to care for their parents. She adds: "Whether adult

---

[13] Sharon Jayson. June 26, 2007. Caregivers Cope with Stress, Mixed Emotions about Aging Parents. *USA Today*:
[14] Ibid.
[15] Ibid.

children have day-to-day caregiving tasks or periodically swoop in from afar, the ever-mounting difficulties faced by their elderly parents keep life out of balance. Emergencies and interruptions become commonplace as this legion of empty nesters, retirees, and the Sandwich Generation still raising kids navigates the uncharted waters of today's increased longevity." [16]

Jayson describes "complex families"—the issues of stepparents; how remarriage affects obligations to older parents; and older first-time parents having fewer children resulting in having older parents sooner and fewer brothers and sisters to assist. She also includes "long-distance care" where adult children oversee care from a distance, which can increase stress and anxiety because they can't observe firsthand; guilt for not being there for their parents when needed; and the emotional tug-of-war that goes with this.

She concludes her article with results from an interesting federally funded health and retirement study, completed by Douglas Wolf, professor of aging studies at Syracuse University. Wolf found adverse health consequences for those who don't share in daily caregiving. Jayson quoted Wolf as stating: "If you have a parent who needs help and you're not providing help, then your mental health score goes down. If you have a parent who needs help and you do provide help, your mental health score goes down. It's no worse to be a caregiver than to not be a caregiver."[17] This is a really meaningful article and I suggest checking it out:

"Caregivers Cope with Stress, Mixed Emotions about Aging Parents" by Sharon Jayson, in *USA Today* June 26, 2007.

---

[16] Ibid.
[17] Ibid.

(http://www.usatoday.com/money/perfi/eldercare/2007-06-25-elder-care-emotional-support_N.htm)

What We've Learned

- Some things you can control; some you can't.
- Choices are important for everyone, and so is respect.
- Being honest with your feelings, both good and bad, is a key to sanity!

Quotes

"I invite you to recognize the emotions that caregiving has evoked in you; to embrace the inner strength that comes from dealing successfully with difficult situations; and to try to move beyond the frustration, the sadness, the isolation, and the other difficult emotions that so often come with being a family caregiver."

—S. Mintz

"Begin the process of managing guilt by telling the truth about what you regret."

—Joy Loverde

According to Loverde, guilt may stem from regrets we have experienced about the past and relationships. We may feel the guilt for regretting not doing something kind or thanking our parents for something in the past.

"No matter how much you love your parents, it's going to disrupt your life."

—Roberta Satow,
a sociology professor at Brooklyn College

"The costs associated with caregiving are enormous. It's time for legislators to take note and to take action to help America's family caregivers."

—National Family Caregivers Association

TIPS AND TOOLS

- "Everyday Heroes: Juggling Work, Guilt, and the Slacker Sibling An Interview with Joy Loverde"

  http://www.mycarecommunity.org/Default. aspx?tabid=336

- Jayson, Sharon. 2007. Caregivers Cope with Stress, Mixed Emotions about Aging Parents. *USA Today.*

  http://www.usatoday.com/money/perfi/eldercare/2007-06-25-elder-care-emotional-support_N.htm

- Loverde, Joy. *The Complete Eldercare Planner, Second Edition: Where to Start, Which Questions to Ask, and How to Find Help.* New York: Three Rivers Press, 2000.

- Mintz, S. Finding Normalcy in a Caregiving Life. *Take Care: Self-Care for the Family Caregiver.* National Family Caregivers Association Newsletter, Winter, 2008.

- New Study Reveals the High Financial Cost of Caring for an Older Loved One. *Take Care: Self-Care for the Family Caregiver.* National Family Caregivers Association. Winter 2008.

Chapter 5

ORGANIZATION

BOXES, BOXES, BOXES

My husband and I spent a spring afternoon, after my parents had moved to Kansas, going through boxes in the garage, as we did on several afternoons when we could make the time. It wasn't something I was eager to do, but I tried to do a bit at a time. I can't get motivated enough to go through my own boxes of stuff that have managed to make it from move to move without being rearranged, let alone go through my parents' boxes. I must admit, it was with some resentment that I made time to do this. I looked at it, however, as time with my husband, and it could possibly be considered as quality time, particularly when we found something that would unveil a bit more of why I was the way I was.

My parents saved *every* card from every birthday, Christmas, Easter, and Valentine's Day; every pamphlet, every warrantee, every guide and instruction manual. I would make it through an entire box of hundreds of cards—stationery browned, smelly, and curled with age—to find a precious envelope of pictures from former generations or a picture of Mother around age two, clutching her only doll, smiling from ear to ear. (See below.)

Treasures in boxes, boxes, boxes! My mom at age two.

As my oldest daughter came through the garage that day after finishing her shift taking care of Grandma, she observed the many boxes filled with papers—some significant, some not. I vowed to do by best to *not* leave boxes and boxes of papers for her to go through when I died. Fletch and I have our own room of boxes in the basement to go through, left over from our last two moves. Cassie sat down and went through several boxes with me. It was also revealing for her, yet reinforced her current pattern of not saving of every little thing. We made a goal of how many to go through, consolidating several, and making sure we kept treasures and things my mom would enjoy going through, and we placed those things in a special box for my mom.

MORE BOXES, BOXES, BOXES!

The home-care providers in Minnesota, where my parents had lived, helped with much of the packing—some with skill and care, others by literally dumping possessions into boxes. Several things were broken; some were antiques. Some boxes were actually filled with trash! We opened one box that was packed with a bag of garbage—some pretty stinky banana peels!

We tried to divide pictures and gave each family the boxes of pictures from their own family. My younger brother, who had been through a nasty divorce, getting none of the pictures of his children, welcomed these photos. My oldest sister, the family historian, has lovingly made copies of many of the old and frail photos. Her organizational skills have been a gift to this process! My husband would make sure that she had a few boxes to take home with after each visit. My middle sister had dozens of boxes of her own and was preparing a move, so she didn't take many of our parents' boxes, but welcomed the photos and precious items Mother would select for her. For my oldest brother, who visits less often, Mother selects gifts from boxes (like the special Bible that was given to my dad by his parents for his high school graduation), and we pack up photos to send with my middle sister or younger brother, who see him more often. I do feel it is important to keep the communication open and going with all family members, even if it is only one way.

Being economical and watching every penny for Mother, we had to get a bit creative with gifts. Mother loves plants and had many, many given to her after my dad's funeral. For the first year, she took cuttings from the plants and gave each child and nearby grandchildren plants for their birthdays. We bought nicely colored pots, and she helped plant them. It was very special, she was able to assist with this, and it was a gift from the heart. She would also give special rocks and shells from my dad's rock collection. We would put several out on a tray and each month, she would choose which ones to give to each child, grandchild, or great-grandchild. She also had many trinkets, glassware, and plaques with sayings on them. She would select items with the individual person in mind, and we'd help her wrap these up with the rock and shell treasures, and she would select and sign the card for the occasion. I believe everyone enjoyed these special gifts from her.

I utilized some of the old photos for my own gift giving. We would scan and zoom in on old small photos, nicely frame them, and use them for gifts. Sometimes we would crop to only include part of the picture or people. With five children in my family, there were not many photos with just one of us with either parent. We zoomed in on nice photos of a parent and an individual child or photos of us kids.

Here is an old picture—found in one of the boxes—of my brother Don and me. We have leaves in our hands, pretending we were trees! I blew it up and gave it to him for his birthday.

I would advise thinning, thinning, and more thinning out things. I think gradually is best. When I would return home to Minnesota after visiting my parents in the last years before my they moved to Kansas, I would take whatever they wanted to give, even if I had no use for it, to help them thin out things. We tried the three-box approach, labeling them "keep," "yard sale," and "toss," but somehow almost everything ended up in the "keep" boxes. My mother did live through the Great Depression, and saved *everything*. (I am certain many of her digestive problems came from eating food that had been saved in the fridge for too long.) The boxes we went through included stacks of Styrofoam containers, recycled plastic plates and cups, lids of all sizes, and anything plastic. Fletch says it all has to do with the "box in your head"—the "emotional box" filled with memories—that cannot be given or thrown away. It's as if by throwing it away, you're throwing the memory away. I've thought we might try what we used to do with our children's precious art projects made of mud or other materials that would not last—take a picture. We'd still have the memory, but it would last and take up less space. Documentation is important. With the use of digital cameras, computers, flash drives, and disks, we can save and document much more in less space.

There are dozens upon dozens of organizational books that offer helpful techniques, but when it comes to a ninety-two-year-old making use of these techniques, such tips are relatively useless, particularly when organization is not a priority.

We save all of the cards sent from my mom to my dad and vice versa, and pull them out near the birthday and anniversary dates. We keep boxes of letters and cards always at her side, and she spends hours reading through them and having others read them to her. My sister's thought was to go through all the cards, cutting the fronts off to make new cards—a nice recycling idea. I have also thought of trying to sell items on eBay to give my mom more money for care costs (with her permission, of course). We collectively gave her a computer for her ninetieth birthday and have thought we might get her involved in the eBay postings and bids.

Let me share a few rules that we made, as our garage had been taken over by boxes after my parents' move to Kansas. You also have to understand that our garage (or as I call it, our "barnage") usually holds a van, a car, and hay; it also serves as a tack room for the horse and an art studio for Fletch (he makes large wooden sculptures). It now holds my mom's and dad's scooters; my daughter's old wheelchairs; Christmas trees; other assorted items; and shelves and shelves of boxes, boxes, boxes.

We don't have many hard rules in our household, but these are with the rules by which we try to adhere:

- Once a box goes out of the garage, it doesn't go back in. It can go in someone's car or be unpacked, but cannot go back in the garage.

- If you come to visit, you take at least take one box to sort through.

- Consolidating counts—if you narrow down two boxes into one that works too!

ORGANIZATION WITH MENUS—THE SANDWICH IS EVIDENT!

Much of our lives has to do with organization and coordinating. We make menus for two to three weeks, keeping in mind the diet restrictions (my mom now has severe diverticulitis) and preferences (Tally has several). I keep this on my computer for reference when making new menus. Fletch formerly tried to shop one day a week but usually found himself going back for meds or other needed items in between.

When making the menus, we see clear examples of sandwiched accommodations. Fletch is the cook at our house, but I help with the menus. We have to consider each day's events and the schedule for the week.

On Thursdays, Tally is at her apartment, my mom has a caregiver for the evenings, and Fletch and I have a date night. We cook things that night that we both enjoy and that Tally or my mom do not. We include Tally's and Mother's favorites other nights. My mom had always done the cooking, so I think it's a treat for her to have others cook. She loves Fletch's cooking. For my mother, we have to consider her teeth problems. We individualize her plate with whatever the menu is, but we usually choose something easy to chew (not steak), or we food-process her meat. Now, with diverticulitis, she is limited to no seeds, no fresh fruits or vegetables, no pulp—it is very difficult for her, as she loves fresh fruits and vegetables. (I sometimes attempt to hide the salad on the table, to avoid her longing look at the tomatoes she can no longer have.)

ORGANIZATION FOR TALLY

Each semester, we spend time orchestrating Tally's schedule, blending it with Fletcher's and mine. With Fletch and I teaching classes and needing to assist with Tally's transportation, and with some care needed during the day, it becomes a true exercise in organization. I call it organization orchestration. Organizing her supports for each day and then working with the providers' schedules becomes mind-boggling at times, but again, the planning can make or break the success of her day and her semester. Here is an example of one of her semesters' schedules. I included the entire week to give you a picture of the coming, going, transportation, and supports needed throughout each week of the semester.

TALLY'S DETAILED FALL 2008 SCHEDULE (REVISED 8/19/08)

MONDAY

9:00 Up, ready for day
Work on homework
11:30 Lunch, self-care
12:30 Leave for class w/Mom
1:00–2:00 Reading class (instructor's name and class location)
2:00 To orchestra late. Needs transportation – Dad?
2:00 Orchestra (instructor's name and class location)
3:00 Provider #1. Self-care at music building. Needs assistance
Snack (in backpack)
Head for E.S. class:
4:00–6:00 Earth Science. Provider #1 assists (Instructor's name and class location)
6:00 Back home. Dinner w/ Mom or Dad or dinner w/ Provider #1 at apartment
9:30 Shower. Bedtime routine
Dressing, bathroom, tooth brushing, hygiene, ROM - range of motion (to stretch muscles in areas of her body she could not move) check skin for pressure sores

TUESDAY

8:00 Up, ready, self-care, etc.

9:30–11:30 Independent study at preschool on campus; back to Mom's office

11:30 Lunch, self-care on campus (Mom has class at 12:30)

1:15 Dad meets you at Mom's office, transport to orchestra

2:00–3:00 Orchestra. Dad will transport, if needed
(Instructor's name and class location)

3:00 Provider #2.Self-care at music building. Needs assistance

Snack (in backpack)

Head for E.S. class:

4:00–6:00 Earth Science. Provider #2 assists
(Instructor's name and class location)

6:00 Back home. Dinner w/ Mom or Dad?

9:30 Bedtime routine

Dressing, bathroom, tooth brushing, hygiene, ROM, check skin for pressure sores

WEDNESDAY

9:00 Up, ready for day

Work on homework

11:30 Lunch, self-care

12:30 Leave for class w/Mom

1:00–2:00 Reading class (Instructor's name and class location)

2:00 To orchestra late. Needs transportation – Dad

2:00 Orchestra (instructor's name and class location)

3:00 Provider #2. Self-care at music building. Needs assistance

Snack (in backpack)

Head for E.S. class:

4:00–6:00 Earth science lab. Provider #2 assists (Instructor's name and class location)

6:00 Back home. Dinner w/ Mom or Dad?

9:30 Shower. Bedtime routine

Dressing, bathroom, tooth brushing, hygiene, ROM, check skin for pressure sores

THURSDAY

9:00 Up, ready, shower

Work on homework

11:30 Lunch, self-care on campus (Mom has class at 12:30)

1:15 Dad meets you at Mom's office, transport to orchestra

2:00–3:00 Orchestra. Dad will transport at 1:40 from Mom's office

3:00 Violin lesson

3:30 Provider # 1 meets Tally after violin lesson in music building, walks back to apartment

Self-care. Needs assistance

6:00 Back to apartment and overnight with Provider #1

When chooses, bedtime routine

Dressing, bathroom, tooth brushing, hygiene, ROM, check skin for pressure sores

FRIDAY—NO CLASS

9:00 Up

Work on homework, sometimes on campus

Independent study, journaling, work on Internet classes

Back home

12:00 Lunch

1:00 Self-care

Work on homework, stretch out and ride Midnight [Tally's horse]

Needs assistance, three adults (two side walkers and one leader)

5:00 Self-care

6:00 Dinner

10:00 Start bedtime routine

Dressing, bathroom, tooth brushing, hygiene, ROM

Transfer to bed. Needs assistance

SATURDAY

9:00 Up, ready

Shower

Work on homework. Needs assistance

Weightlifting, ROM. Needs assistance

12:00 Lunch

1:00 Self-care

Work on homework. Needs assistance

Stretch out and ride Midnight. Needs assistance, three adults (two side walkers and one leader)

5:00 Self-care

6:00 Dinner

10:00 Start bedtime routine

Dressing, bathroom, tooth brushing, hygiene, ROM, check skin for pressure sores

SUNDAY

9:00 Up, shower, ready

Work on homework. Needs assistance

Weightlifting, ROM. Needs assistance

12:00 Lunch. Needs assistance with food prep

1:00 Self-care. Needs assistance

Work on homework. Needs assistance

4:00 Stretch out and ride Midnight. Needs assistance, three adults (two side walkers and one leader)

5:00 Self-care

5:15 Dinner

10:00 Start bedtime routine, dressing, bathroom, tooth brushing, hygiene, ROM, check skin for pressure sores

* * * * *

CAROL'S SCHEDULE

EL 310:

Mon. 2:00–3:50 PM   (Class and location)

CED 326/327

Tues. & Thurs. 12:30–1:50 PM   (Class and location)

Tues. 3:30 – Meetings (location)

Work on Web classes (Class and location)

* * * * *

FLETCH'S SCHEDULE

M/W   3:00–4:00 PM (Class and location)

T/R   12:00–1:00 PM (Class and location)

* * * * *

CONTACTS

Tally's Cell: _____   Carol's Cell: _____

Fletch's Cell: _____   Mikelle's Cell: _____

Tally apartment phone: __   Russells' home phone: __

ORGANIZATION FOR MOTHER

Planning ahead for Mother makes a big difference in my stress level, particularly when it comes to scheduling providers. I try to plan two months in advance, at least in draft form. Each semester brings on new schedules for our providers, most of whom are also students. This is *very* time-consuming, but planning ahead makes it work better for everyone. (More information about hiring and scheduling providers can be found in chapter six.)

We have a general schedule for my mom, although it's is more of a sequence than exact timing of the schedule.

MOTHER'S DETAILED SCHDULE

Gladys Deye's Schedule
(More of a sequence of the day; times are flexible)

8:30-ish Wake up, to commode (5 min)
    On commode (10–20 min)
8:50 To living room, transfers, ROM (15 min)
9:05 Make breakfast, give meds, Maalox, eye drops, ear-

drops, heat to neck (30 min+). Has been eating at table or tray Music or *Little House*

9:35–11:00 Eating breakfast, with assistance (90 min) Could read devotions, book, music or *Little House*

11:00 To bathroom, transfers, toileting help, help brush teeth (40 + min)

11:40–12:55:

On shower days, head massage, shower, hair washed (1hr. 15) Other days, maybe games, devotions, or rest

12:55–1:20 Get dressed, do hair, put on hose (30 min)

1:20 Hand exercises (OT recommended 2 times each day)

1:20 Make lunch, cut up, get meds, Maalox, etc. (20 min)

1:40–3:10 Eating lunch. During that time clean, vacuum, dust, do dishes, laundry, pick up bedroom, living room, general upkeep (90 min)

3:10 To bathroom, transfers, toileting help, help brush teeth (40+ min)

3:50 Assist taking outside, working on a project, games (45 min–1 hour)

4:50 Resting

5:30 To bathroom, transfers, toileting help (20–30 min)

6:00 Make dinner, cut up, get meds, Maalox, eye drops, eardrops, heat to neck (30 min+)

6:30–8:00 Eating dinner with assistance (90 min) Hand exercises (OT recommended 2 times each day)

9:30 To bathroom, transfers, toileting help, help brush teeth (40 + min)

10 or 10:30-ish Clothes off, in pajamas, eye drops, Vicks on toes, evening meds, back rub, foot soak & foot rub

(all recommended by dr. for circulation), sponge bath
if not shower (1 hr–1½ hr.)
To bed.

- She enjoys watching *Little House* and movies, but please try
  to do games, reading, etc., so she isn't watching TV most
  of the time. Thanks!

* * * * *

Night support: Usually up 2–3 times or so at night. Help with
commode, transfers, toileting help (approximately 20–30 min
each time)

Not included:

- Shopping
- Going to appointments
- Going to church or Bible class
- Transportation
- Setting up meds
- Pick up prescription from clinic, take to Wal-Mart, wait at
  least 20 min. for pick up – All takes about 1 hr.
- Assisting control of environment (TV on & selection; mu-
  sic; lights; locking doors; opening blinds)

Total approximately 13 hrs. 30 min. (*not* including night
support)

MEDS LIST—READY TO GO!

Keeping current lists of medication, allergies, and general condition needs to go with the person whenever and wherever he or she goes. This list should be in the backpack, ready to go and easy to access. This is the first thing the EMTs will need when you call the ambulance or head for the emergency room. The computer helps! My daughter Cassie put together this list of meds, primary health problems, surgery history, and allergies, so we would have it ready in the backpack of my mom's wheelchair, so if she had an emergency, the information was there and at hand. We also made copies of her identification and insurance cards, so she would have that information without having the original with her. We updated it, as needed, assuring the last date of revision was listed. Here is an example of that list:

MEDS LIST, ETC., FOR GLADYS M. DEYE
Gladys Deye's Meds (Oct. 1, 2007)

Name	Amount	Time
Lisinopril	10mg (1/2 tab)	8 AM
Klor-Con M10		8 AM & 5 PM
Prilosec OTC	20 mg	8 AM & 5 PM
Colace	100mg	8 AM & 5 PM
Maalox	15cc	with meals
Lanoxin	0.125 mg	8 AM, MWF
Evista	60mg	8 AM
Sprionolactone	25mg	8 AM, MWF
Glucosamine/ Chondroiton		12 noon & 5 PM (holding)
Calcium 600 + D		8 AM & 12 noon
Lasix	80mg	8 AM
Coumadin	1mg	5 PM (holding)
Zinc	50mg	12 noon
Citalopram	20mg	8 AM
Lovastatin	20mg	5 PM
Cranberry		5 PM (holding)

Multivitamin	daily	12 noon
Fish Oil		12 noon (holding)
Super B-complex		12 noon (holding)
Meloxicam	7.5 mg	8 AM
Oxycodone	10mg ER	9 AM & 9 PM
Oxycodone	5mg	for breakthrough pain
Creon		3x/day

Primary Health Problems

Atrial Fib., ASHD, LEE edema, acute renal failure, compression FX, osteoporosis, hyatal hernia, diverticulitis, chronic UTI, rt arm break

Past Surgery History

Both knee replacement
Hysterectomy
Umbilical hernia repair

Allergies

Pentothal
Sulfer
PeNi
Latex
Talcum powder
Iodine

PILL, PILLS, PILLS

Observe closely, how your loved one is doing with medications, both organizing and taking them. This can be a key to checking how he or she is doing with memory and other skills of daily living. Taking small steps in assisting is better than taking over and crushing the self-esteem and desire for independence.

Our nighttime provider is certified in medication dispensing, which has been a godsend and has saved me many hours of making sense of the meds, as my mom takes different medication on various days throughout the week.

We've learned that the multiple and mega-pills that my

mom takes go down much easier with applesauce or yo-gurt—or even ice cream—than with fluids. Mother used to gulp down numerous pills, then stick her tongue with a "la-la-la" to show that they were gone. This did entertain our girls when they were younger, but as Mother got older, this "pill trick" was more difficult for her. That was when we got the idea of using something smooth to aid the swallow. I first used bananas, but she didn't particularly care for this. Then we tried applesauce—and it worked beautifully! Now she takes great pride in carefully arranging five or six pills at a time in her overflowing spoon of applesauce. It does take some fine-motor control, which is more difficult some days than others, but it's much easier than just gulping down the pills.

Mother taking pills with applesauce—it works!

General Fact Sheet

Another piece of information that I kept with Mother, particularly when we infrequently used the adult day services at a local retirement center, was a fact sheet about her. An example is below:

Gladys M. Deye
(pronounced like "die")

Carol L. Russell – Daughter
Home phone: _____
Work phone: _____OR call _____ **& they can find me**
Emergency Cell: _____

Need to know:

- Torn rotator cuffs in both shoulders, so hold under arms if needing to assist with transfer

- Cracked vertebrae in neck

- Knee replacements in both knees (twice)

- Needs wheelchair for mobility but cannot roll self due to her torn rotator cuffs

- Needs help with transfers; definitely stand by or use gait belt for safety

- Needs help in bathroom with wiping, & we put Prep. H on each time, even if no bowel movement

- Can feed self, but needs help serving food and cutting up meat or anything not soft

- Needs lots of water. Likes ice chips with straw & spoon

- Likes tea with milk & sugar with meal

- Takes Maalox after each meal

- May need Tylenol if headache or pain in shoulders

- We'll take care of other meds at home

* NEEDS TO HAVE FEET UP AS MUCH AS POSSIBLE, DUE TO BETTER CIRCULATION

- Loves to meet people, tell about children/grandchildren/ great-grandchildren

- Husband, Armin, was a minister; married for sixty-four years, passed away

- 2+ years ago

- Wrote a cookbook. She's working on signing over 600 of them, for sale $12.95

- *Sweet, sweet, sweet lady!*

* * * * *

Here's another general list for care at home, when orienting new providers:

Reminders for Gladys Deye's Care

General

- Please keep the air conditioner at 78°.

- Do not turn off the icemaker.

- To save on water, please wait to run the dishwasher or clothes washer until a full load is ready.

- Any time Gladys is sitting in the blue chair, make sure the chair controller is out of her reach; she has been known to try getting up unassisted, which obviously is dangerous!

- While Gladys needs a good amount of rest, she loves to go outside, play games, or listen to books. Please take advantage of this and try to get the TV off as much as possible.

- Gladys' favorite show on TV is *Little House on the Prairie*. It is on M–F at 9 & 10 AM, as well as 2 & 3 PM on channel 312.

- At bedtime, be sure to raise both of the railings on the side of the bed.

- Please open blinds in the AM, unlock back door, and open blinds on door (that way, I know she's awake). In the evening, particularly on hot days, close front blinds, as the sun gets pretty warm.

Mobility and Joints

- Torn rotator cuffs in both shoulders, so hold under arms if needed, to assist with transfer.

- Cracked vertebrae in neck, so we use blue roll pillow behind her neck while in chair in bed.

- Knee replacements in both knees (twice), so watch for weakness with transfers

- Needs wheelchair for mobility but cannot roll self due to her torn rotator cuffs

- Gladys only uses her wheelchair (pushed by provider) for mobility. The walker is used to assist with transfers. Any time Gladys is transferring, be sure to use the walker to help her turn to get to her wheelchair. After holding on to walker to balance her standing, use your hands gently under arms, being ready for possible fall. If she is having an especially tired day, use the gait belt while she transfers.

- Gladys needs her brace on her right arm for all transfers and sleeping (broke it last year and had pins put in). While in chair or eating, you can take it off if she wishes. Be sure to put it back on again for any transfers.

- **NEEDS TO HAVE FEET UP AS MUCH AS POSSIBLE, DUE TO BETTER CIRCULATION**

Dressing

- Try to get Gladys dressed every day; she usually has more energy and a better mood when dressed.

- Gladys likes picking out her own clothing for the day (can be given 2 or 3 choices). We try to get dressed in the bedroom so she can enjoy Tweety's company during this time (dressing and doing hair).

- Be sure to remember to insert toe separator on each foot before putting on the support hose.

Meals

- Please do not give her knives, as she is on blood thinner and it is not safe. Cut whatever she needs cut.

- Medication times: breakfast, lunch, supper, bedtime (9:30-ish). Meds set up in pillboxes.

- Give meds before meals. Keep an eye on her; just to be sure none fall on the floor or in her chair. Try to be sure she finishes them before starting her meal.

- Takes Maalox after each meal.

- Before breakfast on MWF, take Gladys' pulse, as her pulse must be at least or more than 60 beats per minute in order for her to take her Digoxin (if pulse is less than 60 bpm, hold the Digoxin—little yellow pill).

- Friendship meals are delivered M–F at 11:30 AM. Please label and date meals, freezing when appropriate.

- When serving delivered meals, put approx. half of the meal on a plate, reheat and serve, saving the rest in the fridge. Watch for anything with seeds or fresh fruits, vegetables, or food with seeds. These bother her diverticulitis.

- Can feed self but needs help serving food and cutting up

meat or anything not soft. If she is eating particularly slowly, offer bites. If she is working more than about an hour, assist or put away or throw food. Food out for longer may not be safe to eat.

- Re: dishes. Please save and rewash all hard plastic plates and white interlocking plates. Please be mindful of things that should not be washed in the dishwasher (e.g., paring knives, watermelon plate, etc.).

- Gladys likes a cup of hot tea with milk and sugar (use about 1 teaspoon; be sure spoon is dry) with almost every meal. We make the tea in bulk, so please make more tea when the bulk is getting low. We use two tea bags for a pitcher.

- Gladys is not to eat fresh fruit, fresh veggies, or any type of food with seeds, due to diverticulitis.

Bathroom
- Please use only one (1) glove per bathroom visit.

- After helping Gladys to the toilet, let her have some privacy by closing the door to a crack, so you can still monitor how she's doing. She will ring her bell when she is ready for help. Check in on her, and peek to be sure she's doing okay.

- When Gladys is finished, she needs help wiping (use toilet paper first, then wet wipes), and then apply Prep. H to anal area (for hemorrhoid) and lotion to buttocks for circulation.

Other General Info:
- Loves to meet people, tell about children/grandchildren/great-grandchildren

- Husband, Armin, was a minister, married for sixty-four years, passed away 2½ years ago
- Five children: _____, _____, _____, _____& Carol
- Wrote a cookbook; she's working on signing over 600 of them, for sale $12.95
- Used to paint, before three strokes, has just started drawing again. Please encourage.
- *Sweet, sweet, sweet lady!*

* * * * *

The following lists the nighttime routine to orient for providers and offer reminders:

Night Routine for Gladys

Gladys is usually ready to go to bed by 10:00 PM, so usually around 9:30 she has a light snack, possibly tea, Maalox, and her bedtime oxycodone ER 10mg. Her bedtime routine begins with the bathroom, then getting undressed, giving a backrub, and then dressing for bed.

Gladys has a foot soak at night (fill a pink tub, adding approx. ½ C. vinegar, a dash of mineral oil, and a dash of ivory soap). These amounts are less than the given "recipe," but they seem to work well. Fill the tub with the ingredients, and then finish filling with warm water. She likes to test the water before putting her feet in; sometimes the temperature needs adjusting. Her skin is *very* sensitive, and she is also very ticklish on the bottom of her feet. Soak feet for approx. 5 min. per foot; doctor's orders.

At this point, usually she likes to get into bed. Once in bed, be sure to give Gladys eye drops and put Vicks on her toenails before putting gripper socks on her feet. She likes the bed at an angle, her round blue pillow behind her neck, and two small flat pillows (or one normal pillow) under her feet.

She likes to say her prayers at night and may need a cue to remember to do this. You can pull in a chair beside the bed. She sometimes likes being read devotions or another book before falling asleep, so please ask if she would like this.

Before I leave her in bed, I make sure both railings are upon the side of the bed, her Kleenex is close to her right, and the tray is right at the side of the bed, equipped with a fresh glass of water, the doorbell, and any other assorted things (e.g., nail file, Chapstick, etc.). Also, be sure that the garbage can is close to her bed. Gladys likes the lamp next to her bed to be on the lowest setting. Be sure to cover Tweety with two pillowcases. The doors to the living room should be closed in both the bathroom and bedroom. The bedroom door is left cracked about six inches, so that you can check on Gladys. Make sure the phone is on the charger, keep the lights in the living room low, and if you have the TV on, please keep to a low volume. Gladys will ring the doorbell if she needs anything in the night. If she needs to use the bathroom at night, we usually utilize the commode in the bedroom, right beside the bed, to reduce transfers.

* * * * *

Also, we have found that making a checklist for daily direct care and household tasks helps to see that things are completed, and then we have a record of who did what and when, so when a new provider comes on duty, he or she knows what has been done. Below is an example of this checklist (modified to fit the page).

Mrs. Deve's Daily Care List

Date: PLEASE INITIAL AND MAKE COMMENTS IF NEEDED.

TASKS	Mon	Tue	Wed	Thu	Fri	Sat	Sun
Morning Care							
File nails							
Range of Motion AM-1x/day : • Arm stick exercise • Ankle rotations • Knee bends							
Foot soak & massage w/ lotion							
Tight socks 4–5 hrs. a day							
Brush hair							
Dressed							
Daytime Care							
Neck & shoulder heat therapy 3x/ day, more as needed							
Shower 2x/ week							
Eye drops 3x/ day							
Meds 3x/day							
Fiber choice 3x/day							

Maalox after every meal & bedtime & if pain in chest												
Prep. H & lotion w/ BR												
Emitrol if nauseated												
Vicks on toe nails 1x/day												
Backrub before bed or nap & baby lotion on legs before bed												
Brush teeth												
BMs												
Blood Pressure 2x												
Weight												
Recreation												
Read books												
Read devotions												
Check e-mail												
Piano: five-finger exercise												
Go outside (if nice), Scrabble, read, dominos, etc. See Daily Activity Options on Dottie's Schedule												
Hand Putty Therapy/Art Supplies												

Daily Household Chores for Ms. Deye

Date:

Chore	Mon	Tue	Wed	Thu	Fri	Sat	Sun
Wash dishes							
Vacuum/Dirt Devil/sweep							
Dusting							
Take out garbage							
Laundry with Ms. Deye as needed							
Change sheet 1x/week							
Make bed							
Straighten rooms							
Clean bathroom							
Meals, snacks, etc.							
Water plants (outside daily)							
Feed Flippy 2x/day (1 pellet)							
Check/fill humidifier							
Canary care: change water & paper daily & food as needed							

We would also post notes on the refrigerator or other locations for various needs. My mom had much trouble with diverticulitis, which is an inflammation of the diverticulum (small pockets in the wall of the colon). She really had to watch her diet—or I should say that we had to watch it for her. Here is an example of the note posted on the refrigerator so all would see and be reminded of what she should not be eating.

* * * * *

Please be sure my mom does not have anything that will irritate her diverticulitis. This means nothing with:

- seeds, nuts, peelings, or pulp
- fresh fruits or fresh veggies (even cooked veggies bother if they have any seeds or peeling, such as peas, corn, green beans, baked beans)
- pickles, peppers

even hot dogs need the casings off.

She *can* eat applesauce, well-cooked carrots, canned fruit or fruit cups (we take out the pineapple).

If you have question about an item, please call me.
Thanks!
Carol

* * * * *

I found it easier to leave a note for all to see, even if it was only one or two providers who needed to see it. We also assigned certain things, such as bathing or watering plants, to certain providers. Our wonderful nighttime provider did the plant watering inside, so we had only one person in charge of the plants to avoid over- or under-watering. We assigned bathing only to those who had been trained and had experience with this type of assistance. It is not worth taking any chances, as falls can happen easily during this routine.

WHAT WE'VE LEARNED

- However painful or time-consuming it is to organize information and schedules, it pays off. You will get better at it. Use the tools noted under Tips below, and consider the examples offered in this chapter. You can always make adjustments, but if you have the plan in place, you will be better prepared.

QUOTE

"Our ducks didn't come—nor do they fit—in a row!"

This one is mine. Getting our "ducks in a row" is a figment of our imagination. You just do the best you can and try to take care of yourself in the process. Although we have developed "resourceful ducks," they still don't seem to fit in a row. I know we do too much, and our plates are overflowing. We try to set our priorities and know that we have to say no to some things and some requests.

TIPS AND TOOLS

Seek out resources and tips for organization. Start somewhere. Know that some things will be more organized than others, but do not give up! Prioritize what needs to be organized and start there. Here are some resources and tools for various areas of organizing your sandwich. Here are a few websites to get you started:

http://organizedfamilies.com/

http://www.internetbasedmoms.com/freebies/organize.htm

http://www.squidoo.com/homeorganizationtips

Elder-Care Checklists

http://www.aging-parents-and-elder-care.com/Pages/Elder_Care_Checklists.html

This wonderful source provides well-designed checklists, very helpful for new caregivers or when conditions are changing. This includes excellent Web sites with the best checklists, including:

Elder Care—First Steps

Seniors and Driving Checklist

Getting Started—What kind of help does your loved one need?

Home Alone—Are They Okay?

Home Safety Checklist

Care Interpreter Living Arrangements—What is recommended for your loved one?

Prescription Drug Reference Checklist

Alzheimer's Living Facility Checklist

Assisted Living Facility Checklist

Nursing Home Checklist

Family Caregiving 101
http://www.familycaregiving101.org/
A "how-to" site by the NFCA with advice on time management, asking for help, navigating the health-care maze, and communicating with insurance companies and hospitals.

Chapter 6

Teaming and Collaboration

Teams and Systems

Working with Agencies and Systems

Fletch and I have worked with many teams throughout our life together (over thirty-three years). The most focused and prioritized teams have been on behalf of our daughter with special needs (e.g., Individualized Family Service Plan (IFSP) teams; Individual Education Plan (IEP) teams; vocational rehabilitation teams); now we're teaming on behalf of my mom. We have worked with both functional and dysfunctional teams. We have participated on various teams involved with social services, educational services, and medical services that deal with both ends of life's spectrum. We have insisted on accountability. We have challenged, promoted communication, asked for accountability, trained teams, and asked questions. In fact, we've been told we ask too many questions, but asking questions has allowed us to gain more knowledge—even to learn what others don't want us to know or perhaps what they themselves don't know. We have filed complaints (both in special education and the Americans with Disabilities Act), we have mediated several issues and have been through two due processes on behalf of our daughter. We are strong advocates for both our daughter and Mother. We believe in equal access and equal rights. We are not willing to let the system take care of things, as many times, the system does not really "take care."

TEAMING ESSENTIAL: GOOD CORRESPONDENCE WITH THE DOCTOR

We are very blessed to currently have a doctor for Mother (and formerly for my dad) who was willing to team with my youngest brother, who is an internist. This was actually part of the criteria for choosing a doctor when they moved to Kansas. We are able to share information via e-mail and fax, so I can get my brother's input on various aspects of my mom's medication, treatment, and general health. This means a lot and gives me some peace of mind. Although we do many medical procedures for our daughter, I do not have a medical background and do not have the knowledge or experience to feel comfortable about making some decisions.

We have always made lists when going to the doctor with our daughter, and we do the same for my mom (and did for my dad). There are some great resources for checklists and suggested questions to ask when taking your loved one to the doctor.
Here are a few:
https://www.hnfs.net/res/tricare/beneficiary/healthy%20living/pdf/-559753496/Going%20to%20Doctor.pdf
www.guidesmith.org/going-to-the-doctor/

Get to know the nurse of your family member's doctor. This person is an essential link for communication, prescriptions, and other medical procedures. Small gifts for both the nurse and doctor are kind gestures. We do this at holiday time. (We also give gifts to providers; this is discussed in chapter seven).

It is important to keep up-to-date with your parents' doctor visits, and go with them if you can. This may take some communication and discussion, as it may be perceived as letting go of some independence and control. This can be difficult for some folks. I think it is significant to remember that our parents are from a generation that not only revered physicians but also had unquestioning, unwavering faith in what the physician had to say. It was as though doctors should not be questioned, and second opinions were not considered. We learned early on, regarding Tally's medical care, that doctors are human and can make mistakes and that questioning and asking for a second opinion are necessary steps in getting the best care for your loved one.

My parents also resisted letting us know—or they didn't remember—what the doctor had to say when they were more independent and went to the doctor on their own. Someone should be designated the health-care power of attorney and have the paperwork completed. (Everyone should have a health-care power of attorney.) Most hospitals require this paperwork, so if your family member has been hospitalized, you have probably already completed a health-care power of attorney form. A living will should also be completed so there are no questions about care. You will also be asked about DNR (do not resuscitate) wishes and forms. (More information about these legal issues and forms can be found in chapter nine.)

Web MD is a wonderful Web site that offers a complete checklist for going to the doctor. (See: Ask the Dr. Checklist, http://www.webmd.com/default.htm. Once on the website, search for "ask the doctor checklist.") This resource includes tips on what to collect before the doctor visit, such as medications, if you have been to the doctor before for this problem, and your medical records. There also is an outline of what to say during the visit, including stating the main problem, symptoms, and the history of problem. It suggests that you record the visit, tells what might happen next, and offers a look at care at home. If you need medications, tests, or treatments, specific questions to ask are noted, such as why it is needed, risks, alternatives, and how to prepare for tests. Other questions are suggested at the end of the doctor visit regarding return visits, phoning for results, danger signs, and sources for additional information.

Web MD also offers another step-by-step list for going to the doctor, which includes the following:

- Observe the Problem
- Learn More about It
- Make an Action Plan
- Evaluate Your Progress

The site also offers other helpful information about which medical information or records to keep with you, information needed in an emergency (e.g., meds, list of health issues, allergies), medical history, records to keep at home (e.g., copy of your advance directive, living will, power of attorney, records of insurance claims and payments), and ways to organize all of your medical information. Suggestions include use of technology, computers, and flash drives to store and back up this important information; binders or notebooks for hard copies; and use of software to create a personal health record.

Another excellent resource is found at

http://assets.aarp.org/external_sites/caregiving/home-Care/talk_to_health_pros.html.

The Web article found here, "Talking to Health Pros: Issues to Consider," is provided by AARP. Family members who care for older parents are encouraged to have good communication with health professionals (doctors, nurses, pharmacists, therapists, social workers). It comes down to three facts: asking the right questions to assist your parent in making educated decisions; giving health professionals the information they need to assist with recommendations; and demanding quality care.

This AARP article also covers communication barriers between health-care professionals and older patients that can result in misunderstandings of treatment and conditions, serious health problems, mismanaged medications, etc.

http://assets.aarp.org/external_sites/caregiving/home-Care/talk_to_health_pros.html

Some basic issues discussed on this Web site include:

- Patient attitudes: Older patients are less likely to search for health information. They may trust the doctor, and so they will not ask questions, ask for details, or get a second opinion.

- Physician training and demands

- Ageism: This covers stereotyping—expecting older people to be frail, confused, depressed, overly talkative, needy, or quarrelsome. Sometimes older patients feel invisible at a medical visit, as the health-care professional speaks exclusively to the adult child.

The above source also includes how adult children can respect their parents' wishes, how much the parents want to communicate with health professionals, and how much they want to tell you about their health. Suggestions for adult children include:

- Talk frankly about the importance of communication for safe and effective care.
- With the parents' permission, talk with their doctor or nurse yourself.
- Encourage them to ask lots of questions. Bring a tape recorder to the doctor visit for answers to the following questions:
  - What illness do I have?
  - What are the drug and nondrug treatment options?
  - What is likely to happen with and without treatment?
  - What costs can we expect?
  - Does our insurance cover the treatment?
  - What is the name of the medicine you are prescribing? What is its benefit?
  - Is a generic drug available?
  - What are the risks and side effects?
  - How often should I take it? For how long?
  - What foods, other medicines, or activities should I avoid while taking it?
  - Do you have any written information I can take home?
  - If I think of questions later, how can I contact you?
- Give lots of information (e.g., medications, hospitalizations, allergies, lifestyle issues, etc.).

- Talk to other health professionals. (e.g., nurses, pharmacists, social workers, dietitians).
  - Do your own research.
  - Be a strong advocate for your parent.
  - Use legal tools.
  - Be a team player.

TEAMING 101: TOOLS FOR COMMUNICATION AND TEAMING

I teach communication skills and conflict resolution in all of my higher-education classes. These are important skills, and a few tools can enhance and foster positive communication.

Techniques That Dissolve Communication
- Ordering
- Threatening
- Preaching
- Lecturing
- Focusing on self
- Judging
- Denying
- Laying blame

Language of Resolution Techniques
- Encouraging
- Clarifying
- Flip sides – try to ake the other person's point of view

- Reflecting feelings – state the emotion, for example, "it sounds like you're feeling…"

- Summarizing – summarize what is said and check for accuracy

- Validating – validate feelings or efforts, "that is upsetting" or "you are frustrated"

- Reality testing – what might happen if you really did this, or tried that

A great book that offers conflict resolution and negotiation techniques is, *Getting to Yes: Negotiating Agreement without Giving In*, offers principles of negotiation. A book summary can be found at

http://www.colorado.edu/conflict/peace/example/ fish7513.htm.

CONFLICT RESOLUTION—REMEMBER PRINCIPLES OF NEGOTIATION

- Separate people from the problem. This means separating relationship issues which can involve difficult emotions, from the issues related to the problem at hand.

- Focus on interests, not positions. This means keeping the focus on what people really want and need, rather than extreme positions.

- Invent options for mutual gain. This means searching for new solutions to the problem, working towards a win/win outcome, rather that assuming that one side will win and the other will lose.

- Insist on using objective criteria. Sometimes the negotiation process can be simplified by discovering outside, objective criteria. Brainstorming ideas, looking at the problem from a different perspective, or doing some research on how others may have resolved a similar problem are ways to consider objective

These simple principles will assist when using the following communication and problem-solving tools. Productive, positive communication and creative problem-solving can result.

SODAS is a tool that my family often has used in problem solving situations. I have also added a SODAS sheet that can be copied for easy use, or make your own.

SODAS

State the problem: Sometimes, everyone's agreeing on just what the real problem might be is a key to the solution. There are often different perspectives on the problem. Saying it out loud or putting it in writing clarifies just what needs to be done and may bring up possible solutions.

Options: Come up with at least three possible solutions. Additional solutions should be recorded, but starting with three options makes this more manageable.

Disadvantages: List negative things that could happen.

Advantages: List the advantages of each of your options.

Solution: Choose which option seems best, and write a plan of action to solve the problem. What will you do, when and how you will do it, and how will you know if it worked or if you need to try another option?

One More Step: Follow through with the plan, assess success and return to other options if needed.

- Everyone's input and participation is important to this process. All ideas must be considered, and no single person should be "calling the shots" or naming all the options. Some situations may require a mediator or facilitator of this process.

Using a preprinted sheet for all participants is helpful. Having a larger copy for recording input for all to see is also important. Here is a sample:

SODAS

State the Problem: _____
_____
_____
_____

Options: _____
_____
_____
_____

Disadvantages: _____
_____
_____
_____

Advantages: _____
_____
_____
_____

Solution: _____

_____

_____

_____

- Follow through with the plan, assess success, and return to other options if needed.

Communication is essential, whether verbal, nonverbal, or via written word. Another tool that I use in all my classes and try to practice in my daily communications and with my family has to do with giving and receiving feedback (which is often negative). Feedback can be offered and received with respect and grace. It can also preserve family relationships. If we put off sharing feedback, the conflicts can grow and become less manageable. The following is a guide for giving and receiving feedback, adapted from the book *Getting to Yes.*

FEEDBACK

Feedback is a valuable communication tool. If you haven't yet tried it, do so today! Remember to respect and practice the guidelines for assisting with communication. We tend to be a society of interrupters. Giving feedback can be used in almost any situation, as there are conflicts and differences of opinion in every relationship. I encourage you to use and share this tool. (See "How to Give Feedback" in chapter one.)

Remember that when receiving feedback on the phone or via e-mail, you may not be prepared for it—it might take you by surprise. It's important, then, to "keep your cool." When reading e-mail or a letter, it's easy to misinterpret the contents and conclude something which may not have been the writer's intent. When you respond, be aware of your tone of voice and choice of words, and use paper and pen to make notes, perhaps checking off how you want to respond or the points you want to emphasize. If you are angry or upset about the message and need to think about it, you might want to pause, call back, or have someone else read your reply. I *always* have Fletch read or listen to my message to make sure I have said what needs to be said, while keeping the tone positive, yet direct. Again, tactfulness and a positive attitude is important!

"TEAM GLADYS"

GLADYS' CIRCLE OF SUPPORTS

Envisioning my mom's supports in nested circles gives a better picture of the various levels. The inner circle are those people immediately in her life—those family members who are with her each day. Then come providers who care for her each day; family members who visit frequently (also grandchildren and great-grandchildren) to give some care; other family who may call or visit less often; and finally, other professionals (doctor, nurses, therapists, pastor, etc.). We have used the "circle of friends" for years with our daughter. It also works well viewing the social fulfillment or social needs of our aging parents. I suggest taking a look at the Web article "What is a Circle of Friends, A Circle of Support?" at http://www.ecac-parentcenter.org/packets/friends/circles.shtml, and then write out your own circle of friends. (A page is available for printing to fill in your own circle of friends at http://www.ecac-parentcenter.org/packets/friends/yourcircle.shtml.)

TEAMING WITH FAMILY

Family meetings are important but are rare in some families. Our family had a few meetings, but they were not always functional. Sometimes it was all a matter of identifying the problem, but some meetings did not even result in identifying the problem. Meetings can also be dysfunctional, particularly if not everyone shows up. Good communication the key to function and making any arrangements work. Whether your aging parent is moving in with you or a sibling, or into assisted living or a nursing home, you *must* talk about it—and soon. Often, we wait too long for these conversations.

Our family meetings were few and often ended with my dad saying, "I'll take that into consideration" or "We'll cross that bridge when we get to it." You may, however, already be at the bridge, no matter how much you try to deny it. One such meeting occurred as my parents were experiencing more limitations. The recurring message was that they *did not* want to go to a nursing home. I felt the need to assist my parents in any way that I could in order to respect their wishes. Commitment is what it's all about.

Having a structured meeting is best. (Refer to SODAS and the feedback tool.) Some families may even need a mediator, monitor, or third party to assist, particularly when there are strong personalities or differences of opinion. Birth order can also come into play here. Being the youngest, I often felt I was not heard, even though I worked hard to speak out, share knowledge, and promote ideas from my professional training and experience.

One sister often talks about "speaking from your heart *or* your head." I say you can do both. You know what your heart believes is right, and you use your head to figure out how to do it.

Here is how one meeting went: Three of my four siblings made it to the meeting. Also in attendance were my parents' power of attorney from their bank and their attorney, to help make decisions. Their options were going to a nursing home or to Kansas, with the plan of building a cottage next to our home. I can still hear the attorney's words to my dad: "Well, I guess you're moving to Kansas!" And they did.

Through the years, my oldest sister, who has been most supportive of my mom's situation here and is closer in proximity (about one hundred miles away), spends at least one day a month taking care of my mom. This gives her visiting time in addition to support of care hours. She and her husband also give Mother financial support each month for paying providers, as do the other adult children. One brother has been very supportive as a medical consult. Another sister calls frequently, and visits once or twice a year, helping when she can.

I send regular updates to all family members via e-mail, which helps a lot and allows for ease of updates in between classes or meetings. My siblings and I may not have always been "on the same page," but I have worked on making sure everyone is informed of various situations, decision-making, and changes.

HIRING PROVIDERS

When we transitioned to hiring individuals from using an agency, it was a major process. (More information can be found in "Transitions" later in this chapter.) I started by putting an ad on the university career service web page. Here is the ad I placed for my mom's caregiver search:

Personal Care Attendant for 92-yr-old woman

- 24-hr care needed for sweet woman who is 92. Basically, care for daily living and personal care needed. Daytime, evening, and overnight hours available.

  Nursing, CNA, LPN, or PT/OT student, graduate student, or experience with caregiving for older individual. A female caregiver is preferred.

  I was surprised to receive nineteen contacts! Of course, I had to screen them all before interviewing, but I did interview most. Before interviewing for providers, you will want to structure your questions and create a checklist or rating scale or some way to assess and select the best match for your loved one. Insist on résumés and references, even if you know the person or if a family member, friend, or acquaintance has referred him or her.

  Here are a few suggestions for screening and preparing for interviews:

- Look at résumés first
- Many good applicants may not have experience, other than with family members' care, but that speaks a lot to where their priorities and hearts are.
- *Get references—contact them!*
- Have your list of questions, and rate applicants on several areas.

  Here are the ones I used:

- Observe the connection between the applicant and your parent; rate it on a scale (1–5 or 1–10).

- Leave the room for a few minutes to see the interaction between the potential provider and your loved one.

After several rounds of interviews, here is the checklist I developed. (I wish I'd had it when I started interviewing.)

Interviewing Checklist for Providers

Interview for Mother's providers:

Name: Date:

Why do you want this job?

Credentials/experience?   1   2   3   4   5
Comments:

Connection with Mother: 1   2   3   4   5
Comments:

Time alone with Mother   1   2   3   4   5
Comments:

Initial impression: 1   2   3   4   5
Comments:

Enthusiasm   1   2   3   4   5

Professionalism   1   2   3   4   5
Comments:

Smoke?   Yes   No

Anything hinder your being here or being on time?
(e.g., transportation, childcare, meetings, etc.)

Days/hours available
Need:

Tues 9 AM–5 PM   Yes   No

Thurs 9 AM–5 PM   Yes   No

Thurs 9 AM–5 PM   Yes   No

Fri 5 PM–9 AM   Yes   No

Sat. 5 PM–9 AM   Yes   No
&going to church?

Sun. 9 AM–5 PM   Yes   No
References:

A NOTE ABOUT SMOKING

I will never understand why so many who are in the Certified Nursing Assistant and Personal Care Assistant professions are smokers! We didn't want to support this, but we did finally put a bucket of sand outside by the front door, so they could dispose of their cigarettes outside, rather than inside, to keep the smell out of the house. Something else to keep in mind with providers who smoke is that smoking includes frequent cigarette breaks. You have no way of supervising this when you are not there—some providers who smoke take many more breaks than the nonsmoking providers; more than would be permitted if they worked in a nursing home or hospital setting. Then there is the clothing permeated with the smoke smell, noticeable as they come in the door. I can even smell it on the furniture where someone who smokes has been sitting. One of my mom's longtime faithful providers is a smoker, and I don't know what we do without her—but I could do without her smoking. If you're loved one is allergic to or can't tolerate the smoke smell, even though there is no smoking inside, you might want to consider this when hiring—the smoke smell isn't just when the person is smoking.

OTHER THINGS TO CONSIDER WHEN INTERVIEWING

When independently hiring providers, you will also want to:

- Check if they're licensed.
- Check if they carry their own liability insurance.
- Find out if the have a federal tax ID number, and be certain they are withholding
- Discuss how you will cover if they are sick or needing time off.
- Check references: do a criminal background check; get driver's license if they are going to transport.
- Be sure to train for individualized procedures, preferences, and equipment.

"Choosing an Agency for In-Home Care"
http://assets.aarp.org/external_sites/caregiving/homeCare/choosing_in_home_care.html

"To remain at home gives older people comfort, control, and independence. And that's especially important when they realize they can't do it all on their own anymore."

This Web site covers areas with which older people might need help:

- Household chores (e.g., cleaning, preparing meals)
- Personal care that is non-medical (e.g., bathing, dressing, transfers, etc.)
- Health and medical care (e.g. nurse, home-health aide, physical therapist)

This resource includes a checklist for the right questions to find the best-quality care available.

"Help Wanted: Tips for Hiring a Home-Care Worker"
http://assets.aarp.org/external_sites/caregiving/home-Care/hiring_home_care_help.html

This resource covers everything you might need to think about when hiring caregivers. First, figure what kind of help your parent needs and how often/how much help is needed for household chores and non-medical personal care.

Next, check the list of specific ways to start the search, ways to advertise, interview, write a job description, know how much you are able to pay, tax issues, review resumes and job history, check references, and include your parent in the interview.

Suggestions for interviewing applicants are given, such as:

- Getting their name, address, telephone number, and social security number (you can ask for proof of identity—if not a social security card, then a driver's license or other photo ID).

- How much experience they've had in home care
- Whether they have any special training, such as working with clients who have dementia
- Whether they are willing and able to perform all the duties you've outlined in the job description
- Why they left their former job
- Why they are seeking a home-care position
- Their expectations of the job
- Whether they drive, and if they have a car
- Whether they have ever been in trouble with the law

Invite the applicant to ask questions about the job and about your expectations as well. Give honest answers. Talk about how you will handle vacation and other time off. Head off any misunderstandings about what each party expects.

Here is a sequenced list of suggested steps within the interviewing, hiring, and "keeping everyone happy" process provided within the above Web site:

- Check references
- Take notes
- Background check
- The hire
- Trial period; give things a test run
- Write out those things on which you both agree:
  - trial period
  - job duties

- salary
- pay schedule
- time off
- start date
- termination policy
- Keep copies of this job contract signed by both of you
- Orient; train
- Drop by unannounced to see how things are going
- Troubleshooting; ensuring that everything runs smoothly
- Keep the lines of communication open
- Termination; sometimes things don't work out.

Theft and abuse should result in immediate termination. Contact the police, as well as adult protective services, if a home-care worker has abused your parent. No one wants this person to work in someone else's home.

Meeting with HCBS/FE

HCBS/FE is Home & Community Based Services for the Frail and Elderly. This is a waiver program for "Individuals age sixty-five or older who qualify for Medicaid benefits may be eligible to receive services through the Home and Community Based Services Frail Elderly program (HCBS/FE). The goal of HCBS/FE is to provide long-term care services in the least intensive care setting of your choice.

Services include:

- Personal care, such as feeding, bathing, and dressing;
- Household tasks, such as shopping, meal preparation, house cleaning, and laundry;

- Health services, such as health monitoring, twenty-four-hour support for medical emergencies, and respite care to temporarily relieve caregivers.
- You must be age sixty-five or older and in frail health.
- You must be assessed by a qualified case manager and determined to need long-term care services.
- Your countable assets cannot exceed $2,000 (a home and vehicle are not included in the total).
- You will be asked to help pay for services if your countable income is greater than the allowable income per month (your local SRS office will help you determine your current allowable income)."

Source: http://www.cilswks.org/hcbs_fe.php

We met with my mom's Social Rehabilitation Services case manager almost a year in advance to make a preplan of when to apply, papers to gather, etc. Finally, she was at the financial level to apply, we planned and prepaid her funeral so her life insurance policy would not count against her. Then we were passed on to the HCBS/FE Area Agency on Aging case manager, who did the actual assessment of hours needed. This started off pretty rough and was very time-consuming. My mom had fallen, had a broken arm, and her other arm was badly bruised; she could not do anything for herself, not even feed herself. Yet when the assessment was done, it was determined that she needed only three hours of assistance a day! Several meetings later, after at least eight hours of meetings, we were able to get assistance for her for eight hours a day. We had to account every minute of her day in order to get the hours that she needed. Fletch and I sat had to justify why she needed help doing specific tasks. I found it appalling that my mother, who could not feed herself, shower herself, or even wipe her bottom, was initially given only three HCBS/FE hours each day. (It got down to a literal minute-by-minute account—they could pay for time for her to get assistance transferring on and off the toilet and with cleaning up, but not for the time she actually was on the toilet!) We ultimately were able to justify more hours, but it took hours of our time to do so.

TEAMING CHALLENGES—WE ASK TOO MANY QUESTIONS

When we ask questions, we expect a response. Sometimes this intimidates people because they either don't know the answer or it may seem as if they don't want to explain how the system works (or doesn't work).

We have learned to document our questions. We typically ask the question, put it in writing and, depending on the issue, wait a few weeks. Then we ask again, in writing (with e-mail, we forward the first e-mailed question). At this point, we often include a CC to appropriate people. Sometimes this has been to the state's advocacy and protection representative; other times, it has been a supervisor or other administrator or state agency. I usually write the e-mail and read it to Fletch, or we'll compose it together. I rarely write an e-mail of this sort on my own. I recommend revision with another pair of eyes and ears. Stating the questions in positive form and not accusing works well.

Creative and effective problem-solving is rare, and people are complacent in doing things the same way they have always done them. We feel that professionals, programs, and systems should be accountable for their work. We check to see if professionals are doing what they say they're doing. We educate ourselves so we know which questions to ask. We work toward collaboration, although effective collaboration definitely depends on the individual team members. I encourage you to educate yourself on various support systems for the aging. Area Agency on Aging it a great place to start. Look at the guidelines and requirements of various elder-care programs, supports, or plans. You must be involved. You must ask questions. There must be checks and balances. You need to know where your loved ones are at any moment of the day, who they are with, and how their day is going. You can't trust the system alone to be there for your child or older parent for support.

TEAMING CHALLENGES

YOU CAN'T SQUEEZE COMPETENCY OUT OF SOMEONE OR OUT OF A SYSTEM WHEN IT'S NOT THERE!

You can't work with a dysfunctional system without there being a dysfunctional approach. We learned this long ago when we teamed with the school districts on Tally's behalf. You can advocate for the services your loved one needs, you can get those services in writing, *but* if the competency of the provider or agency is not there, it's not going to happen regardless of what is on paper.

When Tally was younger, she had a few therapists who really did not know what they were doing—they had never worked with a child with spina bifida, much less with a child in a wheelchair. We would work hours with her team to get and keep the services she needed (e.g., physical therapy and occupational therapy). We would finally get the services written on her IEP, and sometimes the services wouldn't happen, or the therapists did not know how to implement the plan.

Once we learned that not everyone knew what they were do-ing, we also learned that competency could not be magically there because it was written on paper. This realization didn't make it much better, but at least we could admit that we had tried. "You cannot squeeze juice out of a turnip," my mom used to say. You cannot expect more from individuals or pro-grams than they are capable or competent of doing.

Still, there are some very competent individuals working with both the young and old. With a few exceptions, I have found that, overall, college students are more open to learn-ing and to trying new things than older providers. I have also found, however, that some younger college students are not as responsible (e.g., quitting without notice). With college students, you are faced with constantly changing schedules, orchestrating everyone's schedules each semester, and their often not being available during school breaks.

Teaming Challenges—"Some Real Doozies"

Although we've hired some very competent, caring pro-viders, there also have been some unique and unpleasant situations—providers that Fletch call, "some real doozies." I have spent countless hours in caring for my parents, but I've spent even more time and energy on hiring and coordinat-ing their—and now Mother's—hired caregivers. Some issues have been with the agencies we used; some have been with the individual providers.

We have used caregivers who have:

- Pretended to have cancer
- Not shown up for shifts (Once, on the day after I'd given her a holiday gift, the provider did not show up.

Another provider did not show up for her last day of work!)

- Been "fair-weather help" (Some wouldn't come on rainy or snowy days.)

- Not worked on holidays and/or weekends (Although I wasn't notified in advance, one agency assumed that they would not have to send anyone on any holiday. Another agency would not do weekends, even after they said they could cover all hours, all days.)

- Stolen money, meds, and possibly other things (We know one provider stole money from my mom; we could never prove who was responsible for her missing medication. I really don't know what else might have been taken. I started storing Mother's valuable items at my house, letting her know where they were.)

We used a provider for Tally at her apartment who, we later learned, was leaving our daughter's apartment to go help another client! Another of Tally's providers found Tally on campus (when no one was with her) and had Tally sign a timesheet for the provider's hours—we had no idea what was listed on it.

Of course, the majority the providers we used for my mom and Tally were trustworthy and responsible—I don't want all providers to get a "bad rap" from my comments, but you must be careful when hiring and coordinating care for your loved one.

GAPS IN THE CIRCLE OF SUPPORT

"Picking them up sooner rather than later would probably be a good idea!"

I could not believe this message from my oldest brother!

He was talking about our parents, after they had moved to an assisted-living facility near him—only two weeks after they had moved there. The agreement—decided upon at a family meeting—was for them to try it for thirty days, to see how they felt about staying there. When the time came to move things from my parents' townhouse, Mother was not in agreement about the things they were moving—she felt too much was being moved, indicating that they would not be returning to their townhouse. My mom specifically did not want to move two large recliner chairs.

As an advocate of choices—appropriate choices, not dangerous or inappropriate ones—I felt that her choice of leaving these chairs, in the hope that she and my dad would return to their townhouse, was a small gesture; it was a choice that was her right. So I advocated—and the chairs stayed in their home, and my parents did return after a month.

Before they returned, however, several events occurred, including my mom's almost dying from taking Vioxx, and the fact that no one would take my dad to see her during this time in the hospital. After some e-mail exchanges between my two older siblings, my brother let us know that it would be best to pick up our parents "sooner rather than later."

Clearly, my brother and his wife could not handle the stress, family dynamics, and level of care and patience required. I certainly understand the stress, time, and effort, but I have honored—and will continue to honor—the commitment made. It could not continue, however, without my husband's and immediate family's assistance and my extended family's support.

Some Just Don't Get it ... and Probably Never Will

A family member from Fletch's side asked, "Why would you need a provider for your mom when you're there?" I just looked at this person, sighed, and said, "You don't understand!" I restrained myself, even though I wanted to scream at the time (and I'm not a screamer). I wanted to say that helping someone walk, talk, eat, go to the bathroom; and helping with transportation, doctor visits, emergency room visits, bills, hiring caregivers, coordinating schedules, and meeting with agencies is more than a full time job—and I already have a full-time job! Sometimes, though, it's not worth the time and energy to try to explain the level of commitment, time, and love this takes. Most likely, the people to whom it needs to be explained would not understand how the benefits outweigh the emotional, physical, social, and financial toll. Nor would they understand the unseen benefits of seeing your mother every day, seeing her with her grandchildren and great-grandchildren. She is a living piece of history!

Suzanne Mintz, author of the article "Finding Normalcy in a Caregiving Life," shares that some people just don't get it:

"I recall once seeing a young man walking down the street. He was wearing the typical costume of his generation: jeans and a T-shirt. Blazoned across the front of his chest in bold black letters was the statement, 'Normal is Boring.' I read it as he passed by me with the jaunty look of one who believes he is immortal, and I thought to myself, 'He doesn't have a clue. He doesn't realize that normal isn't boring at all. It is the most wonderful thing in the world.' Normal is what those of us who are family caregivers want more than anything else. We want to be like other families that take walking and talking and eating and toileting and swallowing and thinking for granted. We want our loved ones to be well. No, normal isn't boring at all, except perhaps to those who have never experienced the outside-the-norm situations of caregiving." [18]

SEAMLESS TRANSITIONS?

Coordinating everything takes some time, organization, and hard work. When everything is organized, everyone shows up on time, and no one is sick, all goes well. But that is not reality. Life happens! Transitions can be very challenging. In education and special education, we use a term "seamless transitions," which is the idea that if we know the transition is coming, we plan for it in detail, and we organize and make the transition as smooth as possible. From the perspective of a parent of a child with special needs and as a daughter of a ninety-two-year-old, "seamless transitions" are an illusion. There is nothing seamless about it! All, however, is not lost, even though no one—other than someone else who has done it—understands the time, organization, and energy it takes to change schedules and interview/hire/orient providers. As we moved from using agencies to hiring individuals, it was important to take the time to do background checks, check references, and use our instincts. I have misjudged or been fooled in the past, as I tend to trust people. Some of the tips and tools shared in the "Team Gladys: Hiring Providers" section in this chapter can assist with transition times.

---

[18] Mintz, S. Finding Normalcy in a Caregiving Life. *Take Care: Self-Care for the Family Caregiver*. National Family Caregivers Association Newsletter, Winter, 2008, p. 2.

One my most difficult transitions was when our two oldest daughters moved away from the area within two weeks of each other. I was a mess! I wanted to express my appreciation for our daughters and share with other family members just how much their support for Mother/Grandma and Tally meant to me. So I wrote an e-mail to family members, asking that they give verbal thanks to my daughters for devoting over two years of their time to Grandma-care and a lifetime to Tally-care and guidance.

* * * * *

Here is my letter of gratitude and love:
7/16/08

Dear Ones,

I am writing to acknowledge and thank Cassie and Mikelle for their faithful, loving, caregiving for Mother/Grandma and for Tally over the past years. It is bittersweet to see them each spread their wings, as I celebrate their growth but will miss them beyond words. In addition to their normal "launching" from our Emporia area, their part on our support team for Mother/Grandma and Tally could not be surpassed. They have helped Mother stay at home for the past three years, while here in Kansas. (Aug. 1 will be three years to the date!) They cannot be replaced, but I'm interviewing all this week to try to fill in the gaps as best I can.

Cassie's last day with Mother/Grandma is Mon., July 28, before moving to Colorado. Cassie has been working weekly with Mother/Grandma for two years and three months. I'm not sure if everyone is aware that she consistently worked two to four days every week and was backup for nights numerous times, while teaching at ESU and commuting to teach at Baker, and also tutoring and PCA'ing and assisting Tally at ESU classes. She has also assisted with interviews and orientation with new providers for Mother, which helped me immensely. She worked for approximately $2 less per hour than the rest of the providers, as her contribution to Grandma. That was a significant savings for Mother/Grandma over the last two years +. Plus, these were hours and days that she will always remember. She was able to hear *many* stories, helped with her deck garden, assisted with e-mails, watched numerous hours of *Little House*, and—importantly—saved Tweety by diagnosing and treating him when he was losing all his feathers.

Mikelle worked with Mother/Grandma consistently for about 1½ years, and then was backup numerous times as she did more PCA'ing and overnights with Tally at the apartment. She did this while going to school and working at the ESU art galleries. She, too, worked for approximately $2 less per hour than the rest of the providers, as her contribution to Grandma. Mikelle can get Grandma laughing every time she is with her. Just tonight, Mikelle joined us for dinner. We were talking about a potential new provider's name. Grandma said, "That's a funny name," and Mikelle replied, "Well, some people might think Gladys is a funny name too, Grandma." They both laughed.

I am not asking for any donations for gifts; I am just expressing my gratefulness to these two lovely, caring young ladies, who are my daughters. I would ask that you might drop them an e-mail of appreciation for giving their time and energy to help keep Mother/Grandma stay at home over the past three years. It's fun to visit with Mother / Grandma, but the work and specifics of assisting with personal care, dressing, transfers, transporting, dealing with pain, meals, meds, cleaning, etc., is not always easy or fun. And it's different when she's your Grandma.

This change will also mean a void in Mother's/Grandma's world. So, I would also ask that you give Grandma regular phone calls and come visit. Some of you already do this. She so enjoys the calls and visits; they make her day!

I cannot put my feelings into words, any amount of money, or measure in laughter or tears how moved and proud I am to have these lovely, compassionate young ladies as my daughters, and as my mother's granddaughters. They have made "my sandwich generation" much sweeter. They have been the mayo and mustard holding it together, in addition to the pickles, tomatoes, onions, and relish to bring spice, joy, and diversity to my "sandwich experience." I am *so* blessed!

Thank you, a million times over, my dear Cassie and Mikelle!

Written with love, admiration & appreciation,
Carol & Mom

* * * * *

Here is Tally's reflection e-mail after the transition, when her sisters moved out of the area. Writing is important for her—a great outlet and validation of feelings.

* * * * *

Subject: Changes happen but life still goes on

Just thought I would share my thoughts about the changes I've had to deal with in life the last few months.
Love,
Tally

It's nearing the end of summer, and it's hard to look back on the changes that took place or are still taking place over the last few months. As I'm sitting in my new apartment alone, I reflect on what I now recall as one of the best and most difficult summers of my life.

It's hard to believe I will be living alone in my apartment, as Mikelle has moved on to Lawrence to begin the next chapter in her life with her boyfriend, Curt. I'll still get to see her every now and then, but it won't be the same, waking up in the apartment and not seeing her smiling face and her usual "good morning, Tal," as that was regularly the first thing I would I see and hear when I woke up. We've had some pretty awesome times together, just her and me. Looking back at when we first moved in, I feel living with her has been one of the greatest experiences I've had in my life. Sure, we had our disagreements but those passed quickly as we sat down to tacos or pizza for dinner and watched Friends or other various TV shows. We would also spend most Thursday nights playing with her Wii or challenging each other to a round of Guitar Hero.

Cassie is starting a new chapter in her life as well. She has moved to Greeley, Colorado, with her boyfriend, Jake, and puppy, Coopy, to teach and get her PhD at the University of Northern Colorado. My parents, Mikelle, and I spent two days there, helping them move, the beginning of August. I know my dog, Cally, will especially miss Coopy, as the two of them have spent most of the summer's days playing/wrestling together on my parents' deck. Cassie also helped me with some of my classes this past semester. She is also the main reason I was able to pass Intro to Psychology. Thanks,

Cassie! She also took care of my Grandma many days during the week so I was able to see her often.

This summer has also brought some wonderful memories. My family was able to take a much-needed family vacation to Texas to celebrate Mikelle's graduation from ESU. My parents were able to rent an accessible beach house in Surfside, Texas, for a week. This was awesome because not only was I able to be close to the water, but my parents purchased a beach wheelchair so I was able to go "beachcombing" and look for treasures in the sand. I also enjoyed having my sisters wheel me up and down the beach.

In addition to these trips my family went on was a trip to Kansas City to see *Wicked*: the Musical. I had the opportunity to experience this show in Chicago three years ago and had such an amazing experience that I wanted to see it again. My mom knew I wanted to see it again so she helped me make a long forty-five- minute phone call to Ticketmaster and in the end we got fourth row seats and had a "wicked" time to show for it. We also got the opportunity to meet some of the cast members after the show, so that made the show and experience even more special.

As I get ready to start my third year at ESU, it's somewhat hard to believe I've made it this far and am pursuing my dream of attending college. School has never been my favorite thing, but I can honestly say attending ESU has changed my life and I could not imagine attending any other school.

* * * * *

Transition adjustments take time. I plunged into new responsibilities at work, thinking I would be so preoccupied that I would miss our older daughters less. It worked like a Band-Aid—superficially covering the wound but not lasting.

The following is an e-mail sent to our oldest daughter, Cassie, about two months after her move:

* * * * *

Note sent to Cassie, Oct. 2008, after her move in August:

> Hi Hon,
>
> I was working on editing my book and rereading what I had written about you. I started to cry for the first time in a while and realized how very, very much I still miss you. My busy, crazy schedule helps some, but does not hide the ache I sometimes still have. I guess strong bonds come with a price when there is distance. At the same time, I am more than proud of your ambition; so happy you are pursuing your goals! You are so exceptional, and the hard work will be worth it. It can be overwhelming, and you must take care of yourself. I'm glad you have [your boyfriend] to support you as well!
> Love you always,
> Mom

* * * * *

WHAT WE'VE LEARNED

- You can't squeeze competency out of someone or out of a system when it's not there!

- Some just don't get it—and probably never will.

- When hiring providers: *get references; contact them!*

QUOTE

"The most basic of all human needs is the need to understand and be understood. The best way to understand people is to listen to them."
—Ralph Nichols

"Alone we can do so little; together we can do so much."
—Helen Keller

"People have been known to achieve more as a result of working with others than against them."
—Dr. Allan Fromme

TIPS AND TOOLS

Web MD offers a complete checklist for going to the doctor. See "Ask the Dr. Checklist" at http://www.webmd.com/a-to-z-guides/ask-the-doctor-checklist-ask-the-doctor-checklist

The American Health Information Management Association (AHIMA) sponsors a Web site where you can search for paper-based, software-based, and Internet-based personal health records. See www.myphr.com/resources/phr_search.asp, then search for "examples of personal health records". There you will find descriptions of what should be included, tools and services for ways to keep, and best access to your personal health records.

"Talking to Health Pros: Issues to Consider"
http://assets.aarp.org/external_sites/caregiving/home-Care/talk_to_health_pros.html

This source covers communication barriers between health-care professionals and older patients that can result in misunderstandings of treatment and conditions, serious health problems, mismanaged medications, etc.

Some principles of negotiation are offered, excerpted from a great book titled *Getting to Yes*. The following Web site has a book summary: http://www.colorado.edu/conflict/peace/example/fish7513.htm

HCBS/FE is "Home & Community Based Services for the Frail & Elderly." Although this is a Kanas website, it offers information about both the Kansas and Federal HCBS program. See http://www.cilswks.org/hcbs_fe.php

"Choosing an Agency for In-Home Care"
http://assets.aarp.org/external_sites/caregiving/home-Care/choosing_in_home_care.html
This resource includes a checklist for the right questions to ask when looking for the best-quality care available.

"Help Wanted: Tips for Hiring a Home-Care Worker"
http://assets.aarp.org/external_sites/caregiving/homeCare/hiring_home_care_help.html

"Building a Caregiving Team"
in NFCA's Quarterly Newsletter, *Take Care*, Summer 2008
Eight suggestions for family caregivers to build a caregiving team are offered, including: talking with your family, identifying needs, enlisting a family member or friend as coordinator, willingness to accept help, being creative, communicating changes, using technology, and expressing gratitude.

Chapter 7

APPRECIATING THOSE WHO HELP; THOSE WHOM YOU TRUST!

Although we have had experiences with providers who demonstrated that they could not be trusted, we also have had experiences with some wonderful, trustworthy, dedicated providers, doctors, nurses, therapists, and other health-care providers who deserve great kudos and to whom we are most grateful! We have tried to thank them in various ways, trying to get creative but often getting gift cards (usually to Bath & Bodyworks). Gift cards really seemed to be the best, as the providers could choose what they wanted.

I did ask other family members to contribute to the holiday gifts, as my mom did not have the money, and I felt it was not totally my family's responsibility to give gifts to those who cared for our parents. I would send out e-mails before the holidays and ask for contributions, then get gift cards according to the amount contributed. Sometimes it works out well; sometimes it doesn't.

Here is an example of my e-mail to my siblings, soliciting contributions for provider holiday gifts:

Holiday Gifts for Providers, 2008

Hi all,

As I am working on my book chapter, "Appreciating Those Who Help, Those Whom You Can Trust," I am reminded that it is that time of year to thank the providers who take care of our mother. In the past I have purchased Bath & Body gift cards for each provider. The amount for Patty has been larger, as she has done more hours and has been with Mother for three years now (can you believe that?). Anyway, I welcome suggestions for gifts and contributions. This year, with the economy as is it, we are working on either functional or consumable gifts for my family. Although a gift card to Wal-Mart (our only big store) might be the most practical and economical, I have been hesitant in the past to do that, as several providers are smokers, and I didn't want to see the gift card "go up in smoke" or add to lung damage. We only have two providers who smoke, so perhaps this is not as relevant this year. What do you all think?

Here is who we have, with approximate hours (some covered by HCBS):

_____- About 75 hrs/wk

_____- Currently 30 hrs/wk (in Jan. will be 8 hrs/week)

_____- 8 - 24 hrs/wk

_____- 8 - 20 hrs/wk

_____- 8 - 28 hrs/wk

_____- 8 - 20 hrs/wk

If I could have any gift contributions by Dec. 12, then I could purchase whatever we get by the next week, which is finals week. Five of our providers are students, and some will be going home, so I'd like to do this before they leave. If you could let me know via e-mail the amount you would like to contribute and then get the contribution to me by Dec. 12, it would be most appreciated. I am only sending this to siblings, as you can check with any of your family members who might want to contribute with you. I will do the same with my family.

On behalf of Mother, thank you for recognizing the importance of these people in our mother's life and her safe, caring environment!

Love,

Carol

* * * * *

At holiday time we also tried to have my mom work on something she could give. Last year we found cute Grandma-looking angel ornaments to make (from Oriental Trading Company). She did some of the gluing, and the providers and I did the rest. The hot-glue gun was not the easiest for her to manipulate—she had never used one before—and I don't think we'll do that again. It was nice for her, however, to give something that she had helped make. She gave these to providers and family members as well.

Tally, too, would thank her providers. She has always been grateful to those who help her to be a little more independent. We have worked on supporting her taking on more of this herself. When her sisters were her providers (and she had a bit more money, as she was still living at home at the time), she bought them some rather large, lovely gifts or gift certificates. She has since then had other trusted providers and has thanked them with Bath & Body gift certificates, taking them out to lunch, or given other small gifts. The fun thing about taking them out for lunch is that she gets to give the gift and be part of the going-out process, which is good for her.

My sister had some great ideas for gifts and thank-you gestures from my mom. Several ideas took time, which I did not have, but I tried to allocate others to follow through. My mom has a jungle of plants. The second year she was here, we took cuttings from various plants, and she gave each of her children and grandchildren a plant in a nice pot. These cuttings were from plants from my dad's funeral, so they were especially sentimental. This year, my sister brought a large number of purple (my mom's favorite color) plastic pots and glued the front of old Christmas cards to the pot, and we're planting more cuttings. Mother can then give these to providers, the man who delivers her meals daily, her doctor, therapists, etc. Poet Nancy Henry wrote a particularly touching poem, "People Who Take Care," that really says it all—it's in her book *Hard* (Musclehead Press, 2003) and also can be found on-line at http://writersalmanac.publicradio.org/index. php?date=2006/02/11. I encourage you to share it with those who take care of your loved ones.

THE POWER OF A SIMPLE "THANK YOU"

My mother is a kind, loving, and gracious woman. She has always given of herself to others and put others before herself. I'm not sure this is always the healthiest for self-esteem or self-concept, but I have admired this in her and see this in myself at times. Being a minister's wife, she would often hide her tears, feelings, needs, and sometimes opinions out of respect for her husband, the church, or her position as a minister's wife. I did not agree with her not speaking her mind and would get frustrated with the gender-bias treatment she received, as did the females in our family and females in the church. Through all this, however, she has been gracious and grateful. She did learn to manipulate some people and situations through quiet, passive actions, but I believe this was a coping mechanism to keep her sanity. I hear gratefulness when she thanks me for the little things: heating her tea with her meal; reheating a meal she has been working on for some time; opening her mail and reading it to her; assisting her with putting her pills on her spoon of applesauce when she's having a shaky day; bundling her up to go back to her house after having dinner at mine; helping her in the bathroom, etc. I hear her thank her providers for the little things as well. Whenever I visit when a provider is there or during shift change, I always thank them as I'm leaving. When they are leaving after their shift, I thank them again. Each evening after Mother has had supper with us, I roll her back to her house at about 9:00 PM. As I kiss her good night, she says, "Thank you, Carol, for everything!" That means the world to me! I need no other thanks, payment, or compensation!

Tally takes after Mother in many ways. She relates to her grandmother on a different level than the rest of us—literally. She knows what it means to have a little assistance to be able to do more. It doesn't bother her to ask for help, and she always does it with a "please." She sees asking for help as a sign of strength—one of our mottos. She also sees the power of politeness and gratefulness. As I was writing this paragraph, I heard her in the bathroom, knocking on the side of the shower stall—her signal that she needs help with washing her hair. I stopped writing and went to help her, and after I finished, she thanked me for washing her hair. (She also thanked me for cutting my nails so it wouldn't scratch her!) She is grateful for many things, the little things.

It really made me think about how much thanking is in the lives of those who depend on others for assistance with daily needs. Those who are constantly on the receiving end of help, also need to to help others. I have found it important to find situations, even small gestures, where Tally and Mother can be of help to us, so I can thank them. I ask Tal to help hook a bracelet or ask Mother to help with baking. I have to plan ahead for the time it takes for them to perform a small task (especially baking), but I believe it can positively impact the feeling of contribution, self-worth, and self-esteem. My mom does not have money to spend on Christmas gifts for the family, but over the last three years, she has given various little trinkets to her children and grandchildren. Last year for my birthday, she gave me a lovely Christmas angel. She worked on a homemade card with the help of my sister. It was lovely, made and given with love.

Mother, giving me a Christmas/birthday angel

What We've Learned

- Surround yourself with positive people. I have always taught this to my children. When you surround yourself with positive people, you will produce positive things.

- Treating people positively and with respect usually results in reciprocal respect and positive attitudes.

- It's all about attitudes!

Quotes

"Generally, appreciation means some blend of thankfulness, admiration, approval, and gratitude. In the financial world, something that 'appreciates' grows in value. With the power tool of appreciation, you get the benefit of both perspectives: as you learn to be consistently thankful and approving, your life will grow in value."

—Doc Childre and Howard Martin

"To be trusted is a greater compliment than to be loved."

—George MacDonald

"It is an equal failing to trust everybody and to trust nobody."

—Old English proverb

"People of high self-esteem are not driven to make themselves superior to others. They do not seek to prove their value by measuring themselves against a comparative standard. Their joy is being who they are, not in being better than someone else."

—Nathaniel Branden

TIPS AND TOOLS

- Appreciate those who care. Gifts of appreciation, even if small, are a kind gesture that lets others know you value them and their work. Never forget the power of a simple thank you.

- Include other family members when giving gifts to providers. Let family members know the good job the providers are doing and the responsibility the family members have for their loved one.

- "Family Caregivers Recognized" Several organizations recognize family caregivers. This article notes the importance of recognizing and thanking family caregivers. Also noted is, "Family caregivers provide $257 billion worth of "free" caregiving services each year".
http://www.state.il.us/aging/1news_pubs/pr110103.htm

- Positive Attitude Quotes – I believe quotes support our daily efforts, and give us energy to keep on going. This is a great site for quotes that help confirm, validate, and authenticate what we're doing.
http://lucymacdonald.typepad.com/positive_perspective_quot/

Chapter 8

TECHNOLOGIES AND ASSISTIVE TECHNOLOGIES

We rely on technology every day for learning, entertainment, shopping, moving, interacting and communicating, daily living skills, sleeping comfort, dressing, bathing, safe positioning, playing, safety, and independence. Some technology is used by choice and convenience; some is essential for individuals who need a piece of equipment for daily living. It is a powerful tool that can open the door to independence and quality of living. "Assistive technology (AT) refers to both high- and low-tech tools that allow people of all ages to be more independent."[19] High technology refers to devices such as voice synthesizers, Braille readers, switch-activated toys or equipment/appliances, and computers. Simple, low-tech tools are equally important for the young and old, such as special handles on utensils, toothbrushes or paintbrushes, and pillows and bolsters that make positioning safer and more comfortable. Assistive technology can help individuals be more independent in communication, accessing the environment, being social, moving, self-help skills, and safe and comfort-

---

[19] Mulligan, S. A. (2003). *Assistive Technology: Supporting the Participation of Children with Disabilities.* Young Children on the Web

able positioning, and it can promote their health and safety. There must, however, be a good match between the tool and the individual, so the device matches the individual's abilities and meets the individual's need in the environment. "The right match of assistive technology can create magic when it allows a child (or adult) to be more independent and expressive." [20]

TECHNOLOGIES AND ASSISTIVE TECHNOLOGIES IN "OUR SANDWICH"

My family all chipped in to buy Mother's laptop for her ninetieth birthday. She had never written an e-mail and was confused about how this thing worked. She thought everyone could read anything she wrote, so the idea of writing something that all could see was, at times, uncomfortable. Still, she learned how to use it and began, with assistance, to communicate with her children and grandchildren. Family pictures were shared. Cassie, our oldest daughter, would often look up interesting facts and information with Grandma, such as the largest tomato or lemon, or the meaning of various terms on the Food Network or animal channel. Whenever Grandma would want to know about something, Cassie would help her look it up on her computer.

I compiled the following list of assistive technology equipment that my mom and Tally use. Many are essential for daily living needs and used numerous times each day. Each must be maintained for functional use. Below the lists are photographs of examples.

---

[20]   Mulligan, S. A. (2003). *Assistive Technology: Supporting the Participation of Children with Disabilities.* Young Children on the Web

List of Assistive Technology for Mother
> Computer
> Automatic-dialing telephone
> Headphones for phone for better hearing
> Grasp-holder for utensils, paintbrushes
> Adaptive easel for painting
> Bars by toilet to assist with transfers
> Bath seat
> Railing down the side of the bed, so she won't fall out of bed
> Wheelchair
> Walker
> Lift in van
> Power scooter
> Hospital-type tray for chair or bed
> Lounging chair with lifting action
> Hoyer lift – used to transfer an individual from bed to wheelchair (See http://www.youtube.com/watch?v=EP2myQVns9s for a demonstration)
> Deck garden that she can reach from her wheelchair (she grew tomatoes, green peppers, radishes, strawberries, onions, flowers)

List of Assistive Technology for Tally
> Lower Tech:
>> Loop scissors
>> Dysum (to keep from slipping off of seat; can also use nonskid shelf paper)
>> Water bottle attached to wheelchair
>> Holder for reacher on wheelchair
>> Wheelchair gloves

Calculator
Pencil grip
Non-latex balls
Transfer board
Lower railing on steps, study pillow/box tray
Remote for TV, lights, Christmas tree lights, etc.

Higher Tech:
Supportive seating aids
J-seat specialized cushion for individuals with pa-
ralysis, to reduce chances of pressure sores when
sitting or moving out of a wheelchair
Ankle foot orthosis; knee/ankle/foot orthosis
Caster cart
Stander
Reciprocating Gait Orthosis with reverse walker
Stool for adult assisting
Hydraulic bath seat
Leg braces
Alpha-smart – a portable word-processing keyboard
used in Tally's elementary years
Personal care items
Adaptive clothing
Thistle trike (hand tricycle)
Hand bicycle exerciser
Laptop computer for schoolwork, social interaction,
entertainment
Textbooks on CD, so she can read while computer
"reads," for better comprehension
Small tape recorder to tape class lectures
Power wheelchair
Manual wheelchair

Beach wheelchair (goes on sand and in water)
Shower wheelchair
Reacher to pick up things from floor
Cell phone for emergencies, calling for rides, etc.
Lift in van
Ramps and decking around three sides of our house
Tray to scoot under wheelchairs
Roll under sinks, under which a wheelchair can fit
Roll in shower to use with a shower wheelchair
Wheelchair lift to the basement
Side-opening oven door

Technology also made it possible for Cassie to continue working on Web classes she was taking, while teaching part-time in an adjunct faculty position at the university where I taught, in addition to teaching at a local liberal arts university. Technology also allowed me to communicate information and updates on a variety of levels to various groups, agencies, and family members, such as:

- Communication with siblings about my mom's updates, health, finances, pictures, etc.

- Health and success updates on Tally

- Making appointments

- Ordering supplies

- Communication with systems, agencies, providers for both Tally and my mom

- Communication with doctors/clinics

- Communication with brother (physician) for second medical consult
- Also a great "paper trail" for various needs
- Wonderful tool for advocacy

Technology also allowed my mom to paint again. She had enjoyed some art classes before she was married, and then took up painting again after most of her children had grown and left home. She quit painting after having had three strokes. After two years in Kansas, we located a magnificent art therapy graduate student who used adaptive techniques and technology that allowed my mom to paint again. The art therapist offered an adapted easel that supported the canvas at a level that my mom did not have to raise her arms (she had torn rotator cuffs in both shoulders). We also used a wedge to appropriately angle the canvas on the table. The art therapist also offered paint brushes with larger grasping sections when needed. Mother worked for many hours on each painting, and delighted in being able to create, once again. Below is a photo of Mother working on one of her paintings, and well as several other photos of other assistive technology used by Mother and Tally.

Mother painting with wedge supporting canvas for better positioning

Mother with art therapist, using adapted easel

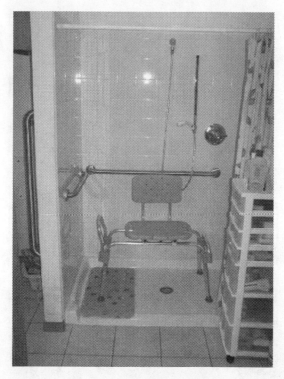

Mother's accessible shower

Mother's toilet areas, with grab bars and space to get
her wheelchair close enough for transfers.

Tally's accessible shower. She uses a shower wheelchair
that she transfers into and rolls into the shower.

Mother's Roll under sink, under which a wheelchair can fit in the
bathroom. Tally has one as well. The pipes under the sink must be
insulated to ensure that the heat won't burn legs when rolled under.

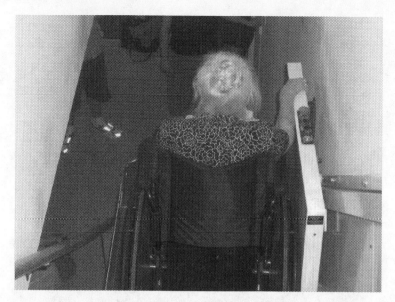

Our wheelchair lift to the basement. This allowed my parents to stay in the downstairs bedroom while waiting for their house to be finished. Tally also uses this to get down the rec room.

Here is Mother's raised garden for her deck. We simply used upside-down pots, bolted to one right-side up, to raise it to easily access while in a wheelchair.

We have also spent much time and effort trying to educate others and advocating for accessible environments. Because we travel with two wheelchairs and two vans, we need to plan ahead to be sure that where we're going is wheelchair-accessible. Below are pictures of where our advocacy has resulted in wheelchair lifts in various locations.

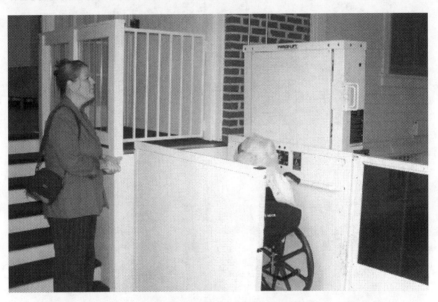

Here is a lift in a business for which we advocated and went through a mediation process for over two years. It was finally installed, and we went to try it out with my mom.

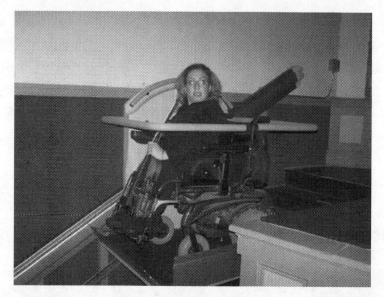

This sleek, quiet lift was installed in a performance auditorium for Tally and others who might be performing on stage.

Mother and Tally both needed accessible vans with lifts. We could not transport them in the same vehicle, so we had two accessible vans. Here is a photo of Tally getting her new van lift, and with Tony Cruise from United Access in Kansas City.

MAKE USE OF THIS *VERY* HELPFUL RESOURCE!

The Assistive Technology (AT) for Kansans Project provides information and referral, advocacy, acquisition and maintenance of devices, peer counseling, and public awareness services for Kansans with disabilities. This state program was particularly helpful to us for years, as both my mom and daughter used assistive technology for independence, safety, and access. We were like a one-stop multipurpose visit for them. They could visit both my mom and Tally in one trip. The AT for Kansans Project provided us with assistive technology assessments, loan of equipment, training, advice, and funding assistance. When Tally was in elementary school, middle school, and high school, they also attended Individualized Education Plan (IEP) meetings and vocational rehabilitation meetings to present assessment results and validate the importance of specific AT devices for learning, mobility, safety, and independence for our daughter. Supports are important for us to survive and manage our daily stress with managing care and assistance. The AT for Kansans Project has been a major part of our supportive teams for both my mom and my daughter. If you live in Kansas, it's a simple number, no matter where you are in the state: 1-800-Kan-Do-It. It is worth the call. They are wonderful people, and in spite of the economic cuts, they are still there to help you. The following Web site includes many links to assistive technology resources for the young and old:

http://www.independenceinc.org/at.html

There are assistive technology programs in every state— you only need to look for it and ask for it. The following link has a complete list of the state Association of Assistive

Technology Act Programs, including contact information and Web sites:

http://www.ataporg.org/atap/.

A great source for an assistive technology and transition manual (from high school to college or work) can be found on this site: http://www.ataporg.org/atap/.

WHAT WE'VE LEARNED

- With a little assistance (from another individual or with the help of technology), you can do a lot more. Assistive technology can make a difference in the life of your loved one, as well as in yours. As the caregiver, it can save your back!

- No doesn't always mean no. If insurance says no to an item, try getting your doctor to write a letter. Sometimes we would write the letter and have the doctor edit and send it. We were able to get various helpful items covered by insurance by appealing the first decision. Appealing does take time, but if it is an item that can make a difference in your loved one's life, it will be worth it. Be sure to look at other sources of funding. Your state's assistive technology project people can also be helpful with this.

QUOTE

"Try before you buy!"

—Motto of the Assistive Technology for Kansans Project

There are resources to try out an item before purchasing. This is particularly important with high-ticket items. Always check with your insurance company for coverage.

TIPS AND TOOLS

• Assistive Technology for Kansans Project:
http://www.independenceinc.org/at.html
This site includes many links to assistive technology resources
for the young and old.

Disability Related & Assistive Technology Web Indexes:
  Ableize, a United Kingdom Directory of Disabled Information Mobility Aids and Services

• Ableize is a comprehensive UK and Ireland resource of
  disability and mobility information. Find disability and
  disabled products and services, sports and the arts, plus
  children's needs, education, social care, and mobility and
  walking aids. The directory contains the largest disability
  categories in the UK.
  www.ableize.com

• Assistive Technology–NE Kansas Education Service Center
Lots of links to disability=related and assistive technology
Web sites.
www.nekesc.org/kids/at.html

• The Boulevard
A disability and health-care site dedicated to providing valuable information about quality products and services available
to health-care professionals and individuals with disabilities.
The Boulevard has links to companies in nineteen categories, including accessible vans; adaptive clothing; adaptive
computer equipment; assistive devices for daily living; free

catalogs; lifts, ramps, and transfer devices; scooter and scooter lifts; and wheelchairs, cushions, and accessories.
www.blvd.com/

• disABILITY Information and Resources
These pages were created and are maintained by Jim Lubin, who is completely paralyzed from the neck down and dependent on a ventilator to breathe. The pages provided here are meant to serve as a resource to provide useful information; therefore, they do not contain a lot of useless, pretty graphics which take a long time to load. These pages do not require Netscape or Explorer for best viewing.

• Disability On-line—the information directory
There are over two thousand links in this directory.
www.disabilityonline.com/

• Disability Resources Monthly (DRM) Guide to Disability Resources on the Internet
People with disabilities often need information to achieve their goals and their independence—information about legal rights, financial resources, assistive technology, employment opportunities, housing modifications, childrearing and educational options, transportation and mobility services, and more. Disability Resources, Inc., is a national, nonprofit organization based on Long Island, New York, which has provided information about resources for independent living since 1993. The organization developed this Web site in 1997 to help people quickly locate high-quality Internet resources on-line. www.disabilityresources.org

- DO-IT Programs' Links to Other Resources
A continually growing list of resources related to disabilities
www.washington.edu/doit

- Esmerel's Collection of Disability Resources
This includes lists of many disability-related resources; literally hundreds of well-organized links.
www.esmerel.org/

- Internet Resources for Special Children (IRSC)
The IRSC Web site brings together valuable information for parents, educators, medical professionals, etc., who interact with children who have disabilities.
www.irsc.org/

- Seaside's Disability, Assistive Technology, and Related Links
Lots of links.
www.seaside.org/linx.html

- The WebABLE! Internet Accessibility Resource Database
This is the WebABLE! database for Internet resources related to disabilities and accessibility. WebABLE!'s renowned list of resources is searchable, based on topic, and specific to your location.
www.webable.com/

- The Yahoo Index
Society and Culture: Disabilities
www.yahoo.com/Society_and_Culture/Disabilities/

Carol L. Russell, Ed.D.

- Assistive Technology Act of 1998, 105-394, S.2432
http://www.section508.gov/docs/AT1998.html

- The Assistive Technology Act of 2004
http://www.afb.org/afbpress/pub.
asp?DocID=aw060109&Special=33

Chapter 9

FINANCES!

FINANCES: IT'S A BALANCING ACT!

If you Google "taking care of elderly finances," you'll find 810,000 Web sites. This chapter is filled with information from Web site articles, various resources, and personal e-mails dealing with our parents' financial situation. They tell the story.

As reported in an *ABC News* story, "Shouldering the Burden of Elder Care," there are an estimated 34 million Americans who care for an older family member. Reporter David Wright tells a story of a twenty-eight-year-old woman who takes care of her mother, who has a brain tumor. She "spends nearly $3,000 each month on expenses. She works part-time, and almost her entire paycheck goes to the home-care nurse who takes care of her mom while she is at the office." She states, "It is not really a sacrifice. I just love her, and I want to be there for her, and I don't ever want her to feel like she is alone."

"A study from the National Association of Caregivers says the whopping costs of home care average more than $5,500 a year. That's $400 more than the average household spends on health care and entertainment combined. The bulk of those funds are spent on just the basics: food, transportation, and medical care and supplies. When the aging relative lives in another city, the costs run even higher. On average, long-distance caregivers spend nearly $9,000 a year." [21]

"This is the first time that research has been done on this issue of the financial out-of-pocket costs of caregiving," said Gail Gibson-Hunt of the National Association of Caregivers. "And we think it's important, because we want Congress to actually do something about it. Over the last five years, Congress has tried several times to give tax breaks to family caregivers, but none of the measures has passed. Elder care is an issue that affects more and more Americans each year. An estimated 34 million Americans provide some care for a family member, age fifty or older. And as the baby boomers begin to retire, that number is going to climb even higher." [22]

Another article, titled "New Study Reveals the High Financial Cost of Caring for an Older Loved One," from the National Family Caregivers Association's *Take Care: Self-Care for the Family Caregiver* (Winter, 2008), states that half of those caring for an older loved one spend an average of 10 percent of their yearly income on caregiving expenses. Other key findings of this study include:

- 34 percent of respondents used some of their saving to cover this cost.

- 23 percent of respondents said they cut back on their own health-care spending.

- Expenses cited were 42 percent (household goods, food/

[21] Wright, *ABC News*, (2007).From: 2008 *ABC News* Internet Ventures http:// abcnews.go.com/WN/WorldNews/story?id=3888689

[22] Wright, *ABC News*, (2007).From: 2008 *ABC News* Internet Ventures http://abcnews.go.com/WN/WorldNews/story?id=3888689

meals); 42 percent (travel/transportation); 40 percent (medical co-pays and medications); 31 percent (medical equipment/supplies); 21 percent (clothing).

- 53 percent of respondents did not work; 37 percent quit their jobs or reduced work hours.

- Respondents spent an average of 35.4 hours of caregiving per week; 19 percent caregiving for more than three years; 32 percent for more than five years.

- Respondents were making the following sacrifices: leisure activities, vacations, saving less or not at all, using their savings, cutting back on basics (clothing utilities, transportation, groceries) and personal medical or dental expenses.

- Respondents reported heightened stress or anxiety (65 percent); difficulty sleeping (49 percent); increased financial worries (43 percent); depression or hopelessness (37 percent); new or increased health problems (26 percent).

- Time was listed at the most significant sacrifice, although most considered it as a labor of love and were doing it willingly.

According to the NFCA, "This study is significant in that it quantifies what family caregivers have been saying for years: the costs associated with caregiving are enormous. It's time for legislators to take note and to take action to help America's family caregivers" [23]).

A comprehensive article regarding finances, "Aging Parent and Senior Finances," from Agingcare.com, states, "As anyone who cares for an elderly relative can attest to, growing old is expensive." The article offers some practical advice

---

[23]   Take Care: Self-Care for the Family Caregiver, NFCA Winter Newsletter, 2008

on finances, money, insurance, and legal issues as helpful resources. It suggests:

• Organize Your Finances
Medical treatment and caregiving can be costly. This makes good financial planning even more important.
http://www.agingcare.com/Featured-Stories/95008/Organizing-Your-Finances.htm

• Finding Benefits and Services
Acquaint yourself with programs that can pay directly for certain caregiving needs, prescription medications, and health-care facilities.
http://www.agingcare.com/Featured-Stories/95011/Finding-Benefits-and-Services.htm

• Understanding Reverse Mortgages: the Pros and Cons
This financial option for seniors is becoming increasingly popular. It uses the equity from one's home to increase cash flow. It's important, however, to be clear on the positive and negative aspects of this option.
http://www.agingcare.com/Featured-Stories/95604/Understanding-Reverse-Mortgages-The-Pros-and-Cons.htm

• Social Security: A Primer
Social Security, at some point, will touch the lives of nearly all Americans. It is important to understand the program and what your loved is entitled to.
http://www.agingcare.com/Featured-Stories/95236/Social-Security-A-Primer.htm

• Asset Protection for the Caregiver and the Elderly
Having the foresight to make arrangements for your own long-term care saves the family emotional and financial distress.

http://www.agingcare.com/Featured-Stories/95666/Asset-Protection-for-the-Caregiver-and-the-Elderly.htm

- Insurance

Insurance policies are often billed as a safety net, but it's important to carefully assess what the policies actually offer and where there are holes.

http://www.agingcare.com/Featured-Stories/95020/Managing-Insurance-Policies.htm

- What You Should Know about Long-Term Care Insurance

Long-term care insurance may be worthwhile if the premiums are affordable and the buyer has significant assets to protect.

www.ucu.org/longtermcare.htm

- Navigating the Medicaid and Medicare Maze

Medicaid and Medicare can be a godsend for the elderly, but the rules are confusing. Get basic information about each program.

www.agingcare.com/.../95024/Navigating-the-Medicaid-and-Medicare-Maze.htm

- An Overview of Medicare Prescription Drug Coverage

If your loved one is on Medicare and needs prescription drug coverage, there are two plans to choose from. Find out how to evaluate which is best for your loved one.

www.workworld.org/wwwebhelp/medicare_part_d_prescription_drug_coverage_overview

- Medicare: Protecting Your Loved One's Interests

Thus far, Medicare Part D has had its share of surprises and glitches. Following these tips may help you avoid pitfalls and resolve any problems that crop up.

www.agingcare.com/Featured-Stories/95020/Managing-Insurance-Policies.htm

LEGAL

What Is a Durable Power of Attorney and Why Do Caregivers Need One?

A durable power of attorney enables the caregiver to handle specific legal and financial responsibilities on behalf of the elderly person.

http://www.agingcare.com/Featured-Stories/94967/What-is-a-Durable-Power-of-Attorney-and-Why-Do-Caregivers-Need-One-.htm

Advance Care Directives

Advance care directives help ensure your voice is heard in the event that you or the person you care for become incapacitated and are unable to make decisions or let your wishes be known.

http://www.agingcare.com/Featured-Stories/94984/Advance-Care-Directives.htm

Do-Not-Resuscitate Orders

Complex medical procedures have the ability to keep people alive longer than they could naturally expect to live but with a greatly reduced quality of life.

http://www.agingcare.com/Featured-Stories/95007/Do-Not-Resuscitate-Orders.htm

A great source on "Tax Tips for Family Caregivers" can be found in the National Family Caregivers Association's *Take Care: Self-Care for the Family Caregiver* (Winter 2008). It covers areas, such as:

Tax Tips

- Medical Expense Deductions: General Principles
- Special Expenses (e.g., medical equipment)
- Nursing-Home Care
- Nursing, Therapeutic, and/or Aid Services
- For Whom Can You Claim Medical Deductions?
- Where to Get Help

ANOTHER FINANCIAL RESOURCE

"How to Pay for Long-term Care without Breaking the Bank"—there is a lot to consider and think about regarding financial planning for the elderly.
www.gilbertguide.com/2007/03/01/financial-planning-for-the-elderly-a-personal-perspective/ - 34k

Also see "Caring for Elderly Loved Ones"
http://moneyfitness.com/mc6/topic.php?b=24544978-0-&c=463&h=506,3,2

Taking proper care of your parents as they age can be difficult unless you are prepared. This site includes information on:

Taking Care of Elderly Parents
Helping a Parent Find the Right Housing
Home-Based Health-Care Services
Living with the Family
Other Housing Options
Nursing Homes
Helping a Parent Find the Necessary Health Care
Medicaid
Paying for Custodial Care Out of Savings

If You Are Paying to Support Your Loved One
Managing Affairs in the Event of Incapacity
Being an Agent for an Incapacitated Loved One
Going to Court to Help Your Loved One
Checklist for the Terminally Ill

Taking Care of Elderly Parents and Raising Children: Balancing Roles
http://www.associatedcontent.com/article/280807/taking_care_of_elderly_parents_and.html

---

Senior citizens are particularly vulnerable to financial distress once they're living on a fixed income and experiencing cognitive decline. The following site offers information on how caretaking children can help:

http://health.usnews.com/articles/health/2007/11/02/taking-care-of-your-parents-protecting-their-finances.html

* * * * *

I have shared the following e-mails regarding finances, particularly when my mom was running out of money. These are self-explanatory and present the sense of urgency at this time. Her home in her former location finally sold (and we were giving my mom and dad loans until it sold). I have removed the amounts and names of people and agencies for confidentiality.

The following e-mail with an agenda for a conference call occurred early on, regarding finances before a family meeting, before the move:

From: Carol Russell   Sunday, October 9, 2005, 12:16 PM
To: Siblings
Subject: Conference Call Today at 5:00

Dear siblings,

After returning from our presentations in Western Kansas (totaling fourteen hours of presentations, over nine hours of set up/clean up, and ten hours of driving in three days), we are pretty exhausted. However, it was refreshing to see how well everyone did without us, yet the planned coordination was essential. I am grateful that Dottie was able to be here and was able to get out and do some fun things with the folks. She will send an e-mail with details, I'm sure, and I know it took some coaxing to get Papa out. Thank you, Dottie! They enjoyed it. Cassie and Mikelle helped with Tally and arranged their schedules to transport her and take care of her needs.

I hope you can join us for the conference call tonight at 5:00. Dottie had sent the numbers; I'll check and send them again when I locate them.

Here is the agenda, with some of the details:

- Overall health: Dottie & Carol
- Overall finances: Carol & Fletch
    - Approximate figures:
    Checking: _____
    Savings: _____

- Also, two life insurance policies _____
  More is paid into these than they are worth
  Need to reanalyze these
  Probably need to cash these to prepay funeral costs

- Car and burial plats: these do not count as assets for Medicaid

- House not sold, reduced by $_____, from $___to $___

- Bottom line: With cash, they have a little over two months for provider care (@____+ per month) and meds (which run $_____ per month)

- They are running out of money, which is why they moved here. If their house does not sell, we will try to get Medicaid but may need some help with a loan in the meantime.

- We already have a loan to them for $_____. We cannot loan them any more. We have made the interest payments but cannot really do this any longer. There is still more to finish on the deck and stain the place. Fletch can do this but has to work a bit at a time to fit it in. We cannot really hire anyone at this point, as they are running out of money.

- When the house sells (depending on what it sells for), after realtor fees and paying off the loan, they will have approximately $_____ for provider, meds, medical, etc.

- Meds: Carol, with help from Don & Jon?
  - Protonix $_____/ month
  - Prilosec OTC would be $_____/ month

- Pharmacist said Prononix is a bit stronger but not that different, and if Prilosec worked, it's worth it. That would save them $_____/ month

What do you think, Don?

What other meds might a generic work for and be cheaper?

- Townhouse: Dottie?

The realtor has not contacted us; we've called her each time.

Dottie said she could call for updates

Should we lower the price again?

- Medicaid: Carol

Papa is on the Senior Care Act for some of his hours.

I have called to get an appointment for an assessment, but have not heard back, as it was just before we went out of town. I will call again tomorrow.

- Funeral Plans: Carol, Dottie, and Kathy?

Prepaid funeral expenses will not count as assets under Medicaid for up to $5000 prepaid for each. This would be helpful to do before the Medicaid assessment. We need to:

  - Sell the _____ plats (from where they moved)
  - Buy local plats _____ or elsewhere?
  - Set up arrangements with Pastor _____ (he has a checklist they use, but we do not yet have it)
  - Set up and prepay wishes through a funeral home (up to $5000 each)

- Car: Fletch?

- In January, insurance is due. Theirs has been about $400/6 months

  - If put on our family insurance plan, could be about $200/ 6 months
  (They would still own it)

  - Registration also due in Jan., $450–500

  - Worth about $8000–9000

- Other?

Love,
Carol

$*****$

This part of an e-mail shared needed items for Mother/Grandma in 2006 that would be functional and would save her some money on daily needed items:

"Steph asked that we resend the list of some Christmas ideas for Mother/Grandma. I thought maybe some others might want it, too.

Grocery $

Cracklin' Bran ($3.50/box)

Juices (cranberry or cran-grape or cran-raspberry)

Crackers, cheese, summer sausage

Chicken noodle soup

Paper products (TP, paper towels, Kleenex)

Non-latex gloves

Wet Ones

Advantage nutrition drinks

Baby lotion

Maalox, vitamins (multi, calcium w/D)

Prilosec OTC

Fruit (pineapple, oranges, and watermelon are her favorites)

Easy-to-chew chocolates or treats; choc. covered cherries are a favorite (we try not to do a lot of sweets, but she does like them)"

* * * * *

Here is another e-mail about Mother's depleting finances. I tried to keep family informed and updated:

July 23, 2007

Dearest family,

Each day we are blessed to have Mother with us. She is doing very well, health-wise, this summer, after a rough spring with acute intestinal problems, her last six teeth out, adjusting to lower denture, and her two different meds' severe allergic reactions. I think we are on top of it now. She is in good spirits in spite of the heat these days. Some days she gets out in the morning but mostly in the evening when it's cooler.

She still attends church every Saturday evening and Bible class on Wednesdays (the ladies that lead it were on vacation the past two weeks). She joins us on different outings when it's not too hot and she feels up to it.

She has loved the visits from family and friends. Her visit from a dear friend was a highlight this summer, as were visits with children, grandchildren and great-grandchildren. Thank you all for taking the time to visit her, she so treasures your visits.

It was a bit scary, putting her last savings into her checking account last week. She will soon be out of money. We have been able to stretch her money over the past two years. Mother and I discussed what to do with her cookbook money (which accounts for years of her peddling her cookbooks). She wanted to use it for her funeral. I told her that her insurance policy would cover that. (I have to have her policy designated to a specific funeral home, with a preplanned funeral, itemized expenses before the Medicaid meeting.)

We will be meeting with the Medicaid representative and then a screening appointment, which is still TBA. The screening is the crucial meeting, as they decide, depending on her needs, how much and what kind of services would be provided. I have asked Cassie, Mikelle, Patty (her main providers, along with me), and Dottie to be there, and Jon would like to be included for the experience.

Something I learned in the last few months is that she would have to pay approximately two-thirds of her income (retirement income from Papa and her social security) each month to be on HCBS—Home and Community Based Services for Frail & Elderly—which is the Medicaid program she would be on. This program is a state-funded program that enables a person who is older, with limited income, to stay in her home and not be forced to go into a nursing home for care. Yes, it sounds very strange to have to pay for the program, but we have to weigh the cost with the benefits. If they will give her hours for nighttime care and some during the day, pay for her meds and insurance, it will be worth it. If not, I'm not sure what I'm going to do. (This is where I take a long s-l-o-w deep breath,) She will, even with HCBS supports, not have enough to cover her care costs each month, as they will not cover twenty-four-hour care. I will know more on what exactly is covered after the screening meeting and will let you all know. We will cover her care costs if she is totally out of money before Sept. 1, and also until

Medicaid services are in place. I understand that this can be up to forty-five days after the application, so we may need to stretch even more than we do already.

This fall is going to be an absolute zoo for us. I hope I can get this all set up and rolling soon. My teaching load is exceptionally full, teaching two grad classes and three undergrad classes; Fletch is teaching three classes (two new ones); Tal is taking five classes and will be part-time living with Mikelle (but the supports, schedule, and transportation still have to be set up). Cass will be adjunct for two new classes (critical thinking and a psych class). We're excited to help sponsor Mikelle's senior art senior show in Feb. or March. Tom, Fletch's dad, will turn ninety in November, and we're helping to organize a birthday art show (Tom and family) at Baker's Russell-Holt Gallery, Nov. 17. We're trying to get a new van (as ours is slowly deteriorating and is often in the shop or "Fletch's shop"), and we're working on funding for a lift. We still have a Medicaid appeal going for Tal, and an ADA complaint and mediation on behalf Mother on a local business' nonaccessibility.

That's the update for now.

Love you all,

Carol

* * * * *

The following parts of an e-mail to family describe issues of theft by a provider, an ADA (Americans with Disabilities Act) mediation, and application plans for Medicaid:

From June 21, 2007
"Hi all-

What a week we've had! Mother/Grandma is feeling pretty good and has been involved in making this world a better place this week. Besides getting her doctor and dentist appointments in, she was also involved in the following:

- We just finished meeting with the sheriff deputy over the provider (from an agency) who stole a money order from another provider (also from the agency) on these premises. We were suspicious of some meds, cash, and possibly some supplies taken as well. This was back in March, and the person no longer works for Mother/Grandma.

- Last week Mother/Grandma accompanied us to a two-hour mediation over a local business' nonaccessibility and unsafe elevator. The owner apologized to Mother/Grandma for putting her in what she felt was an unsafe situation and agreed to have an ADA consultant come to make recommendation, and will hopefully make changes. His attorney was not as agreeable. Anyway, some progress. The mediator was great and thanked Mother/Grandma for coming and making a difference, also sending her a sweet card.

Okay, so the main reason for my e-mail is to report that I will be officially applying for Medicaid on Mother/Grandma's behalf in August. We have stretched her money for two years and will now look for supports. The Medicaid process is quite complicated, and minimally supportive (may only be three hours of care/day). We are looking for additional supports.
Love,
Carol"

* * * * *

This e-mail was after Mother's oral surgery, a drug allergic reaction, and update on Medicaid:

From May 21, 2007
"Hi all~

Mother/Grandma recouped pretty well from the oral surgery and goes in again tomorrow for a final fit of her lower denture so she can wear it while eating. She was feeling so well on Thurs. that we finished her deck planting (five tomato plants, four peppers, a strawberry, onions, radishes, flowers), and she even rode on her scooter. Then we had some other complications. Yesterday she broke out in a rash all over her back, legs, stomach, rear, etc. It was pretty much driving her nuts. After calling Don (thanks, Don) we gave her a Benadryl and used hydrocortisone all over. This helped a little, but she was so restless, she got up and fell. She was so quiet that Patty didn't hear her. She has been getting up over the last two weeks at times without ringing the bell, in the bathroom, too. So I'm not sure if she's remembering or gets up in her sleep. Anyway, she's okay, but her back hurts even more than it did. The rash really worried us when we remembered that we found a tick on her head on Fri. We went to see Dr. S today. He said it was a drug allergy. He gave her a steroid shot (forgot the name) and recommended Claritin, so she won't be as drowsy, especially during the day. If she's not doing better by tomorrow, we'll go in again and check her back again. She was *very* fidgety all day, a little better tonight. She has also been much more confused lately.

On another note, the Medicaid meeting Fletch and I went to last week on Mother's behalf was not great. Of her $____/ month income, she has to pay $_____+ (more than half) to be on HCBS

(Home & Community Based Services). Unless they assess her, and she gets more than five hours of service a day, it's not worth paying into it. We can't officially apply until she is down to $2000 in assets, which by my calculations will be around Aug. or Sept, a little later than I had originally predicted (I had said June or July). I have some more calculating to do, and she will need to have the assessment for need (which they won't do until she applies), but that's the direction we're headed.

The other thing Medicaid requires is a prepaid funeral (itemized), and her life insurance policies to be directed to a specific funeral home (right now, they're directed to a non-specific funeral home). So, I would really like some help with the specifics. Maybe we could work on that a bit when you come this week, Dottie.

She *loves* getting phone calls.

Anyway, that's it for now.
Love you all,
Carol"

＊ ＊ ＊ ＊ ＊

Here is another update of Mother's health and finances:

"From: Carol Russell
Sent: Sunday, October 22, 2006 12:49 AM
To: Siblings
Subject: Update on Mother—long/important

Dear family,
Mother is doing very well and has good care! She really looks good and is in good spirits and health, better than she

has been in years. We do enjoy her so and are blessed to have her doing well. We do work hard, taking care of her on a daily basis.

This week started with a Monday 8:00 AM call that Mother's afternoon provider (who had just been with her a little over a week) was quitting. After several calls over two days, I was able to get an afternoon person from the new agency, and I left work early on Tues. to orient her for Wed. afternoon. Bible class is on Wed. and Mother so enjoys going. Fletch and I are both involved with classes and Tally's schedule at the time she needs to leave, so we cannot transport her. Wed. AM, I got a call that the new afternoon provider cannot lift her wheelchair. I tried calling LCAT, the city transportation system, and they were booked during that time each week. Then I arranged for the provider leaving to get her chair in the car, I would meet them at the church from work at 1:20 to meet them to help unload, and then they'd call me again for reloading, and when they got back, Fletch would be back here to unload.

That's what my life is like these days, besides assisting Tally with her freshman year at ESU and an overload this semester of teaching five classes and executive director of the campus preschool. Please know that I am not writing for sympathy or praise; I'm just giving you the picture of life for us these days.

With that "picture" comes more concern for Mother's financial situation. I have also had trouble finding providers and agencies. The stress the past few weeks has probably caused my recent shingles. I had written you all two months ago, Aug. 20, about my concern for Mother's financial situation, and the savings difference we have made. I was talking with _____ yesterday, expressing my concern, and she asked if we had a "Plan B." I told her we were past Plan B and now on C, D, or E. So I decided to list the plans that have been, are now, and will be. Here are the facts:

Plan A:
Winona Quality Living:
Was $_____ +/month

Plan B:
Move to Emporia
Local agency, 24 hrs.day:
$_____ / month

Plan C:
Patty, Cassie, Mikelle, Tally, Fletch & myself, along with limited local agency:
$_____ / month

Plan D (currently):
Local agency was not doing well, provider checks were bouncing, water and electricity had been turned off, the director and asst. director quit, etc. So, changed agencies after two weeks of filling in with temporary help.
* Now, with Patty, Cassie, Mikelle, Tally, Fletch and myself, along with (new agency):
$_____ / month

Plan E:
We're looking at all possibilities: We visited the adult day services in Emporia with Mother last week. We are looking at the _____ adult day services for days when someone is sick or Cassie has teaching commitments. We've also talked

about possibly a few days a week to save money. It's $7/hr and includes lunch, snacks, activities, administering meds, has a chapel, Bible class, and area to rest and put her feet up. She said she liked that one best and it was also recommended by Pastor _____ .

- If we were to use the adult day services, along with Patty, Cassie, Mikelle, Tally, Fletch and myself, I think we could get the cost to:
  $_____ /month.

Fletch and I met with the Medicaid representative last week. She can apply when she is down to $4,800 total assets. If she qualified for Medicaid, she could be under the HCBS (Home & Community Based Services) program for the "frail & elderly." The brief assessment and estimate that was given us was that she could only get three hours a day, which was very disappointing. We will try to get more information and appeal this if needed, but it does not look good. I had heard (from another care agency) the most they would cover is eight hours a day, but her initial screening estimated only three hours a day, which will help some, but not that much. Medicaid would, however, help with meds.

So, as I said in August, she would be out of money. we're looking at somewhere between March and May, depending on how Plan E works.

Plan F, G, etc:
With Plan E (above):

- Approximately $_____/month minus her $_____ of SS and retirement leaves her $_____ short for care each month.

- HCBS, if implemented for three hours a day would be

about $____/mo, leaving $____ short for just for care expenses each month. (Again, we will appeal this.)

- Other additional expenses not included above:
- health insurance @ $240/mo
- meds average $250–$300/mo until she'd qualify for Medicaid
- her electricity $100/mo
- car costs: cost of gas, insurance, registration, upkeep of car

- We would offer to pay her utilities (water, TV, phone, trash, gas heat—about $120–150/mo
- We would also offer to pay for her groceries, about $100/mo (in addition to already covering her evening meal each night, with leftovers).
- I will try to do more hours. Besides her power of attorney business and case management hours, I currently do about twenty-five hrs./week of care. I am doing more on the weekends now, as I cannot find weekend care. So I will probably be increasing to about–thirty-five to thirty-eight hours/week. I cannot do any more than the hours in the day. Obviously, I cannot quit my job to care for Mother.

Even with this, she will need additional help! When her money is out, she will need help from each of us. Somewhere between May and June, she will need approximately $\_\_\_\_\_-$____ additional funding each month. That's about $___ - $_____/mo from each of her five children, or that's approximately 3.5 nights of care, or four days of care per month from each of us. Mother needs our help. We will, of course, continue what we've been doing, and do more wherever we can, but there's only so many hours that we each have in the day.

Fletch and I talked, and we are willing to cover this for her until July, which will be two years of her living in Kansas. At that time we are asking, on behalf of Mother, for your monthly contribution or time for her care. This could be each month or multiple days in a row (e.g., in summer). The folks gave generous $ gifts to each of us, as children, and a generous amount of $ to each of our children for years for Christmas and also emergency loans when needed. It's our turn to give back. Mother knows I am asking for this on her behalf.

Please think of useful gifts to her for Christmas:

- Grocery $
- Cracklin' Bran (about $3.50/box, and all she wants for breakfast)
- Juices (cranberry or cran-grape or cran-raspberry
- Paper products (TP, paper towels, Kleenex)
- Advantage nutrition drinks
- Baby lotion, Maalox, vitamins (multi/calcium w/D/ Prilosec)

We also plan to sell Papa's Rascal and wheelchair and a few other things for additional care money for Mother.

If there is concern that we've "already been paid" for Mother's needs by the addition here, let me share the following. If we had been paid for our hours (at local rates, not Minnesota rates), the cost of the addition has been covered by:

- In-kind care hours each week
- Backup provider when others are sick, late, or didn't show up
- Finding agencies and orienting new providers

- Case management hours
- Power of attorney hours, including paying bills
- Maintenance hours
- Shopping, often more than once a week, getting meds
- Food, evening meals
- Assisting at appointments (dr., dentist)
- Countless calls for care, program information, working with agencies, hospice, visiting day services, etc.
- Emergency room visits (the first six months was frequent)
- Meetings with agencies
- Appointments arranging, planning, and supervising building of addition
- Land for building addition
- Took out equity loan on our home to build the addition and paid for the loan interest the first few months
- Worked with realtors in (former location) until the townhouse finally sold
- I would be happy to share these specific figures with anyone interested.

- On another topic:

Mother is compiling a list of her things with names of who to give them to. For less complication, she is putting only her children's names on them, and then as children, we can give things to our children. So if there is something you are really wanting, please let her and me know so we can record it on the list.

Sorry this is so long, but it all needed saying. I've been working on this off and on most of the day (after working with Mother this morning). As Mother's power of attorney, I'm letting you all know the state of things and Mother's need for our help. I am checking again, but this figure is less than the nursing home costs I have seen. Please give your input and I will share with Mother. We have to talk about this. We look forward to hearing from each of you. I will keep you posted with any new information.

Love you all,
Carol"

Toward the end of the e-mail above, I listed many of the things we do. I don't think awareness of what we really do is understood by many, unless they are here and actually do some of the caregiving, doctor visits, shopping, med runs, etc. There are times that I feel the need to list and somewhat justify all of the things we do, many go unsaid, unwritten.

Below is an e-mail from when we were changing payroll agents to save some money. The following e-mail was sent to the director of local agency we were leaving, due to paying half of night support that another agency paid ($20/night versus $10/night).

9/13/08

Hi _____,

Thanks for returning my call. As I mentioned, due to the increased cost of living, and her increase of HCBS client obligation, I have to look out for what is financially best for my mom. Changing payroll agents, will result in a savings of $300/month or $3600/year. We are planning to transition payroll agents for my

mom, effective Oct. 1, for both daytime hours and night support. I have contacted my mom's case manager, _____, who will be contacting you. I have notified most of my mom's providers and will let the rest know this week. Hopefully, it will be a smooth transition. Please let me know if there is anything else you might need from us.
Thanks,
Carol Russell

* * * * *

"12/15/07

As Mother's POA, I need to share the following summarization.

In looking back, I wanted to again share these figures for twenty-four-hour care:

- Former location agency: $_____+ per month / $_____/yr
  (They did not charge double for them both but did also use up Mother's long-term care insurance in addition to the above figure.)

- Local agency: $_____ per month/$_____/yr
(They did not charge double for them both.)

- Another local agency: $_____ per month / $_____/yr
(Although not used for a year)

- Current arrangement, with the coordination of Medicaid hours, a few hours from agency, other hours from Cassie, Patty, and other caregivers and my in-kind hours:
  $_____ per month/ $_____/yr

As you can see, this last figure is $200,000/yr., less than the beginning figure of twenty-four-hour care in their former location!

The alternate would be a nursing home, which with Medicaid (MA) coverage only, is not a reasonable alternative. I will not let this happen. The state-funded nursing home in town is not a place I would even take Mother to visit. (If you haven't been in a state-funded nursing home lately, try stopping by.) The other options (higher quality nursing homes) would entail additional funding from family in addition to MA. I don't know the exact amount but could look into it for comparison. You cannot get the "top of the line" nursing home for MA funding. A nursing home is not an alternative for Mother, which is what I have always felt for them both. Mother deserves the dignity, care, respect, and loving environment after all the years she has cared for everyone else.

Love,
Carol"

* * * * *

The following e-mail includes the latest Christmas list. Christmas '08 was an economically challenging Christmas. We, as a family, decided to give only functional or consumable gifts or artwork/homemade gifts. My niece always asks what Grandma needs. Here is my reply to her:

"Hi _____,

You are always the first to ask—what organization! In fact, I looked back on my developing organization chapter in my book, and there was the list I had sent in the past. I had to tweak it, as she cannot have fresh fruit, nuts, or fresh veggies, so here we go.

These are things that we often cover when she's out of money each month. Your mom and dad often bring things from this list as well, when they visit. I'll send the list to others as well.

- Grocery $
- Cracklin' Bran ($3.50/box)
- Juices (cranberry or cran-grape or cran-raspberry)
- Crackers, cheese, summer sausage
- Fruit cups
- Applesauce (she takes her pills 4x a day with applesauce)
- Paper products (TP, paper towels, Kleenex)
- Non-latex gloves
- Trash bags
- Softsoap refill
- Wet Ones
- Advantage nutrition drinks
- Baby lotion
- Maalox, vitamins (multi, calcium w/D)
- Prep H
- Maalox
- Prilosec OTC (we get the generic version at Wal-Mart)
- White vinegar, Ivory soap (for foot soaks)
- Easy to chew chocolates or treats but no nuts
- Phone calls—she loves to hear from everyone!

That's all I can think of for right now. We plan to buy some things for reorganizing. We're getting new blinds for the deck doors; a big shelf for plants so we can clear the floor and she can see her fireplace; and I think we're going to get a small purple Christmas tree, as the other one was not turning well, and we had trouble with the lights last year.

Love,
Carol"

* * * * *

WHAT WE'VE LEARNED

- It's a balancing act! Start talking about finances and long term care plans early, if your parents are willing. If not, have the discussion with the rest of the family. Someone needs to know the finances. Look for "red flags" such as un-paid bills, unreasonable purchases, etc. Organize. Seek out resources, find programs for which they are eligible, check insurance coverage, learn about Medicaid and Medicare, designate a durable power of attorney, and have medical wishes understood (a living will, DNR, etc.). You don't have to pay an attorney to complete these forms. They are available on-line, and all you need is a notary.

- It's also important to keep all family informed. If you do this, no one can say they didn't hear about something or were not aware of the situation. It gets to be like an electronic newsletter. This does take time, but technology helps. I could not do this without e-mail and computers.

QUOTE

"All parents know about sacrifices, but now, their children are learning about them as well."
—David Wright, *ABC News*, in "Shouldering the Burden of Elder Care"

"It's our turn to give back, not to turn our backs."
—Author unknown

TIPS AND TOOLS

Aging Parent and Senior Finances
http://www.agingcare.com/Finance/?gclid=CJLay4y205ICF
QurPAod6ksrnA

Caregiving Statistics and Cost Savings
http://www.asktransitions.com/infobase/infobase.html
This Web site includes:

- Who provides most of long-term care?

- How much money is spent by caregivers?

- How much money can a company save by educating their employees?

- Empower yourself with the facts and figures about aging and caregiving.

Caring for Elderly Loved Ones

- http://moneyfitness.com/mc6/topic.php?b=24544978-0-
  &c=463&h=506,3,2

Money-Saving Tips for Family Caregivers: Simple Steps to Cut your Expenses in NFCA's Quarterly Newsletter, *Take Care*, Winter 2009, p. 3 - 4

Shouldering the Burden of Elder Care
From 2008 *ABC News* Internet Ventures
http://abcnews.go.com/WN/WorldNews/story?id=3888689

Chapter 10

R-E-S-P-I-T-E

RESPITE: Taking Care of the Caregiver

I do not practice what I preach on this topic. I think back to the most salient example of this with sad reflection. Twenty-one-plus years ago, I was sitting by the side of my newborn baby in the neonatal intensive care unit, stroking her angelic face after three surgeries in her first week of life. I could not leave her side. After a strenuous labor and delivery, not taking care of myself and staying by her side, I found myself with a bladder infection, yeast infection, and hemorrhoids! I don't know what else could go wrong on that end of my body! The nurses urged me and almost kicked me out of the NICU, telling me I needed to take care of myself so I could better take care of my baby. I did but only when nearly forced by others to do so. I was not thinking too clearly at that time, but I appreciated the message to first take care of myself to better support for the days and weeks ahead for my newborn daughter.

I have heard repeated advice, take care of the caregiver; you cannot take care of someone else unless you take care of yourself; put the oxygen mask on yourself first, then help others; patch yourself, then patch others. This is true, but you sometimes need reminders and gentle—or stronger than gentle—pushes to do so.

Respite can be defined as "a brief period of rest and recovery between periods of exertion or after something disagreeable." Rest and recovery certainly sounds inviting. As I've said, respite should not be running to Wal-Mart and spending a half-hour looking for sales while you wait for your mom's prescription to be completed, but the moments of respite are needed, and integrating some relaxation moments and techniques throughout the day can offer some sanity. I used to teach Lamaze classes, so the slow, deep breathing comes in handy when stress is high and days are so busy I can hardly breathe. At the end of this chapter, "Tips and Tools" offer Web sites that list quick relaxation techniques to give you a breath on busy, crazy days.

Respite can also bring with it some guilt, which can cause the "resentment/guilt yo-yo." I have mentioned our Thursday night "date nights" that we started last year. Tally stays at her apartment, with assistance, and we have a provider for my mom that evening. We do not always go out; we often cook in. We talk and talk and talk. Sometimes we walk down to the pond with a bottle of wine or champagne. Sometimes we just take a walk or watch a movie. The together time is nice. I highly recommend a weekly (at least) time to spend with your spouse.

We in the Sandwich Generation experience stress on a daily basis; it's almost a way of life. Our mental health is at risk, as is our physical health. According to "Caregiver Stress," produced by the National Women's Health Information Center U.S. Department of Health and Human Services, Office on Women's Health (http://www.mental-health-matters.com/articles/article.php?artID=725):

- Approximately one-fourth of families in America are caring for an older family member, an adult child with disabilities, or a friend.

- Surveys quote that more than seven million persons are informal caregivers to older adults. Caregivers include spouses, adult children, and other relatives and friends. Other surveys found that almost twenty-six million family caregivers provide care to adults (aged eighteen or older) with a disability or chronic illness, and five million informal caregivers provide care for older adults aged fifty or older with dementia.

- Various studies show that more than half of caregivers in America are women.

- Twenty hours per week is the average amount of time that caregivers spend on caregiving. More time is required when the person cared for has multiple disabilities.

- Caring for a person with disabilities is physically demanding. This is especially true for older caregivers, who, according to surveys, make up half of all caregivers.

- One-third of all caregivers rate their own health as fair to poor.

- Caregivers often worry that they will not outlive the person for whom they are caring.

- Caregivers frequently suffer from depression and are more likely to become physically ill.

I found several sources with tips for caregivers. One well-organized list is from an article titled "Top Ten Tips for Caregivers" from the National Family Caregivers Association. (http://www.americanheart.org/presenter.jhtml?identifier=3039889)

This list includes suggestions such as taking charge of your life and not letting caregiving be the central focus; being good to yourself by taking quality time for yourself; watching for signs of depression and getting professional help when needed; accepting help from others; educating yourself about the condition of your loved one; being open to technologies that foster independence; trusting your instincts; grieving losses; dreaming dreams; standing up for your rights; and seeking support from other caregivers. Strength in knowing you're not alone.

For formal respite care programs, see http://www.aaaphx.org/CAREGIVER+RESPITE. It is important to look at both formal and informal help. You cannot do it alone!

See: http://www.aaaphx.org/node/37 for a "Caregiver Quiz" that will help you determine if you need a little help. The Area Agency on Aging provides questions related to caregiving; for example, about feeling stressed or run-down; missing work; needing a break; if you have a limited social life or loneliness; not eating well; or showing signs of depression.

It refers you to the Area Agency on Aging to help find solutions. They have a twenty-four-hour Senior Help Line at 602-264-HELP (4357) or toll-free at 1-888-264-2258. They have important information about services that can help caregivers and those for whom they give care.

On Vacation: Where the Sidewalk Ends

I've always enjoyed Shel Silverstein and have read his books to my children for many years. His books are really for all ages. *Where the Sidewalk Ends* (1974) has always been a favorite and has represented much of our lives, in that one's creativity comes out "where the sidewalk ends." This point really hit home as we were on our first vacation together in three years. We went to Branson, Missouri. Branson is like a mini Las Vegas, with every type of show, shop, fireworks, candy, T-shirt, and souvenir—along with beautiful scenery, lakes, and rivers. We took in the more natural, less costly and less commercialized fun. My sister Kathy, via her Resort Condominiums International (RCI) timeshare, treated our family to a getaway. We were able to have coverage for my mom's care by my older sister Dottie (and team), so I was secure in knowing that she would be well taken care of while we were gone. It also gave my mom a little time away from us, with a different pace and many activities to do with Dottie.

We hit the sidewalk's end, literally, one night, and it clearly illustrated for me our journey, our collective creativity/problem-solving, and our general approach to life. We live with a philosophy of not "if" but "how" to do something. We had spent a couple of "dream days," with all three of our girls together. We swam, fished, shopped, saw beautiful scenery, dined on crab legs, and toasted each other. It was wonderfully delightful, truly quality time! At the end of the second day, we went to see the dancing, musical, fire-shooting, colorful fountains down by the river's edge at Branson's Landing. We enjoyed the first show so much that we stayed for the second. By that time it was pretty dark, and the fog was moving in over the landing. All five of us walked along the new sidewalks—Tally had her power chair. It was an eerie, dream-like feeling with the waves of fog around us, our dancing shadows against the fog on the riverside, classy new lampposts with speakers that played great music, and "doggy waste stations" here and there along the lovely, new, clean, wheelchair-accessible path.

We were headed back to the car, walking and wheeling along together.

I was reminded of a comment Mikelle, our middle daughter, made many years ago. She had observed and lived our advocacy for accessible environments for almost her entire life, as she was two years old when Tally was born with spina bifida. Mikelle wasn't more than nine when she said, "Mom, you just want the whole world to be pavement!" I replied, "No, I just want pathways."

There in Branson, we were on one of those lovely pathways together—no one needed an alternate route. It was a totally inclusive experience. Suddenly, there it was—the sidewalk's end. There was orange plastic construction fencing, making a barrier to our inclusive experience. We hadn't seen it in the dark, or we would have turned around. Yes, it would be a great accessible experience once construction was complete, but for the moment, we were "in a pickle." To the right, there was a hill and a curb that could not be maneuvered by Tally's power wheelchair. To the left was the railing of the riverside. Being the quick-action–prone person that I am, I was ready to head back the mile we had just walked to get to the street over the curb, where the road and path had split. Fletch, being the creative problem-solver, looked around and noticed some bags of woodchips piled up by a little waterfall under construction. He quickly brought several of them over to the road's curb, and we collectively pushed Tally up the slippery slope to the curb and safely over the makeshift curb made of bags of woodchips. I imagined what the workers might wonder the next day, when they saw their bags rearranged. We have often taken the "path less traveled," and we literally did that night.

BUTTONS—TO PUSH OR NOT TO PUSH

As with most families, we know each others' "buttons" and can push them if we choose. We had an agreement to try not pushing each others' buttons on this trip. Our time together is too precious for that. I promised to try not being so controlling (although I think there is a difference between being controlling and being a good planner to get things done). I guess my suggestion to not push each others' buttons could possibly be considered controlling, but then, it's also a matter of respect. On this topic, Mikelle said to me, "I know the buttons. I just chose not to push them." I believe family respect is choosing not to push the "buttons" that we know are there.

THEN THE VACATION ENDS!

We returned from our somewhat normal vacation to find that one of the caregivers was moving—the next day! And then the reality hit. Thank God for my sweet daughters, who could help fill in temporarily (because it was summer) until I found someone else to replace the provider who was leaving. I knew this backup would not always be available—I was (and am) the permanent backup. I cannot let my guard down or totally relax, but vacations—planning and anticipating— helps keep me sane.

MIKELLE'S GRADUATION VACATION—TO THE BEACH!

We told Mikelle we would take her on vacation some- where (within reason), and she chose to go to the beach. This is very unusual, as we have not had the funds to finance trips, other than work-related or to visit relatives. So we started sav- ing for and searching for an accessible beach house that also allowed pets (Cassie's Cooper, a miniature schnauzer, and Tally's Cally, a bichon/shih tzu). The puppies had to join us, as did the boyfriends, of course. This took some research; Cassie and I started searching. There were not many accessible beach houses, let alone any that were pet-friendly. The thing about accessibility in rentals is that you have to be extremely specific with your wording and asking questions. We learned that "accessible" could mean only being able to get in the front door. "Fully ADA" meant not only entrance accessibility but that the bathroom door was probably accessible as well—it did not necessarily mean there weren't other barriers (steps to deck) or that there was a roll-in shower. One place was even going to charge if we used the elevator! We finally found a lovely accessible beach house, with a ramp all the way down to the beach. We tried to rent a beach chair, without luck, so we ended up buying one. Tally was able to join us on the beach, collecting pounds of seashells. We took turns cooking each night, and it was lovely—a real vacation.

Tally's beach chair that we purchased to use for our rare family vacation to the Gulf in Texas after Mikelle's graduation. It truly allowed us to all be together on the beach, collecting shells, enjoying the sun and waves.

CHECKLISTS, CHECKLISTS, CHECKLISTS!

Sometimes I feel like my life is made up of checklists. We have checklist for what to take, which includes medical supplies, and wheelchairs (manual, power, and beach wheelchairs), besides all the other things, including the dog and kennel. We also have to be sure things are taken care of at home. This checklist is for the providers who take care of my mom, in addition to caring for our house and the horse and lamb. Having these organized checklists helps to prevent some of the worry when we're gone.

Carol L. Russell, Ed.D.

RUSSELLS' CHECKLIST

Daily Job	SAT	SUN	MON	TUES	WED	THURS	FRI
WATER PLANTS with hose: *Between houses *Flower garden pots (by fountain) *Around cherry tree *Roses * Mound by jeep (Tally's corn) * New fruit trees * Mother's deck							
Feed Beta "Mr. Bucket" 2x/day, 1 pellet							
Feed Midnight & Dilly 2x/day	(T)	(T)	(T)	(T)	(C)	(C)	(C)
Pick up mail & paper: Mail – 2:00: PLEASE PUT MAIL IN BASKET ON OUR TABLE. DO NOT HAVE MOTHER OPEN BILLS, AS THEY CAN GET LOST AT HER HOUSE. Paper – evening Also, expecting UPS deliveries, check our back door							
As Needed: *Push water our of gazebo roof. * Be sure to put cushions back in storage bin (as rain or cats may damage them).							

CAROL'S EMERGENCY CELL: _____

MIKELLE'S CELL: _____

THANK YOU!

Day-to-Day Respite

Respite cannot wait until the once-a-year vacation. Weekly and daily respite of some sort is needed for sanity. Again, the National Family Caregivers Association's brochure, titled "Share the Caring," is helpful, with suggestions for creating an action plan for a caregiver who may need support or for a friend or family member who would like to help. The "Help I Need" and "Help I Can Offer" checklists offer ways family caregivers can ask for help and ways others can assist family caregivers. Examples of "Help I Need" includes: a night out with friends; dinners prepared; a weekend away; someone to ask how I am; pick up prescriptions and other health-care items; and help with paying the bills. Under "Help I Can Offer" are suggestions that coincide with the "Help I Need" column, such as dinner and movies on me; a meal prepared a certain number of times a week; a weekly phone call; run errands; or a check for a certain amount of dollars. There is also a section at the bottom of the page to personalize where help might be needed or offered. Some weeks I would give anything for a weekend away or someone else to do the bookkeeping or pay the bills. Dinner and a movie sounds great as well. See the National Family Caregivers Association's Web site or go to www.thefamilycare-giver.org/pdfs/326503_SharetheCaring_broch.pdf

Try to build mini-breaks, mini-respite into your life; it is essential. Incorporate relaxation techniques, a massage, imagery—whatever works for you—into your life. Here are a few Web sites for quick reference on managing stress and finding respite in your daily life.

- Stress Management for Healthy Living Quick Mini-Relaxation Strategies
http://www.csupomona.edu/~jvgrizzell/kin370/extras/quick-relaxers.html

Ten Relaxation Techniques by Steven Gillman
http://ezinearticles.com/?Ten-Relaxation-Techniques&id=182965

Quick Relaxation Techniques
http://www.law.uidaho.edu/quickrelax

What We've Learned

- You cannot do it alone, so don't try. Accept—and expect—help.

Quote

"Put the oxygen mask on yourself first, then help others."
—Author unknown

"Laughter jiggles the toilet handle of life"
—Al Schmidt

"Family respect is choosing not to push the 'buttons' that we know are there, no matter how tempting it may be."
—C. Russell

Tips and Tools

"Top 10 Tips for Caregivers" from the National Family Caregivers Association
http://www.americanheart.org/presenter.jhtml?identifier=3039889

There are formal respite care programs. It is important to look at both formal and informal help. You cannot do it alone!
http://www.aaaphx.org/CAREGIVER+RESPITE

Caregiver Stress
From the National Women's Health Information Center US DHHS, Office on Women's Health
http://www.mental-health-matters.com/articles/article.php?artID=725

Care Management Techniques You Can Use
www.nfcacares.org/pdfs/CareManagmt.pdf

Family Caregiving 101
A separate "how-to" site by the NFCA, with advice on time management, asking for help, navigating the health-care maze, and communicating with insurance companies and hospitals.
http://www.familycaregiving101.org/

Strength for Caring
A site for family caregivers from Johnson & Johnson, with original articles written by experts, along with how-to materials.
http://www.strengthforcaring.com/

End of Life Services

Several resources offer guidance on locating end-of-life care and respite for family caregivers. The following may be helpful:

- www.hospicefoundation.org

  The Hospice Foundation of America offers an informative article that explores myths about death and pain and offers insights on grief.

- www.cms.hhs.gov

  The Centers for Medicare & Medicaid Services provides information about coverage, eligibility, and benefits for hospice reimbursement through Medicaid.

- www.nahc.org

  National Association for Home Care and Hospice has an extensive Web directory that allows an individual to search for home care and hospice by location, payment types, services offered, and more.

- www.nhpco.org

  The National Hospice and Palliative Care Organization Web site provides information on choosing a hospice, Medicare and Medicaid, and basic hospice facts.

Chapter 11

Advocating

Making a Difference!

We have advocated whenever we could. Prioritizing our advocacy efforts was difficult at times. We have advocated for everything from wheelchair-accessible buses to accessible playgrounds; from elevators in schools to wheelchair lifts on stages for orchestra concerts. This need for advocacy increased when my parents moved here, as we then had three family members using wheelchairs. This is certainly part of our lives in our continuing sandwich.

When attending my brother's wedding, we had another advocacy opportunity. As shared earlier, although the location of the wedding was accessible, the reception was on a riverboat, with no access to the top floor, where the reception took place. Whenever I find myself in these situations, I think about whether to make a fuss or let it go. When Tally sees the situation we're in, sometimes she says (talking low, with her teeth clenched), "Mom, just *don't* say anything!"—even though she knows I will. Then I ask myself, would my feedback make any difference, or would I just be a "whiner"?

We ended up carrying both my mom and daughter in their

wheelchairs up a steep dozen steps to the party. Although the upstairs was also very tight and not accessible, my mother delighted in being able to be present and enjoy her son's wedding reception. At the end of the evening, those carrying my daughter down almost fell, which was quite frightening.

We usually check on accessibility prior to anywhere we go. This is essential when traveling with two people who use wheelchairs. Over a month before the wedding, I had e-mailed, checking on accessibility. We were assured that they would do everything they could to assist and make things accessible.

I wrote them after the wedding. This is an example of one of many advocacy letters we have written for various issues:

"Hi _____,

We returned from a lovely wedding weekend for my brother aboard one of your vessels. Our celebration was dampened by the nonaccessibility of the experience. The wedding ceremony on the docked boat was accessible, with a great bathroom and plenty of room for wheelchairs. However, as we looked at the boat for the reception and dance—they were serving on the top floor—*no elevator!* When we asked staff what was the plan, and they said, "Oh, we can serve them on the main floor." I said, "But the party and dance are upstairs!" There was little response.

You had stated, "We make every reasonable effort to assist and accommodate passengers with special needs." No staff assisted us carrying both my ninety-two-year-old mother and my twenty-year-old daughter up and down the stairs for the reception (I'm guessing because of liability). No staff asked us if we were all right after doing so. On the descent, one family member started to slip when carrying my daughter down. It could have been much worse than scraped elbows. No one asked if we were okay getting down, either.

What I am most frustrated about is that this was not disclosed to us before that time, even after e-mailing to ask about it. The setup could have been downstairs, with overflow upstairs. Even when contacting you before the wedding, it would have been helpful to have been told that the upstairs was *not* accessible. You did tell us about the thresholds, which we handled with help, but not about having to carry folks upstairs to be part of the party. It took an extensive amount of planning and effort to get my ninety-two-year-old mother there from Kansas. It is also frightening to be carried up and down a steep flight of stairs (no matter what your age)—I encourage you to try it sometime.

In addition, we had asked about a recliner or some type of chair for my mother to be able to put up her feet during the four-hour trip. No staff had heard of the request.

The staff was friendly but didn't seem to know what to do with us. We did have assistance during food serving, and a staff member found a crate for my mom to put up her feet, after my request. Those were the only accommodations. After getting my mom and daughters up, I went down to tell staff if there was an emergency, they had better be up there to help us get them out.

I will look into the ADA requirements for vessels; I am very curious. I cannot believe that they are exempt from ADA. I would suggest being up-front with your consumers about the nonaccessibility. Even after contacting you with the topic, we did not receive the full information. I would also suggest that you work with the staff on ways to accommodate and assist. I will let you know if I learn anything from contacting the ADA Tech Center.

In advocacy for accessibility,
Carol Russell"

MORE MAKING A DIFFERENCE!

Sometimes opportunities for advocacy come to us. We were recently asked to testify to the Kansas State Legislature regarding Home and Community Based Services waiver programs on behalf of my mom and daughter, who are both on HCBS waiver programs. HCBS provide services beyond those covered by the Medical Assistance or Medicaid program that allows individuals to stay in a community setting instead of a nursing home or a Long Term Care Facility (LTCF). The waivers include:

DD Waiver: for individuals who qualify with developmental delays

PD Waiver: for individuals who qualify with physical disabilities

FE Waiver: for "Frail and Elderly" who qualify

We could not make it that day, but I wrote the following testimony via e-mail:

From: Carol Russell
Sent: Tuesday, October 21, 2008 9:18 AM
To: _____
Subject: Waiver Programs Feedback

Hi _____,

As much as we would like to be there today, our absolutely c-r-a-z-y schedules, with our own jobs, assisting our youngest daughter, Tally, who is at ESU and on the PD waiver and caring for/coordinating care, etc., for my ninety-two-year-old mother, Gladys Deye, on the FE waiver. To have been there, all three of us (Tally, Fletch, and me) would have had to miss classes, and I would have had to pay for more care for my mom to cover the hours I would have today. We have so much we could share—time is our biggest challenge. We would be happy to talk with someone via phone appointment or write more when we have a weekend to do so. I will give some highlights of what we would share:

Tally is on the HCBS/PD waiver. She has spina bifida, along with several other significant health issues. She has had many case managers through the years (she had been on a DD waiver while in public school). We have worked with each to develop a plan that fits her needs. There are never enough hours. We assist her and coordinate her schedule (which is the major key), help find and train appropriate PCAs, transport her, etc. She could not do this on her own. She does what she can, but if we were not overseeing or dropping her at the campus dorm door, she would not be succeeding. She currently has a 3.8 GPA and is almost a junior. She has her own apartment. Her PCAs support her and greatly add to her success. She needs assistance with most self-help; meal prep; cleaning; dressing; laundry; etc. (We can give much more detail, if someone needs it.) More hours are always needed if we are to work toward more independence from her parents. If we were not coordinating the whole picture, I don't know where things would be for her. It is frightening to think about!

My mom, Gladys, is ninety-two and is on the FE waiver since she ran out of money. She needs help with all things. We also assist her and coordinate her schedule, we help find and train appropriate PCAs, transport her, do much of the care, assist with everything else. My main feedback is that we had to literally go through every minute of her day to get the hours that she needs. My husband and I sat through many meetings, justifying why she needed help doing this or that. It is appalling to me that we could see a woman who could not feed herself, shower herself, or even wipe her bottom being given three hours a day of FE/PCA hours. It literally got down to minute by minute—they could pay for time for her to get assistance transferring on and off the toilet, and with cleaning up, but *not* for the time she was on the toilet! We were able to justify more hours, but it took hours of our time to do so. Some thing is wrong here—and we'd better figure out our supports for the elderly, as there will be multiple times more of us in the years to come!

I would like to add that if you were expecting folks to take time off of their jobs and pay for travel expenses to come to such a group, a stipend would be in order. This is time you are doing your job; for others, it is their volunteering of time. I have worked with many state committees through the years, and some support for time and travel has been allowed.

This all comes down to time. We are "sandwiched" in our time right now. We work as a team to make this work, and the support of HCBS FE & PD Waiver do help with the puzzle. We would be happy to share more; we have much more to share if anyone wishes to listen. Thank your for your time in reading this and addressing the feedback. We wish you a productive day!

Thank you,
Carol, Fletch, & Tally Russell

THE AMERICANS WITH DISABILITIES ACT

The ADA (Americans with Disabilities Act) was written in 1990. We're still working on implementing and honoring it. The problem is that there are no ADA police officers, so individuals who need the accommodations, their family members, friends, and advocates end up doing the "policing." We end up being the complainers, the squeaky wheels, the advocates. For more information on ADA, see www.eeoc.gov/types/ada.html.

Also see ADA 2008 Amendments:
www.2keller.com/blog/americans-with-disabilities-act-ada-amendments-act-of-2008.cfm

THE OLDER AMERICANS ACT

According to the Aging Network (http://www.enoa.org/network/oaa.html): "Of the nine million Americans over age sixty-five who live alone, two million say they have nowhere to turn if they need help."

The Aging Network Web site notes that the "Older Americans Act Potential Services," through the 670 area agencies on aging under the Administration on Aging, will have some combination of the following services:

- Access Services
  - Client Assessment/Health Maintenance

- Care Management
- Information and Referral
- Transportation
- Community-Based Services
  - Day Care
  - Congregate Meals
  - Legal Assistance
  - Senior Center Programs
  - Employment Services
- In-Home Services
  - Home-Delivered Meals
  - Home-Health Services
  - Chore Services
  - Homemaker
  - Telephone Reassurance
  - Friendly Visitor
  - Energy Assistance and Weatherization
  - Emergency Response
  - Respite Care
- Services in Institutional Care
  - Preadmission Screening
  - Ombudsman

They also offer a summary of the Title I Older Americans Act

- An adequate income in retirement in accordance with the American standard of living

- The best possible physical and mental health without regard to economic status

- Suitable housing designed and located with reference to special needs available to the older American at an affordable cost

- Full restorative services for those who require institutional care, and a comprehensive array of community-based, long-term care services to sustain older people in their communities and their homes

- Opportunity for employment, with no discrimination because of age

- Retirement in health, honor, and dignity, after years of contribution to the economy

- Pursuit of meaningful activity within the widest range of civic, cultural, and recreational opportunities.

- Efficient community services, readily available when needed, with emphasis on a continuum of care for the vulnerable elderly and access to low-cost transportation.

- Immediate benefit from proven research, knowledge of which can sustain and improve health and happiness.

- Freedom, independence and the free exercise of an individual's initiative in the planning and managing of his or her own life.

This all looks pretty good, but how it truly "comes out in the wash" is another story. You don't get your elder loved ones the services handed to them "on a silver platter." You may have to ask, and ask, and ask again; advocate for the services, spend hours researching and having meetings, and still you will learn more each time you search. Using your communication skills, taking notes, and making agencies accountable for what they say is constant. I like to use the reflective tools, such as, "So I hear you saying …" or "Let me get this straight; this is what you just said …" or "Does this mean this?" or "Are you really saying …?" I have been blessed to have Fletch come to all the important meetings regarding my mom. Again, he is an exceptional partner—not many sons-in-law would do what he does. We had much experience from our advocacy and meetings with the school districts throughout Tally's education. We learned again that you cannot let "the system" take your loved one. You have to be involved, educate yourself, communicate, and advocate. Our wheels "squeak" pretty well as a team.

THE OMBUDSMAN PROGRAM FOR ELDERLY

The Ombudsman Program is mandated under the Federal Older Americans Act to receive, investigate, and resolve complaints made by or on behalf of persons in nursing homes and assisted living facilities.

According to its Web site (http://www.acombuds.org/About_Us/about_us.shtml):

"The Ombudsman Program promotes principles of consumer empowerment, prevention and quality care by responding to complaints from, or on behalf of, older persons receiving long-term care services, and by providing resident and public education, including information and referral assistance to the network of long-term care services. The Ombudsman Program has a unique role. While it works cooperatively with regulatory agencies and other programs such as Adult Protective Services, its efforts are focused on complaint resolution and empowering persons to resolve complaints themselves, when appropriate."

One such program is Ombudsman, Inc., an independent, nonprofit organization in California. It implements the state's Long-Term Care Ombudsman Program, a free and confidential service that maintains and improves the quality of life for residents in long-term care facilities. This site lists a summary of the ombudsmen roles:

- Ombudsmen actively work to protect the rights and dignity of residents in long-term care facilities.

- Ombudsmen provide an ongoing presence in facilities to promote the highest quality of life and care on behalf of the resident.

- Ombudsmen investigate complaints made by, or on behalf of, long-term care residents and advocate on behalf of the resident.

- Ombudsmen investigate reports of elder abuse that occur in long-term care facilities or adult day health-care centers and report such cases to licensing entities and law enforcement agencies.

The Ombudsman Program helps:

- Residents in nursing homes
- Residents of board and care facilities
- Residents of adult day health-care centers
- Members of the resident's family
- Government and private agencies

The Ombudsman Program can assist in resolving concerns about:

- Elder abuse and neglect
- Resident's rights
- Quality of care
- Appropriate placement
- Transfer and discharge from care facilities, including assistance with appeals
- Dietary concerns
- Medical care, therapy, and rehabilitation
- Medicare and MediCal benefit issues
- Durable power of attorney for health care

This is a fantastic protection program for older individuals and their families. The only problem is that it does not protect the individual in his or her own home. I have contacted a few people at the state level about this. They agreed that it is needed, particularly with the number of older individuals getting care at home. At this time, however, it was not covered. Discussion occurred, but I have little hope right now, with the economy the way it is. The economy is an excuse, but where are our priorities, even when the economy is bad? Shouldn't we still have the health, safety, and quality care as a priority for our older population, no matter where they are housed?

One last resource for the advocacy topic is an article titled "Family Caregiving and Public Policy: Principles for Change".[24] Advocates and the NFCA got together to draft this Statement of Principles. More than forty national organizations have endorsed these principles. The eight principles are listed below are quoted from this article:

---

[24] "Family Caregiving and Public Policy: Principles for Change" in the Winter 2008 issue of *Take Care*: National Family Caregivers Association (vol. 16: no.4).

- Family caregiver concerns must be a central component of health care, long-term care, and social service policy-making.

- Family caregivers much be protected against the financial, physical, and emotional consequences of caregivng that can put their own health and well-being in jeopardy.

- Family caregivers must have access to affordable, readily available, high-quality respite care as a day component of the supportive services network.

- Family caregivers must be supported by family-friendly policies in the workplace in order to meet their caregiving responsibilities. This would include flextime, work-at-home options, job-sharing, counseling, dependent-care accounts, information about what referral to community services, employer-paid services of a care manager and more.

- Family caregivers must have appropriate, timely, and on-going education and training in order to successfully meet their caregiving responsibilities and to be advocates for their loved ones across care settings.

- Family caregivers and their loved ones must have afford-able, readily available, high-quality, comprehensive services that are coordinated across all care settings.

- Family caregivers and their loved ones much be assured of an affordable, well-qualified, and sustainable health-care workforce across all care settings.

- Family caregivers must have access to regular, comprehen-sive assessments for their caregiving situation to determine what assistance they may require."

What We've Learned

• People, in general, are not aware of the American's with Disabilities Act of 1990, nor do they take the responsibility to know or act on it. There are not "ADA police officers." We, as family members and individuals with physical needs, are the ADA checks and balance.

Quotes

"Whining is only acceptable when you're whining to someone who can make a difference"

—Marilyn Hamilton, the creator of Quickie Wheelchairs

"Choose your battles!"
(I don't know who first said this, but it's good advice!)

Ombudsman perspective on the job

"The handshake and thank you from a family member after a two-hour care plan meeting—$500.

That beautiful smile lighting up the face of the resident that you just promised to come back and chat with again real soon—$50,000.

Filling out monthly reports and progress notes—$5.

The look on the administrator's face when you tell her that you personally have observed the facility in making a mistake that she considered nothing more than complaining by family member whose expectations were too high—priceless.

Ah, the power of ... an ombudsman!"

—Carol Schmidt, Maryland LTCO volunteer

TIPS AND TOOLS

ADA
www.eeoc.gov/types/ada.html

ADA 2008 Amendments:
www.2keller.com/blog/americans-with-disabilities-act-ada-amendments-act-of-2008.cfm

Advocating for the Elderly by Veronica Velasquez
http://www.tricityvoice.com/articledisplay.php?a=3482

Ombudsman, Inc.
http://www.acombuds.org/About_Us/about_us.shtml

Advocating for the Elderly Adult by Cindy Shemansky
Family Caregiving and Public Policy: Principles for Change
TAKE CARE! Winter 2008
Older Americans Act
www.aoa.gov/about/legbudg/oaa/legbudg_oaa.aspx

The Basics: Older Americans Act of 1965
www.nhpf.org/pdfs_basics/Basics_OlderAmericansAct_04-21-08.pdf

Chapter 12

Our Sandwich Continues

The Loss of My Dad

We had the gift of a lovely, long fall with many extended family visits for my dad's last Thanksgiving and Christmas in 2005. We knew he would not be with us much longer. About two weeks before his passing on January 26, 2006, we started him with a hospice program. Hospice was wonderful, beyond words. They suggested that family come to see my dad one last time. Every one of my siblings did make it to say good-bye to him. Family tension still lingered, but he was able to see and talk with each of his children. At the time of my dad's death, I was blessed to have my oldest sister, Dottie, with us. Everyone else had gone home. It was the start of a new semester for me, and I was trying to continue my teaching. I was fortunate to have Web classes that semester, so I could teach mostly from home.

Tally was taking an evening Sign Language class, and I was assisting her in class that semester. One evening, we had learned the slang version of "wow." You sign a "W" on either side of your mouth, while forming an "O" with your mouth. It was pretty funny. I was over at my parents', showing Cassie,

Mikelle, and Dottie what we had learned. We were laughing at how silly we looked doing this slang form of "wow." My dad was watching us intently. He hadn't spoken a word in days. I looked up at him as he observed us and was amazed to see he was making the "wow" sign, too! I ran to get the camera and had a picture taken of my dad signing "wow" with us!

"Wow" in Sign Language: My dad was signing with us, during the week before his passing.

Dottie assisted with everything from singing German songs that my dad loved to giving back and foot rubs to help his comfort and circulation. She prayed the German prayer that he had requested be read to him when dying. He had sent it to us years ago, requesting that we pray it with him when it was his time to go.

DOTTIE'S REFLECTION OF OUR FATHER'S LAST BREATH

As stated earlier, my oldest sister was with us as Papa neared death. Here is an excerpt from her reflection, which specifically describes the time of my father's passing:

Papa passed away, at home, with Mother lying next to him on one side, and I sitting on the other, reading his prayers, singing favorite songs, and saying the German Prayer the he had mailed to each one of his children, at an earlier time when he thought he was near death.

When he stopped breathing, shortly after 7:30 AM, I called to the hospice helper to phone Carol next door. His pulse was gone, and his color that was slightly yellow, turned chalky white, and the tips of his ears and toes started to mottle. Mama kissed him many times, and in the middle of tears said, "Oh. honey, I don't want you to go!"

Then something happened that I never saw before. When the door slammed, the helper yelled, "Carol's here!" Papa gasped and resumed breathing while Carol climbed on the bed, next to his ear, and assured him of her love, and she would take care of Mother, and she could let him go.

I called siblings on my cell to provide a chance to say one last word while he might still be able to hear.

This was a powerful experience for me. I had never been with someone when he took his last breath. I will always remember this and the loving way my mother embraced my father's almost lifeless body. I can remember how I felt after saying good-bye and assuring my dad that we would take good care of Mother.

Hospice was wonderful! My mom was able to caress and kiss my dad, wash his feet once more, and just have time with him to say good-bye, knowing that the vigil was over.

The minister came and prayed with us. No one rushed us or disrupted us. We were together for almost two hours after he passed.

Nature's Way of Grieving with Us

I remember that after my dad passed, I hurried over to tell my family. As I walked out the door, I can recall hearing our guinea hens just cackling very loudly. I thought maybe a dog was after them, so I went to see where they were and found them directly outside the window—where my father's body was just on the other side. They were gathered there, almost as if they were talking to me about what had just happened.

We contacted the funeral home to make arrangements to transport my father's body. As we followed them out the door, I can remember a strong gust of wind and hearing my father's wind chimes that hung just around the corner. We later learned that this wind burst blew off one of the door screens on the deck side of the house. I remember the provider telling me about the times when he had been with someone who died and then opening a window or door and experiencing a gust of wind, as if the soul of the person passing was being released. I do believe we experienced this.

As they moved my dad on the cart and rolled him out the door to their vehicle, my mom, sister, and I were singing, "God Be With You 'Til We Meet Again." A neighbor's dog came running over, put his head on my mom's lap, and stayed with us until the vehicle drove down the driveway. I will never forget what I believe are signs of other living creatures on this earth, responding to our grief, almost understanding our pain and loss.

THE SOUNDS OF GRIEF AND SORROW

I can still recall my mom's first viewing at the side of my father's casket. A sort of subtle, anguished moaning whimper came from her, over and over. It was a sound I had never heard from her, and one I have not heard since. With all that they had been through for over sixty-four years of marriage, with all that she had supported of his life serving the church and endured from his flaws and hurtful behavior, *he* was *her* life. It wasn't until he passed that I really started to see my mother as an individual, with her own thoughts and behavior, rather than constantly referencing my dad to see what to do or say or how to respond. I feel my mom "found herself" at age ninety.

PUTTING GRIEF INTO WORDS

Shortly after the funeral, when everyone had gone home, someone had sent me the following poem, written by Christopher Wiseman in *In John Updike's Room*. I related to it so! Here is the note I sent to my siblings and extended family, along with the poem, "Bedside Manners."

* * * * *

This poem was tough to read. (See below.)
It makes you stop on a busy day to drink in the love,
    the appreciation for the clouds and a sunny day,
    the sunrises and sunsets,
    the moon and stars at night,
    the number of guineas that ran across the yard
    (Papa counted them every day),
Papa's *loud* yell of "*Hello!*" from the deck across the field, so
    loud that

it made Midnight (Tally's horse) jump a bit while Tally
  was riding.
I will miss all those things, but will remember the times,
  the visions,
  the smells,
  the singing,
  the holding of his hand ... until the very end.

Love,
Carol

Poem: "Bedside Manners"
by Christopher Wiseman
from *In John Updike's Room*, published by the Porcupine's
Quill Press.

Bedside Manners
How little the dying seem to need—
A drink perhaps, a little food,
A smile, a hand to hold, medication,
A change of clothes, an unspoken
Understanding about what's happening.
You think it would be more, much more,
Something more difficult for us
To help with in this great disruption,
But perhaps it's because as the huge shape
Rears up higher and darker each hour
They are anxious that we should see it too
And try to show us with a hand-squeeze.

We panic to do more for them,
And especially when it's your father,

And his eyes are far away, and your tears
Are all down your face and clothes,
And he doesn't see them now, but smiles
Perhaps, just perhaps because you're there.
How little he needs. Just love. More love.

~ by Christopher Wiseman (copyright)
Reprinted by permission of the author. Also note that Christopher Wiseman's most recent book is *36 Cornelian Avenue*, published in 2008 by Vehicule Press in Montreal. (Both books available on Amazon.com in the US.)

MY DAD'S FUNERAL

Although small, my dad's funeral was very nice. Family came, and grandsons were pallbearers. The church owned a small graveyard in the country that was only for members of their church (Lutheran) and families. About a week before my dad died, we were able to take my mom and three of my siblings out there. It is right on the edge of the Flint Hills of Kansas, a very beautiful and remote area. My mom thought it was nice. We took pictures of the area and brought them back to show my dad on the computer. He seemed to understand.

We had planned the funeral in the last days of my dad's life. My oldest sister has musical gifts and had been a music teacher for years, so she was very helpful in selecting and arranging the music. My nephew (her son) and our two oldest daughters played a trumpet, cello, and flute trio.

Although there were some very uncomfortable and rude family dynamics during those two days, we made it through. I felt badly for my mom, having to see her adult children exhibit some very childish behavior at a time of her intense sorrow and loss. I know this happens at funerals and other family gatherings, and unfortunately, it dampens and fogs the reason we are there—to honor and celebrate the life of our father. I am so glad we could still be there for my mom after everyone left and can be with her every day for the rest of her life.

We try to take my mom out to the cemetery as often as we can. It is a half-hour drive, so we have to plan ahead; then be flexible with the weather and her health. Here is a photo of Cassie and Mikelle coming out with us one day.

Here is another visit to the cemetery. Tally and Mikelle came this time. I felt strange at times, taking my mom to the place where she'd be buried someday. I asked how she felt about it, and she said it was comforting.

MY MOM TURNED NINETY-ONE THIS WEEK

About two months after my father died, my mom turned ninety. We had a big party, an open house, with family and her new Bible class friends. She didn't even know their names, but my sister, the queen of organization, had all the names of the ladies, made invitations, and invited them when she accompanied her to Bible class one Wednesday. It was really quite sweet. We had lots of elaborate food, a huge cake with ninety candles (one hot cake!), and to her delight, she also had a card shower, with over one hundred cards.

My mom turned ninety-one this week. This year we decided to just have family. We had a great gathering of more than twenty family members, with four of her five children, grandchildren, and great-grandchildren to celebrate. She was in the hospital last week. We do take a day at a time. We're trying to figure out the digestive problem through a process of "elimination." The doctor says it's either the meds combination (as she says, she takes "enough to choke a horse") or something internal. She's been slowing down and is a bit more confused. Some days she doesn't remember that my daughter, who is her caregiver three days a week, is her granddaughter.

She's a *Little House on the Prairie* "junkie." It's quite sweet. It seems to jiggle her memory to share more stories from her childhood. We read the entire series to her and then found that the TV show was on four times a day on the Hallmark channel! She plans her day around the hours it's on.

Part of her extended birthday celebration included a trip to the one-room schoolhouse on the Emporia State University campus. We've been trying to get there since she moved here. She taught in a one room schoolhouse for several years before she was married. She seemed to really enjoy the visit and felt quite at home. It was precious, observing her discover textbooks she'd used, finding a lunch pail just like the one she used to have, seeing books she remembered using, noting the dunce cap and paddle in the corner, recalling all of the answers to "the quiz," and relaying various stories spurred by different objects displayed. We wrote "Happy 91st Birthday" on the chalkboard, and she signed her name under it, and we took a picture. We're going to go back again when we have more time and a video recorder.

Mother's ninety-first birthday. We took her to the one-room schoolhouse. We wrote a happy birthday message on the chalkboard. She decided to sign her name.

Mother turns ninety-one.

NINETEEN AND NINETY-ONE

When my mom turned ninety-one, and we placed the "9" and "1" candles on the cake, and I realized the irony of the numbers of the sandwich I was in—between the 19 and 91. Tally was nineteen and Mother was turning ninety-one. On second thought, they are really the core, the meat of the sandwich, and I'm just the mayo that holds it together or maybe even the bread that embraces them. This is no open face sandwich; it is not me alone. It is a group effort: multigrain, if you will. Whether the bread or the contents of the sandwich, it is a commitment that involves choices I will never regret.

I believe the choices we make do make us who we are. Choices decrease as we get older. If one is younger and has limited abilities, some choices have never been options. Choices, options, and freedoms are what it's all about. A young professor and dear friend of mine in special education used to profess that "It's all about options and freedoms." This has stayed with me and guided me with my caring for young or old. It's also important for those in between young and old.

Granted, some of my own options and freedoms have been limited as I've worked for the options and freedoms of others. I have missed some things and not had the energy for other things (part of that is just age). At the beginning of my sandwiched journey, we were in the emergency room almost every other week. I can remember the first time—I had planned to go out with Fletch for the first time in months after my parents moved to Kansas. We were getting ready to go and had the call from the provider next door that my dad was not doing well. We spent that Friday night in the emergency room.

I feel like I'm constantly on guard; I cannot let my guard down. I remember this feeling with Tally's first year. She had three surgeries in her first week of life and nine in the first year. I felt that if I relaxed, thinking all was well, something still was always lurking behind us: another surgery, another health issue, another agency to deal with, issues to advocate. With planning, there is often a plan A, B, C, D, and sometimes more. Here is an example of plans A, B, C, and D for Easter 2007, written in an e-mail:

"Sorry it's taken us a while to reply. We just weren't sure how Grandma was going to do, and we were trying to figure out Plan A, B, C, and D. She's doing pretty well right now. We would love to come and plan on doing so. Plan A is Dottie is planning to pick up Grandma to stay overnight with them Sat., and she'd go to church with them, and we would come for dinner (not sure about church), and take Grandma back with us. I'm pretty sure Cass and Mikelle are coming too; I'm not sure about Jake. I'll let Cass reply. Plan B is we'd bring her on Easter. Plan C, if she's not up to it, we'd come and Patty might stay with her. Plan D is if she's really not feeling well, then we probably wouldn't come either. I hope we don't have to do Plan D."

MAKING BANANA BREAD ON SATURDAYS WITH MOTHER

On most Saturdays, my mom and I made banana bread. I had brought her a great banana bread for years while they were still in Minnesota. It was a *Good Morning, America* (my favorite news show) recipe from Emeril's recipe competition. It was a wonderful source of potassium and protein for her. I always put in an extra egg, an extra banana, and extra nuts. The recipe is already rich with these ingredients. I found that it was one food that she never refused. A loaf would last her about two to three days at the most!

By the second month after their arrival, I realized we had

not yet made banana bread. It hit me when I saw four black bananas in their refrigerator. My Mother hates to waste food, so this was a good way to not throw away the ripe bananas, while keeping her involved with cooking (which she spent a better part of her life doing and enjoying). She had even put together a recipe book, *Apron Strings by Gladys*. It was a collection of over twenty-five years of recipes from a column she had in the Lutheran Journal (of which my dad was the editor for many, many years).

So, the banana bread had to be made. It was as though the bananas ripening were the cue to not only make the bread but to have some quality Mommy/Carol time. Let me also tell you that when my mother was more active, she and I never did too well in the kitchen together. She often had certain ways of doing things that were different from mine.

Sometimes, one or more of our daughters would pop in to help out. Mother's first job was to always peel and smash the bananas. She could do this without much range of motion in her shoulders. She had torn rotator cuffs in both shoulders. She would meticulously do her job. She carefully peeled each banana and made certain all the "strings" were removed. Each time, she would remind us of the importance of checking to assure that the bottom stem was still with the peeling (not part of the ingredients), as she had learned that tarantulas may lay their eggs in that part of the banana. She would then crack the eggs, checking for any shells. She would sometimes stir, depending on the pain in her shoulders.

It was somewhat new territory. Yet the accessibility of it was familiar, as I had set up cooking with Tally at the same table location. My early childhood and special-education background also helped me with ways to present directions, promote independence, accessible features, etc.

And we would talk. We talked about her life with my dad. We talked about my dad then. We talked about Tally's life. We talked about Mikelle and her artwork. We talked about Cassie and her achievements. We talked about my siblings. We talked about the nuts—in the banana bread and in life. She said she loved to bite into the bread and be surprised by a big chunky nut (we did not crush the nuts; we left them whole or in large pieces). We said it was kind of like life—you'd be surprised by the chunks.

A FALL IN THE FALL—AND ANOTHER SANDWICHED WEEK

Gearing up for the fall teaching semester when teaching at a university takes much time in meetings, class preparations, organizing and redirection of thoughts, and a psychological, physical, social, and cognitive transition from summer to fall schedules. We started off the week with a celebration of my mom's artwork at the twenty-seventh annual "Art Is Ageless" show put on by the Emporia Presbyterian Manor. My mom was in her 91½-year-old prime, proud of her three paintings that graced the wall of the Emporia Art Center. My sister and her husband came, and we all went out to eat and had a great day. My mom had the largest group with her, the five in my family and my sister and her husband, eight in all, including my mom. We snacked on cookies and punch and enjoyed the show of senior artists.

The next day, the reality of the season sent me off to an 8:00 AM–8:00 PM day full of meetings. My sister stayed another day and overnight with Mother. That night, Mother fell. My sister is still haunted by the thud in the night that no one wants to hear. Mother had gotten out of bed to "take a walk"—the bottom bed railing had been mistakenly left down—and she slipped and fell. She went down, breaking her arm, spraining her wrist, and bumping and bruising all over her body.

The entire morning was spent with the home-health nurse, doing an assessment for my mom after returning home from the hospital. The following morning we were at Social Rehabilitation Services for a two-hour meeting regarding her Medicaid application. The afternoon was spent with the Area Agency on Aging screening for three and a half hours, totaling almost ten hours (within two days) of forms, figures, and meetings. My sister came to assist, and we had data to support and validate.

After Mother's fall, we found a great resource on-line to measure pain. You can see this pain scale at http://www. anes.ucla.edu/pain/FacesScale.jpg. We used this often when measuring pain for my mom. This put us all on the same page, with some consistency of the measure of pain she was having.

I Am Not Invincible

Surgery

I had to have surgery. It was not only physically unpleasant, but psychologically, the thought of not being there for those who depended on me was frightening. My thoughts are below, written in an e-mail thank you for support from my immediate and extended family:

* * * * *

Subject: Thanks for your call & support!
Dearest ones,

Thanks *so much* for your supportive calls yesterday. I am

on pain meds for a bit, sleeping a lot, and overall, doing better. I'm feeling pretty hopeful and will feel better with definite lab info. It does put a scare in you, and I do not wait well. I identified, if even for a short time, with those who must constantly live with uncertainty. I have lived "on guard" before, but it's been for others, not for me. I truly value myself and love life, and I also know how many others depend on me. My life is not just for me. We are not immortal, but when others depend so greatly on me for their daily needs, I wish I were.

I am blessed to have my dear sweet family. Fletch and Tally were there to hold my hand in the post-op. It was strange for Tally to be on the other end, watching my IVs, monitors, etc., versus being on the receiving end. Tally was there to get anything I needed. While Fletch went to evening class, Cassie and Mikelle came over with flowers for me, and dinner for Tal (I had Jell-O.)

Thanks again for your loving support. I'll let you know when I know.

Love always,
Carol

WHEN I ALMOST CHOKED

I am certainly not invincible! I nearly choked last night on a spoonful of honey—my home remedy for a sore throat. I couldn't breathe, and my windpipe was blocked, and I was gasping for air. Fletch calmed me down and had me drink some water. But it occurred to me—what if I had died? What would become of my family, my Tally, and my mom? Life is fragile.

BUT WE NEED TO LIVE FOREVER!

The need to live forever is a common feeling for parents of children with special needs, not for a selfish reason but to have someone who will take care of their child forever. According to "Caregiver Stress" by the National Women's Health Information Center US DHHS, Office on Women's Health (http://www.mental-health-matters.com/articles/article.php?artID=725), "Caregivers often worry that they will not outlive the person for whom they are caring." It's a very painful thought, either way you look at it. There is little worse than losing your child; I cannot imagine. Our children are supposed to live more of their lives after we are gone. On the other hand, if there is really no one who can give loving care, assist, manage living arrangements, etc., for your adult child with special needs, that can also be tragic. We try to foster independence and support from our older daughters, but the bottom line is that our country does not have the best programs for those with special needs or for the elderly. The system has serious gaps. There are people who take advantage, abuse, and neglect those who are not as able to defend themselves or who are not as aware of what is happening.

THERE ARE NO SHORTCUTS

Sometimes, you have to go up to go down; you must turn right to turn left or take two steps backward to get one step forward. Sometimes, you must go in the back door, through the kitchen, to get to the table. You have to advocate, even mediate, just to get in the front door. We are used to alternate routes. If you have a family member who uses a wheelchair or walker or has health problems, you understand. Having had three family members who used wheelchairs at one time, we learned to plan ahead, sometimes taking our own ramps. We try to spread awareness where we can. Progress takes time, and having patience for slow-moving progress is challenging at times.

We continue to use the tools: SODAS and giving and receiving feedback (noted in chapter six). Sometimes, it's just a matter of defining the problem or identifying the options.

Here are some notes I made when we were switching to HCBS/FE (Home and Community Based Services/Frail & Elderly) self-direct. This takes some work, but you will have more flexibility. Figuring out how to best arrange hours is a challenge and takes time.

There are two issues that make it worth the time:
    Save some money for my mom
    Have secure care, as my husband and I work
This process, in brief, is outlined below:
    Meetings with SRS for over a year, prepping for ease of transition
    Alerting family more than an year before she was out of money and applying for MA
    Figuring and refiguring
    Trying to explain it to family, at least monthly update of her condition and financial situation
    Some don't care; I do hope they at least feel guilt, but they probably don't, if they don't care. They probably have no conscience.
    Extended family (even in-laws) giving
    Our own dollars (up to $3,000 to 4,000/month during transition), in addition to all of our in-kind hours
    A plan
    Revising the plan (no doesn't always mean no)

> Meeting, meetings, meetings, advocate
> Letters of support from doctor, family, pastor

Question: Am I lengthening the quality of life for Mother but shortening my own life?
Answer: Perhaps

LIFE GOES ON

Our lives are full of transitions, problem-solving, and flexibility. We are in the middle of multitransitions in our family this month. We just left our oldest daughter at her new place in Greeley, Colorado, where she will be working on her doctorate in educational psychology. She had become my support in problem-solving issues with my mom and Tally; she was my sounding board. I not only had extra days and years with her while she finished working on her master's and part-time teaching in the same building on campus where I taught; she was also my daughter, provider, and assistance coordinating care for my mom, and a colleague, as we discussed major issues in teaching methods and strategies and education. It is a very special and unique bond, which not many parents get a chance to have. When I had tears leaving her in Colorado, it was way beyond a mother/daughter bond. Because I took care of an aging parent with the assistance of an adult child, the "sandwich thing" really hit me. Teaching in the same college with my daughter was also a unique experience. I was comforted when seeing the building where she would be taking and teaching classes, meeting her department head and secretary, and looking at campus. I am also comforted, knowing how exciting and challenging her next phase in life will be. She is so ready. I also find comfort that she has found love, and she has a puppy. I am so very, very proud of her, her goals, and her ambition.

Out middle daughter, Mikelle, is also in the process of moving out of the area. After graduating and finding love, she will be moving a little over an hour away. Although this is not the nine-hour trip to see Cassie, it's still an adjustment for us. She too has been a great source of physical and emotional support. She has also helped take care of Grandma on a regular basis and then part-time, as she helped Tally with more supports and independence-building while in her apartment. She spent regular overnights with Tally in her apartment, giving Fletch and I our "date nights," as well as giving Tally a break from us. I think she understands my emotions better than most. She is a very sensitive young lady. She has helped support Tally throughout her life. She was only two when Tally was born. That was a difficult transition for her, with our needing to be in and out of the hospital with Tally most of the first year of Tally's life. Mikelle is a wonderful source of humor, which we need often to keep our sanity. She often reminds me of the reality of issues, and that it's okay to cry.

More "Signs" in Our Environment

I believe in connective signs in our environment and that things happen for a reason. If we allow ourselves to be aware of details—to look, see, hear, and smell details around us—there might be meaningful observations there. Moments in life, some planned, some significant, and some spontaneous, seem almost surreal when they are happening. Your senses pick up sounds, smells, and sights that are embedded in your memory. It isn't until later that the reminders of those senses take you back to that moment. It could be a song playing at the moment something happens; the smell of the air, someone's perfume, something cooking/baking, cologne or air freshener; the place in nature, the road, house or group of people; it can all take you back to that moment.

We took my dad to the emergency room via ambulance two weeks before he passed away. We had just been admitted to the hospice program that day, so we were told to take him home. He hadn't talked much for several days, not more than one-word communications. As I was driving him home in his Cadillac, he turned to me and said, "Nice car ride!" I nearly fell over! That was one of the last full sentences he said to me. For several weeks, as I would pass that specific area of the road, I would hear songs that would send significant chills up my spine: "My Father's Eyes," "Wings of an Angel," "In the Living Years," and "Dust in the Wind." I also saw an eagle a time or two (my dad was always excited about an eagle-spotting). There were often other large birds flying in that area. As I noticed this, I often felt a sense of calmness, knowing my dad was in a better place, without yo-yoing blood sugar levels, insulin shots, pain, or confusion and delusions. This was both strange and comforting at the same time. My husband thought I was crazy, as I would turn the radio on at that location on our multiple trips in and out of town.

HOLD ON TO THE JOY

Some days you want to last forever. Yesterday was one of those days that I did not want to end. When we helped our oldest daughter move to Colorado, we took a day with her up in the mountains. We traveled to Sprague Lake, which had a lovely accessible trail around the lake, with a spectacular view of the mountains. We went to another lake, Bear Lake, and were rained and hailed out. As the almost deafening hail beat down on our large accessible van, I looked back at my three daughters, and it took me back to the camping days when they were little. We always loved adventures together, and everything we did, we did together. It was a warm, lovely, heartwarming day that I will always treasure.

The days and celebrations that Mother was able to be a part of are very treasured. Being the youngest of five children, I never thought my parents would live to see any of my children graduate from high school. My father had a heart attack at Cassie's high school graduation in 2000, before my parents moved to Kansas. After the move, my mom was able to be a part of Tally's high school graduation, Cassie's master's graduation, and Mikelle's college graduation celebrations.

Mother and Cassie sharing a toast at Cassie's master's graduation, May 2006

Mother at Cassie's master's graduation, May 2006

Mother sharing in our celebration of Tally's
graduation from high school, May 2006

271

Mother was able to see her great-grandson, Liam, baptized. It was a very special day. From left: son-in-law Ken, daughter, Dottie, Mother, and great-grandson, Liam

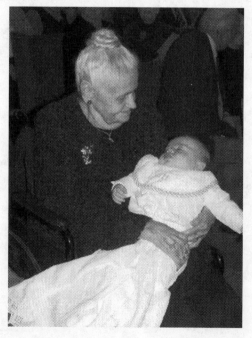

Great-grandma and "Little Lord Liam" on his baptism day. The baptism gown had been worn by most family member for five generations, made by Liam's great-great-great-grandmother.

Christmas 2007 with my mom. She was able to attend
a presentation Cassie did at Union Station.

POWER OF DOCUMENTATION

Pictures, family videos/DVDs, and documentation are
valuable! I encourage you to take lots of picture and document those joyous times. With digital cameras, disks, electronic frames, and computers, there are many ways to document and review those times. The pictures and videos help
with the older person's recall as well. In early childhood, the
Reggio Emilia model offers a great example of the use of
documentation to view progress, remember events and build
on experiences. I think a similar model could work for older
folks as well. Our children, now grown, delight in looking
at our hundreds of family videos from their infant and early
childhood years. It's also an effective way to keep family history. Our goal is to put all the videos onto DVDs. It's a very
lofty goal. Cassie has asked for all the family videos on DVD
as a wedding gift someday. I understand that videos only have

a ten- to twenty-year lifespan (various sources give this range), so preserving them is important. There are many sources on this. Here is one: http://genealogy.about.com/library/authors/ ucmishkin4a.htm.

We took pictures all the time. When my sister comes monthly to visit and take care of Mother, sometimes she brings her grandchildren so Mother can visit her great-grand-children. Here are a few pictures from a day with Dottie.

Mother & Dottie enjoying her deck.

Grandma sharing watermelon with great-grandchild Rylee and daughter Dottie.

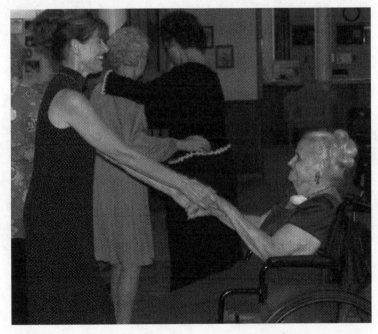

Dottie dancing with Mother at the Seniors Prom, put on by a local retirement center.

Visits from grandchildren and great-grandchildren were a treat for Mother. We always documented the visits. Tally was with Mother several times a week, and we often took pictures of various activities we did together. Once our older daughters moved away, they would visit Mother when they were home. Dottie's adult children and families made arrangements to visit when they could. They also lived about an hour away, which made it easier. Don's son and family also made a special effort to visit to see Grandma, all the way from Northern Minnesota – a long trip. Here are some photos from grandchildren and great-grandchildren visits.

I also have some very special and meaningful private photos. During my dad's last days and hours of life, I asked my
mother if she would like me to take some pictures of her
and my dad. At first she refused, but the next day she asked

if I would do that. It was more than precious. I took several photos of her with my dad, kissing him, caressing him, and stroking his face. Even as my dad was no longer conscious or speaking, he was still able to pucker up his lips to accept her kisses. If was almost surreal for me. I had trouble focusing with tears welling up but was able to document a dear time in my parents' life together.

I'm not a fan of taking pictures at funerals or of people in caskets, but it is a practice that had been in my mom's and dad's families, so we did take pictures at the small family visitation. We also photographed all the flowers and displays we put together. Mikelle put together a lovely slide show of my dad and his life with us that we displayed on a laptop in the back of the church at the funeral. My mom still looks at this. We had a display of old photos as well.

AND IT'S ALL RIGHT TO CRY

"It's all right to cry/Crying gets the sad out of you/It's all right to cry/It might make you feel better!" This song from *Free to Be*, by Marlo Thomas, is one we played at home and in my early-childhood classes years ago. I believe in this, and I don't hide my emotions or tears. It demonstrates the importance and intensity of the situation. Crying might make you feel better, but I believe it makes everyone else uncomfortable. My response to someone else's tears is a hug. So why don't we just do that, rather than turning away, not making eye contact, or making others feel they need to hide their tears? I cried a lot with this last set of transitions. Change is hard, especially when it removes a source of immediate support or security.

It's also important to know when you need professional help—when the tears won't stop. You may need others to remind you about this, and then you still may deny it, and respond, "I'll be okay." In all my studies of the family and family development, I know that keeping busy is a good way to cope with the tears and try to move on. Yet sometimes we do need professional help to be able to move on.

SAYING YES WHEN YOU KNOW YOU SHOULDN'T, FOR THE SAKE OF AN OPPORTUNITY!

At the expense of more stress, more time away from family, maybe even some respite, we might say yes to something we should have said no to. I tried to prioritize commitments and have said no to many things. The following describes "an opportunity" that perhaps was not the best for me. More work can be almost respite (not the healthiest type of respite); then again, it may be an escape.

The dean of my college would often call more work "new opportunities." I have been very careful with my time and have learned to say no to many things, such as: committees, surveys (only doing those I really cared about or felt obligated to do), or joining organizations, particularly if they weren't active, functional, or could make a difference. When asked to run for president of the faculty senate at my university, I struggled with the decision, as it is a major commitment. After careful consideration, talking with family and department head, I felt supported, so I agreed to be nominated. The next fall I was elected second vice president and was honored and overwhelmed. Then, the first vice president stepped down! That fast-forwarded my life a year, not something I needed! I developed a tick in my eye and a deep tissue muscle pull in my shoulder. I had physical therapy and worked on relaxation, and I'm still working on this!

My Brother's Wedding

The following are excerpts from two e-mails written to my brother and siblings about the possibility of my mom's attending my brother's wedding, a ten-hour drive, when she was ninety-two years old. Although this experience has already been shared, the process of planning for this event was worth noting. The first email is from my sister, outlining what it would take to make the trip. We pretty much decided it was not going to work, nor would it be possible for her, healthwise. Then Mother kept bringing up that she wanted to go but didn't think she could and felt no one else thought she could.

Below is the first e-mail from my sister:

* * * * *

Mother said today she really wished she could attend the wedding, but she knew she couldn't because she does not have any money.

On the one hand I would think it would be reckless to do it, even if we could come up with the money and someone's frequent flyer miles. However, eager anticipation and determination to go could make a big difference in her desire to live and take care of herself. At ninety-two, if she would not survive the trip, at least she would be doing what she wanted to do.

It would require paying for her, and a provider to eat and to get to KCI. Prior disability notification to the airlines would make the flight the least challenging part of the trip. The Twin Cities ought to have accessible cab service available from the airport to an accessible hotel room if arrangements are made well in advance. Then somebody would have to help while there, so Patty could have sleep time. Again, arrangements made well in advance could get them from the hotel to the boat, and back again, in an accessible cab.

Then there are arrangements for the trip to the airport, disability flight arrangements, arrival help at the airport, and driving back to Emporia. I suppose it might be possible to drive her van to KCI and park it.

Never say never.

* * * * *

Here is a second e-mail from me, five weeks later:

I need to share with you that Mother has been talking more about possibly going to your wedding. This morning she was asking me about a dress, and I asked if she wanted to see it or wear it to church tonight. She said she wanted to wear it to your wedding!

Well, we talked about what we had talked about before, with the cost, her health, etc. We had pretty much decided it was not the wisest thing to do, from several angles: particularly physically and financially. Dottie had written an e-mail not long ago about arrangements and cost. No one responded to her e-mail. We know Mother probably couldn't make the drive, but to drive, we'd have to take two vans. Our van alone would take about $340 just for gas round trip. Both vans would be $680–$700. We'd also have to put new tires on the other van to go out of town. I don't think the van travel would be good for her health, as she'd be in her wheelchair the whole time.

So, that leaves us with flying (for which we'd need two tickets), hiring a caregiver 24 hrs. each day to fly with and stay with her (depending on if I can find someone who is willing to do that), transportation to the airport, motel stay, meals (for two), etc. We had estimated somewhere between $2000 and $3000 for everything.

We are already putting about $2000 or more per month into her care, utilities, maintenance, meals, transportation, and supplies. That doesn't include the bookkeeping and case management hours I do. We cannot afford another $2000–$3000 to cover her going to the wedding. She doesn't want to ask you, (my brother) to cover it. I told her we may call you to talk about it. I'm sure you would love to have her, and there are many details to think about that are beyond the financial details. I would have to find one of the providers who would be willing to work for 3 days straight (I would assist, of course). There are also several outcomes. Thinking logically, the possible scenarios are below:

- Everything would work out as planned, there would be financial assistance covering her costs, a good provider, she would have a great time seeing most of her children together (probably for the last time in her life), and she would make it home safely, tired, but no trips to the emergency.

- She starts off on the journey and ends up in the hospital there, or ends up in the hospital here when she gets home.

- She doesn't make it to the wedding, dies on the way, dies at the wedding, or dies on the return trip or when she gets home.

I talked with (my sister) this morning, and she talked about how much Mother would look forward to this, but also if something happened, she would be doing something she wanted and chose to do. I agree, yet I'm not sure if it is a wise and responsible choice to give her. I would like to hear thoughts from you, and the rest of her children. This is our mother; I would like to respect her wishes and choices when possible and when they are safe. She knows those around her, cherishes seeing her children, grandchildren, and great-grandchildren and watches the calendar, counting the days until someone plans to visit. I think another reason she wants to go is to see more of her children together before she dies.

Could we arrange a time to talk with Mother when I'm on the phone? Her recall is not good, and she would not remember what is talked about. Please let me know what might be a good time for you. This Wed. evening would be good, between 5:00–9:00 PM. I am booked Sun, Mon & Tues evenings.

Please advise.

Love,
Carol

* * * * *

Responses were, at first, reserved and cautious, which I completely understood. Then, as we started to plan, looking at costs and all the other particulars, one of my mom's providers offered to go; her husband would drive. It was very generous and worked out quite well, overall. As mentioned earlier, we ended up carrying both my mom and daughter in their wheelchairs up a steep dozen steps to the party, which offered another advocacy opportunity. Mother delighted in being able to enjoy her son's wedding, and that is why we made the effort.

* * * * *

Here is the thank you e-mail I sent to my brother and his new wife:

Dear ones,

What a lovely wedding and party! The scenery was beautiful, food delicious, and party was fun. Thanks for your generosity in covering our rooms, and Mother's expenses, as well. The Bath & Body gifts were also very thoughtful. Mother had a delightful time and is totally exhausted. I'm sure it will take her at least the week to recover (Fletcher, too—ha ha). I wish you could have seen her eyes as she gazed up at you two when you were saying your vows and singing your duet. I was holding her hand, and she squeezed my hand at the end of ceremony. She said all of the Lord's Prayer, and sang along on the chorus. She enjoyed all of the interesting historic décor, going through the locks, great food, watching the dancing, and just being a part of the entire celebration. She looked beautiful in her sparkly purple dress, fancy updo of her hair, and the biggest smile.

All the planning, arranging with her provider and husband, even carrying both Tally and Mother up and down the stairs was worth being a part of your celebration of love and commitment together. I'm glad you had a little time off before going back to reality.
It was great to see everyone and be a part of your special day. It was a short but fun time.

Love to all,
Carol

Brother Don & Lindy's wedding with Mother

Earlier that year, Lindy, Don's wife, made a gorgeous historical photo quilt for Mother. Below is a photo of it. It had old photos of my mom and dad in the top rows, then each child's baby picture with five photos of each child's family going down laterally from their baby pictures. It hangs over Mother's fireplace, and she cherishes looking at it each day.

Beautiful photo quilt made by Lindy for Mother.

OLDEST BROTHER AND WIFE VISIT!

I was awakened and surprised one morning by a call from my oldest brother. He and his wife were planning to come by that afternoon (they live nine hours away). Mother was delighted but still didn't believe they were coming. I arranged to work from home that afternoon so I could be around. The provider did some extra cleaning; bless her! I had the provider take one of Mother's pumpkin pies out of the freezer that she helped make before Thanksgiving, so she would have something to serve. Mother said, "Ice cream would be good with that. Do I have some?" I assured her that she always had ice cream in the freezer.

Will wonders ever cease? I was in the last days of writing this book. Maybe there was a reason for my delaying completion. I remember thinking; this chapter may have a better ending. I remember the joy my dad had when seeing my oldest brother for the last time before my dad died. My dad raised his arms high to embrace him, even though he had barely moved his arms for days. I was delighted for my mom that her oldest would soon visit her. I had decided to go over for a bit, take some pictures, and then leave to let them have their visit. I was hopeful that all would go well.

Everything did go well. It was a very nice visit. I didn't get a lot of work done that day, but it was good to have Mother have a visit from her oldest son. I met and greeted them, took pictures with Mother, then went back to my place for a bit (and got a little work done on this book). Later I went back to share pumpkin pie with them. They were very nice with Mother and me, and even gave her a gift before they left. I told Mother it's a good thing she lived long enough to see some hearts soften. I guess time can heal, if you live long enough.

MOTHER CELEBRATES HER NINETY-THIRD BIRTHDAY!

Mother says she never thought she would live this long. We are blessed to have her. Although she has frequent confusion, she still knows us, and we can do fun things together. Tally tells Grandma every day just how cute she is. Some days and weeks get so very busy that I barely see her. However busy I am, I talk with her daily, and that is a gift as well. Knowing we have arranged a safe and comfortable place for her with good care is also a gift. Having her visit Tally's new apartment, plant another deck garden in the spring, and join us at the pond to feed the fish on warm days is also a gift. Not many have this opportunity, particularly if the youngest of five children. Life is special and life is a gift. We treasure each day.

My mom on her ninety-third birthday!

My sister, Dottie, sent the following e-mail after one of her recent monthly visits with Mother. Mother's heartfelt words and prayer says it all:

"Dear ones,

My caregiving visit with Mother, from which I just returned, was so pleasant. We played Sorry, watched TV, went outside, had a shower/SPA morning and sang some old favorite hymns together. The memory that surfaces the most came from the day before, though, when Rachel and I took her out to eat at Shanghai, then to Bible study and the hospital lab.

It was the end of Bible study with nine friends who are elderly, widowed, and devout Lutherans. Caregiver "R" had been pretty quiet until they asked everyone to close by holding hands and expressing one thought for the group prayer.

"R" said all she wanted was to get into grad school, and more urgently, pass her research/statistics test on Monday.

The ladies wanted to know her name and noted what time she would take the test. They said they would all pray for her. If they thought it was too early, they would pray the night before.

However, the one that produced some misty eyes was Mother's prayer. We were all impressed that she could read her Bible passage aloud. Then she touched our hearts with her slow, halting words, 'Dear God, I am so-o-o-o old ... and I keep on living. Thank you. Amen.'

I'm sure I cannot fully convey the emotion in that room with mere words, but I did want to let you know, especially those of you who are contributing substantially to her home care, how much it means to her.

Love,
Dottie"

WHAT WE'VE LEARNED

- Fletch and I cannot do what we do without the other. We are a team. Whenever one of us is sick, it has a domino effect. When everyone is well, on time, and doing his or her part, life is manageable, even good. Some days can be quite good; then again, some require more patience and creative problem-solving.

- Time may heal all wounds—if you live long enough. This thought came to mind after my oldest brother called to say he was coming to visit my mom for the first time since my dad passed away, almost three years ago.

QUOTE

"In this life we cannot always do great things. But we can do small things with great love."—Mother Teresa

TIPS AND TOOLS

A must-have resource is this pain assessment scale: http:// www.anes.ucla.edu/pain/FacesScale.jpg

We used this often when measuring pain for my mom. This put us all on the same page, with some consistency of the measure of pain she was having.

Videos only have a ten- to twenty-year lifespan, so preserving them is important. Do a Google search on "preserving family videos." There are many sources on this. Here is one:

http://genealogy.about.com/library/authors/ucmishkin4a. htm

Chapter 13

REFLECTIONS

Reflection has been the theme of this book for me. It has been a deeply personal reflection process, while also integrating and weaving my professional knowledge and experience. I wanted to include other family members, so I asked each member of my family for their reflections of events over the past three years. I truly wanted honest and open responses and assured them I would not take any of it personally; I felt others could learn from this process in our family. The following e-mail describes, more specifically, my request to my siblings.

* * * * *

"August 2008

Dear sibs,

It was three years ago when the folks moved to Kansas. Mother is currently doing pretty well, with aches particularly on wet days, which we have certainly had much of this summer. It has been quite a journey for us these past years. As you know, I have been writing a book about the Sandwich Generation and hope to have it completed in the next few weeks.

I am asking for your input and reflection, if you wish to give it. I would like our various perspectives. I am not looking for praise or accolades; I am seeking your honest reflections about the process and perspective three years ago, and now.

I have put together a few questions, but you are welcome to go beyond them or in a different direction. I will not change the content, but the editor may edit if needed. If you choose, you can reply via e-mail, hard copy, or if you'd like, I can call you and you can dictate your thoughts.

Here are the questions:

- How did you feel about the plans to move the folks to Kansas at the time (3+ years ago)?
  - What emotions did you feel?

  Did you understand the plan, and how did you feel about it?

  What reservations/concerns, if any, did you have?

  How was the process of family communication at that time?

  What worked well?

  What could have been done differently?

- How do you feel about the process now, about where Mother is?
  - What emotions do you feel?
  - How do you feel about her living situation?
  - What reservations/concerns, if any, do you currently have?
  - How was the process of family communication at this time?
  - What works well?

- What do you think should be done differently?
- How do you feel about your own plans, communication with your children, etc., regarding where you might live as you grow older?
  - Do you see various options?
  - Have you communicated with your children your wishes regarding your choices, as you grow older?

A recent Census Bureau population projection through 2050 is that the number of people eighty-five and older will more than triple by 2050, to nineteen million! What do you think is the future for the aging in our society? What issues do you think are important to talk about, as families and as a society?

I am asking Fletch and our children for their input and perspectives. I know what some of their answers will be, as we have talked about it.

The process and perspective of one family going through this time/these decisions/this communication process is my goal. I believe that others can learn from what has worked well, as well as from our mistakes. I truly value, respect, and appreciate your time to give your input and reflection.

Thanks so much!

Love,

Carol"

* * * * *

Only Dottie chose to respond. Below is her heartfelt and honest response, for which I am most grateful.

Reflections by Daughter Dottie

THEN

A book titled *Die Broke* by Steven Pollan and Mark Levin presented a radical concept that resonated with me. My spin on the idea is, "When you can't take it with you, it makes sense to earn enough money for moderate, balanced, debt-free living, and die without leaving messes for others to clean up." That is why I honored my parents' desire to stay out of institutional living and live their lives like they always did, with some help, of course. Who knows how long they would be around?

My parents lived frugal, meaningful lives. Their charitable contributions and investments were primarily reserved for Lutheran Church Extension Funds and AAL (Aid Association for Lutherans) Insurance. They even purchased long-term care insurance for Mother, since she would probably live longer. They understood that this would be provided in her home so she would not have to go to a nursing home.

They visited many church members and old friends in nursing homes and said they were drugged up, herded about like cattle, and were terribly lonely and unhappy. They were steadfastly adamant in their desire to stay in their own home until death.

Funds rapidly diminished when they paid for help in their home. Profound disappointment with their understanding of long-term care insurance, both in limited help at home and in capping out, called for family intervention. Health professionals, Medicaid, and siblings pointed to nursing homes, even thought the figures show it would be happier, cheaper, and safer to get Medicaid help at home.

An inappropriate attempt to put them in assisted living,

when they should have been in a nursing-home level of care, resulted in frightening mismanagement of my father's diabetes, and a dangerously strange environment for my mother by giving her Vioxx when her old medical records noted she could not tolerate it. Fearing cerebral hemorrhage, should she fall, she was taken off Coumadin, even though she had a history of stroke.

When my mother, in particular, was terribly frightened and felt betrayed, my youngest sister's family and my family moved them back home with full-time care providers. Within the year, their banker (and power of attorney) called a family meeting to say they could not continue living like this. The only suggestion that affordably granted their wishes to stay in their own home was my youngest sister's offer to build a little house for them next to hers and use the sale of my parents' home to pay for it.

God-awful furor arose from brother and sister; old family secrets shocked and hurt all of us; and the bulk of the burden fell on my youngest sister, with extended family help. We moved them to an accessible home that was brought down the highway in two pieces, literally lifted over the top of the Russells' home, and awaited family cooperation to build decks around three sides for wheelchairs.

NOW

Papa passed away, at home, with Mother lying next to him on one side, and I sitting on the other, reading his prayers, singing favorite songs, and saying [his favorite] German prayer.

When he stopped breathing, shortly after 7:30 a.m., I called to the hospice helper to phone Carol next door. His pulse was gone, and his color that was slightly yellow, turned chalky white and the tips of his ears and toes started to mottle. Mama kissed him many times, and in the middle of tears said, "Oh honey, I don't want you to go!"

Then something happened that I never saw before. When the door slammed, the helper yelled, "Carol's here!" Papa gasped and resumed breathing while Carol climbed on the bed, next to his ear, and assured him of her love, and she would take care of Mother, and she could let him go.

I called sibling on my cell to provide a chance to say one last word while he might still be able to hear. Even though moving was hard on him, he often said he was glad they did it because he would not worry about Mother, living next door to her youngest daughter.

Mother is now always near someone who honors her grieving, in spite of horrible sibling conflicts. Slowly, she regained interest in attending her granddaughters' orchestra concerts, art shows, graduations, gardening, bird-watching, enjoying other aspects of nature (sunsets, deer in the woods, a possum on the deck), family celebrations, enjoying *Little House on the Prairie* reruns, listening to books, women's Bible study on Wednesdays, and church on Saturday nights. She is able to do this in spite of chronic pain, infections, and stomach problems that challenge her daily.

A funeral director told my husband that elderly spouses usually do not last longer than a year after their mate dies. Mother is now working on year number three, at the age of ninety-two. Her ninety-year-old, yodeling brother-in-law tells her by phone that they are both antiques. She laughs and retorts that she can still boss him around because she is two years older. If I complain about my own aches and pains, at age sixty-two, her unsympathetic reply is, "You don't know what old is!"

Often she will say, "I just don't know why I am living so long!" Well, Mama, I would say that a few of the reasons include:

You lived long enough to care for Papa to the age of ninety-two. You did this by carefully watching his diabetic food intake, symptoms, foot care, and back rubs. You buffered his frustration with kindness, even though it was very difficult at times. Statistically, by virtue of his health, death could easily have taken him in his seventies.

Your survival impacted the life of a carpenter. As your new little house was being built, Fletch came in and found this man, who had been working on your house, shaking and crouched over on the floor in your new living room, crying. Fletch thought he was sick, but it was that he had recently put his parents in a nursing home and could not believe what the Russells were doing for you.

Even though your short-term memory can be frustrating, you still have the ability to capture our attention with stories. Your recollection of the end of WWI in southeast Missouri is an example of how your family stories are of historical significance.

At the end of WWI, you remember how you saw straw-stuffed overalls, hanging from a tree. A fire was lit beneath it. You cried inconsolably because the man you knew best who wore overalls was your beloved daddy. No one understood why you were so upset. You remembered that your mother could not pick you up, probably because she was pregnant with one of the eight children she bore. So a lady pulled a washtub off the fence, turned it upside-down on the ground for you to sit, and fed you white soda crackers. Later, you learned that they had burned the Kaiser in effigy, and not your daddy.

- You are the only living resource for nieces and nephews to ask questions about family, as you are the only member of your immediate family still living. Your last brother died a few months ago.
- You published a cookbook, *Apron Strings by Gladys,* about which people are still interested today.
- Your oil paintings were presented in two art shows after you turned ninety years old.
  - Caregivers talk about how you warm their hearts with memories of their own mothers and grandmothers.
- You testified at a hearing for accessibility rights in you own town, after a frightening wheelchair experience on an anti-quated freight elevator at Papa's funeral. You, dear Mama, made a difference for others with disabilities in your own little corner of the world, because you had the courage to speak up.
- You perseverance forced all your children to examine the value of a human life and how incredibly important it is to discuss financial priorities. Your children, grandchildren, and great-grandchildren are learning profound lessons in respecting the elderly and that sincere compassion requires thoughtful phone calls, cards, pictures, visits, hard work, and money.
- Your longevity has afforded time for grandchildren, alien-ated by divorce, to reconnect.
- Your friends at Messiah Lutheran Bible Study have joined

you in praying for all of us, as well as for countless other concerns. When I ask you to pray for things like my husband's cancer, my daughter-in-law's pregnancy, and my grandchildren's ear infections, I know you will do it, just like you prayed for us when we served in Vietnam.

- I call you every day, simply because I can. You joke that you are "above ground, vertical, and breathing." How many other daughters my age have the privilege of calling their mothers? Most of them have died. Your laughter is so good to hear when I tell stories about your great-grandchildren. You really perk up when they visit. I love keeping notes of things I want to tell Mother.

FUTURE

The list I've started will continue, even after you leave this physical world. My present attitudes impacted by this experience are:

- Good health is worth more than all the money you can save.

- An attitude of gratitude goes a long way for personal happiness and those with whom you live.

- I'm cleaning my basement, garage, and file drawers with renewed commitment, because I learned that organized living is worth more than gold when you age. It saves my nerves, self-confidence, and my relationship with my children and husband.

- Flexibility helps you live happier and longer. In other words, don't wait until things are just right before you decide to live.

- Be open to working with problems while staying true to

your moral and ethical values. You will have done your part for family integrity and will die with a clear conscience.

- We talk openly to our children about death and money. In addition, we get professional help on managing feelings and finances instead of keeping in a secret.

Finally, I am amazed at my youngest sister and her family. Even though they have "many plates spinning at once," my sister manages problems with assertiveness and grace. The way she works out her family challenges, her profession, her marriage, and personal health is absolutely a work of art. The divine beauty of it is that she uses the lessons she learns to help others with similar problems.

Carol's name was inspired by her birth date—December 26, 1952, the day after Christmas. When she dies, she wants Christmas trees, not flowers at her funeral. If I'm around at that time, which is highly unlikely, I will picture Carol as the angel on top of the tree. Sometimes, it seems like she gives more than is humanly possible. The depth of my gratitude toward her, and her family, surpass verbal expression.

* * * * *

REFLECTIONS FROM MY FATHER-IN-LAW

I was delighted to hear that my father-in-law was willing to give me his reflections on our process. He is an awesome father-in-law, artist, and my former art teacher in college; he is almost ninety-one and still painting every day. His perspective is important to me, in that he is of my mom's generation and has had a very different life (only child, as compared to my mom's being one of eight children) and very different perspective than she. We discussed our plan with him, from the beginning. He was even with us the day my mom and dad's house was lifted over the top of ours, in construction. The following are his thoughts and reflections.

THEN and NOW

To be blunt, I never questioned your sanity, but I have deep and grave questions about parents, particularly me, expecting such a move to take place. I believe in desperately hanging on to independence as long as one lives, because I believe that is living! If you recall, my mother was exactly the same way. Alice and I begged her to come live with us, year after year, but she and we finally understood that her life was not to be absorbed by our life, though she deeply loved us.

I understood your plan with the house and all, but I never could comprehend the complex and expensive reasoning behind it and why a family should become totally divided over the providing of love and care.

I certainly did and do have concerns for Fletch and Carol over the rather chaotic fretting and worry over monthly bills, which I gather are exceedingly high from the standpoint of the rest of the family.

FUTURE

I just want to stay as independent as possible. I want no big sacrifices on the family's part. There is always assisted living, but it would be very nice to plan a clean heart attack, a rather difficult job, but very nice.

I've been thinking back and Aunt Essie comes to mind, with her care for Grandmother (my grandmother). She built a large room on the house, filled it with Grandmother and two other old ladies, and charged them enough to pay for the room, her care, and meals. It seemed to work fairly well in that Aunt Essie always seemed a little demented, in a "'20s girl" sort-of-way.

I think the future of aging will be conducted on a very independent approach—villages on their own, filled with the older generation, hiring individuals from outside the village to help. They would come and go, as to any job. Care hospitals will be run as a business in the village or town. The older group will run the towns, as long as they physically can cope. Businesses will be run and turned to a younger old group—anything but treating each other as old folks!

My father-in-law's reflection reminded me of how different perspectives can be. I can recall my dad also feeling like life would not be worth living if he needed to use a wheelchair. I can also recall Tally (who had used a wheelchair for mobility since age two) telling him that it didn't really matter, as long as he could get from one place to another and that he could live a full life while being seated!

* * * * *

I also requested similar feedback from my immediate family. I added a few questions, including questions about our sanity, then and now. I am most grateful for their honest and open responses and reflections. Here are thoughts from our three daughters and from my dear husband and partner throughout this journey.

From Cassie, our oldest daughter, who did direct care for Grandma for over two years, while balancing two part-time teaching jobs at two different universities and assisting with our youngest daughter as a personal care assistant, as Tally attended her first two years of college. She is incredible! Here are her reflections of the past three-plus years:

THEN:

- How did you feel about the plans to move the Grandma & Grandpa to Kansas at the time (3+ years ago)?

"At the time, I thought that the plans sounded very beneficial for G & G, but I was a bit worried about you both (Mom and Dad) taking on too much, especially Mom. Mikelle and Tally still lived at home, and I know you were still quite busy with trying to get the school stuff organized for Tally's senior year. I admired you for taking on so much, but thought the plan might be a bit ambitious!"

- How old were you, and what was happening in your life then?

"Let's see, I think I was twenty-three and starting my last year of my master's degree. I was looking forward to teaching again, and at the time of the move, Jake and I were getting ready to go to his brother's wedding in DC."

- Did you wonder about our sanity?

"Ha-ha, yes! Well, your sanity, no. I knew you worked very hard with all the planning and looking at the feasibility of the situation. I knew you were doing this in sound mind; thus, not insane. However, I did wonder about how your sanity was going to be possibly changed after the move!"

- What emotions did you feel?

"My emotions were generally pretty neutral. I wasn't living at home; thus, at the time, I wasn't going to be directly affected by the change. I was happy that G&G were going to be provided with what they wished, and I was a bit worried about how this would impact Mom, Dad, and Tally, but overall it was a positive emotion."

- Did you understand the plan, and how did you feel about it?

"I know I understood the plan, because I remember Mom talking over and over how the move was going to go, and the possibilities of care once they were down here. I felt the actual physical move plan was a little haphazard, but I thought the long-term plan was well grounded and made sense."

- What reservations/concerns, if any, did you have?

"The only concerns I had focused on the impact of having G&G so close. Finances were a concern, too, of course. Also, I knew that at the time, Mom wasn't taking a whole bunch of time for herself, and I knew this would probably be even more limited with moving G&G down."

- How was the process of family communication in our own family at that time?

  - What worked well?

  - What could have been done differently?

"I think the communication within our own family was very good. At the time, the communication was primarily face-to-face. We did a lot of family meetings, talking about the situation and the plan of what was going to be done. I believe everything worked very well. I know I felt like I knew exactly what was going to be happening, and was as prepared as possible. I'm not sure doing anything differently would have been beneficial."

- How did you see the communication in my family (of origin) at the time?

  - What worked well?

  - What could have been done differently?

"And now for something completely different. The communication with your family of origin is poor to mediocre at best. I believe (and still do) that you are by far the most effective communicator in the family. Communication is a two-way street, with most of your communication occurring via e-mails and phone calls. I'm honestly not sure anything could have been done differently, with positive consequences. The communication within your family is marred with stubborn egos, mental issues, and selfishness, personality traits that can't be easily changed to benefit communication."

NOW

• How do you feel about the process now, about where Grandma is?

"I feel very good about where Grandma currently is. Many, many times when I was working with her she would tell me, "When you're ninety-one, I hope you have a granddaughter to take care of you!" or some other way of saying how much she appreciated the care she was getting and the environment she lived in. I was lucky to be able to see the consequences of her environment in her mood, interactions, and overall interest."

• How old are you now, and what is happening in your life now?

"I am now twenty-six and working on my PhD in educational psychology at the University of Northern Colorado."

• Did you wonder about our sanity now?

"Every day! I sometimes wonder if you guys are taking

on too much, but I don't worry about you. You are taking more measures to take time for yourselves (like your date nights), and Tally is becoming more independent. Both of these should at least help ease stress and worry in other areas of life. I think you are now better prepared to handle the situation. I wonder if these things (like time for yourselves, Tally's being more independent, etc.) weren't somewhat products of the situation. I'd say positive ones."

• What emotions do you feel about the current situation?

"I'm quite happy with the current situation. I think Grandma is in a good place and has good people caring for her. I think you and Dad have adapted to the station, and taken appropriate measures. I wish I could be there to help more, but besides that, I have positive feelings about the situation, besides mild concern about the financial and emotional side."

• What reservations/concerns, if any, do you now have?

"Not as many! I'm confident Grandma is getting exactly what she wants; thus, my concerns for her are quite limited. My concerns, such as the ones above, would focus more on the impact of Mom, Dad, and Tally."

• How is the process of family communication in our own family now?
  • What works?
  • What can be done differently?

"I think the process of communication is good. Up until very recently, I would rate our communication as stellar! Communication has always been extremely open and honest. E-mail works as a good communication process, but I'm much better at reading e-mails than responding. Phone conversations are great, except when I'm out of minutes (such as now!)."

- How do you see the communication in my family (of origin) now?
  - What works well?
  - What can have been done differently?

"I see communication within your family as flawed and, at least with some members, nonexistent. I kind of chuckled at [an] e-mail, stating that [one family member] had read the e-mail and was afraid that if Gma came, then [another family member] would be coming as well. Just that line alone illustrates many of the communication problems! I guess you at least know that they're reading your e-mails. As I said before, it's impossible to effectively communicate with family members who let egos, emotional issues, and mental problems get in the way. I believe you have done extremely well with what you have been given in your siblings' tangled web; however, I believe that effective communication might be impossible within your immediate family (at least at this time or until some people aren't around!)."

- How do you feel about your own plans, communication with your children, etc., regarding where you might live as you grow older?

"This is prefaced with 'should you choose to have children,' right? I feel quite ill-prepared to be planning where I might live, as I get older. I really have no plans at this time and think much will be dependent on the situation, not just personally but nationally as well. I will definitely try to keep open communication with my children, should any happen to pop up."

• Do you see various options?

"Of course! Lots of options, very dependent on the situation at hand. At this point in my life, I can't really speculate that far!"

What do you think is the future of the aging in our society? What issues do you think are important to talk about, as a society?

"I believe the future for the aging could go one of two ways. Either the government will get on the ball and start reforming how the aging are treated/what kinds of resources are devoted to this population, or the government will wait too long and try the retroactive approach. I hope for the first outcome, but fear the recent history of the government's actions are much more retroactive. I think issues, such as reform of health care and social security, increasing resources for the elderly (social, financial, etc.), and increasing aid for individuals who wish to stay in their own homes (as opposed to nursing homes) are very important issues to bring up. Hopefully, the large influx of the aging in our population will kick-start these discussions and help move toward a society which appreciates and more fully supports its elderly population."

From Mikelle, our middle daughter, who did direct care regularly for Grandma for over a year and filling in when needed. She did this while balancing her last year of college, a part-time on campus, and assisting with Tally as a personal care for a significant number of hours each week. She is an awesome young lady! Mikelle was only two years old when Tally was born and was twenty when Grandma and Grandma moved to Kansas. Here are Mikelle's reflections:

"Being twenty years old at the time, a sophomore in college and still living at home, I was not too thrilled about my grandparents moving in with us. I understood why this needed to happen and knew, in the big picture, it was probably for the best; however, I still was unhappy about it. I remember my parents being concerned about my sisters' and my feelings concerning Grandma and Grandpa moving to Kansas. We had numerous family meetings and talked with each other about how we felt and what could be done to make things go more smoothly. I knew it was going to be a big change for everyone (especially my immediate family) to undergo, not only moving my grandparents but also the emotional, financial, and physical stress that goes along with it. When my grandparents arrived, their house addition was not ready, and they ended up living in our basement (where my mini-apartment was). I felt as if it not only turned my life but my family's life upside down. Luckily this was a temporary solution, and they were moved into their house a couple weeks later. It wasn't until after they moved to their new home and began to get settled that I realized how important this transition was and how happy they both were. I remember coming home from classes and driving up to see Grandpa and Grandma eating popcorn on the deck and watching the birds. I could tell they were both truly happy which, in turn, made me feel this was the right decision.

About a year after this, I moved out of my parents' house and into an apartment closer to school. My grandpa had passed about six months before I moved, then I began to help take care of my grandma. Almost every Thursday night for a little over a year I spent providing care for my grandma. At first, it was a little awkward helping my grandma with personal-care needs, but after a while it became more routine. At times it felt like work, but other times I felt incredibly lucky to see my ninety-year-old grandma once a week for more than a year.

Now, I'm twenty-three years old and not living near my family and my grandma. I feel I have more of an outside view, since I don't see my parents and grandma every day. We still talk frequently, and I see my grandma when I come home to visit. I still worry about my parents' (especially my mom's) stress levels, though with Tally's becoming more independent and Grandma with care providers, my parents probably have more time to themselves now than when my sisters and I were growing up. They even have a weekly "date night"! It wasn't until I moved out of my parents' house and on my own that I began to realize how truly incredible my parents are. They made it possible for my grandparents to live the rest of their days how they wish and that they are happy. If I ever live to be ninety-plus years and have the loving family, support, life, care, and choices my grandma has now, I'll consider myself unbelievably fortunate."

From Tally, our youngest daughter, who is an amazing young lady. With all of her medical, physical and learning challenges, she is driven to complete college, live more independently, and sees people and the world in a very positive light. She has been well supported by her family. Tally also did companion care for Grandma and would call us on her cell phone as soon as Grandma might need something for which

Tally could not physically assist. Tally has taught us many things, many of which prepared us for "our sandwich" and caring for our aging parents. Here are Tally's reflections:

"At first I was upset about the decision. It was going to be my senior year, and I didn't think my parents would have time to help me through my senior year.

- I was excited to have Grandma here for my graduation. If she had been in Minnesota, she could not have been there. It was exciting to walk down the graduation aisle and see my grandma there. She has been a part of other milestones for me, too.

- She got to see my senior orchestra solo, which was a big deal. She had thrown up before she came but came anyway. It meant a lot to me.

- Having Grandma at my graduation and other milestones took away from my frustration of having them move here my senior year, when I thought my parents wouldn't have enough time to help me with everything I wanted to do with prom, graduation, and all my medical stuff.

- When they were in Minnesota, I worried a lot about them and we couldn't see what was happening. When they were here, I was more at ease, since I knew what was going on with them all the time.

- Since the move, there are a lot more positives, one being that we don't have to make the nine-and-a-half-hour drive to see Grandma, Now it takes me nine and a half seconds or less to get there.

- Another positive is that I have gotten a lot closer to Grandma. She's good at Scrabble, but sometimes I think she tries to use words that aren't really words."

Things get pretty crazy some days, with various schedules, providers, and time in general. About life these days, Tally has become more flexible and now has the following attitude, which I quote:

"I'll go with the flow, wherever you go!"

* * * * *

FLETCH'S REFLECTIONS

MY PERSPECTIVE—LIFE IS FULL OF SURPRISES

THEN

"It's often said that we don't know what we have until it's gone. I think that is true of most things we hold dear, but I feel this holds most true for our parents.

Rather than looking at the wishes of Carol's parents, some members of the family appeared to be thinking of themselves. It was an unselfish act and a noble cause to do what we did.

On one of our visits to Minnesota to visit Carol's parents, we noticed a major decline in both of their health. As we saw them rapidly aging, and Carol's mother recovered slowly from a bad fall, we offered to arrange something for them here in Kansas. Papa Deye would reply with his "pat answers" and no discussion, "We'll take that into consideration" or "We'll cross that bridge when we come to it." Well, we finally said that they were about to cross the bridge. There was still no discussion of moving closer to one of their children.

This decision to move her parents down to Kansas wasn't hard for me, but it wasn't totally my decision; we made it together. We did it to honor Carol's parents' wishes to not move into a nursing home. Moving my in-laws to Kansas over three years ago was to provide them with a safe and comfortable place to live.

It's an honorable sacrifice to give back to the human condition by taking care of your aging or sick parents. Losing my mother to cancer when I was twenty-two years old, gave me one of life's experiences that made me face the future differently and redirected my outlook on life. When I was twenty-two and my mother was dying of cancer, I took a semester off from college and moved home to help out. That decision to move home at that time of my life is one I would never regret. The giving of my time and the time spent with my mother, knowing she wasn't going to survive (she was in her mid-fifties), gave me a better understanding of life and what's important.

THE DECISION

The thought of having aging parents living with or near us was not even a remote consideration at the time when I married Carol, over thirty years ago. When the need arose, the idea was formed that we could facilitate a move to be with us. It was not a frivolous decision.

This decision was honoring their wishes to be together and not be committed to life in a nursing home.

THE PLAN

A family meeting took place while Carol's parents were still capable of making logical decisions. I feel that the plan was not totally understood by Carol's father. Their lawyer was also at the meeting, and when options were given of moving to a nursing home or to build a small home in Kansas, the attorney said, "Armin, it's a no-brainer; it looks like you're moving to Kansas!"

The plan itself was easy. With the overall design, practicality of the move, and the house plan, there was little input. It was mainly just the two of us working on the plan. At that point, the rest of Carol's family was looking at assisted living or a nursing home, with the exception of Carol's oldest sister, who supported the belief that they did not have to live in a nursing home. Being the creative person and artist that I am, I liked the process and challenge of being the general contractor of building a wheelchair-accessible "granny shack." I enjoy that hands-on process, but this doesn't just happen, you have to take each step from point A to Z. The process of putting it all together took six months of preplanning, creative financing, hours with general contracting, prearranging twenty-four-hour care and hours of meetings with the builders, the family, e-mails, the care agencies, etc., with very little direct family feedback. We were pretty much on our own during the planning stage.

SACRIFICE

Our lives did not stop. We were both still working and taking care of Tally's needs. Our children were still graduating from high school and from college. Doing this meant Carol was taking on a whole other time-consuming (nonpaying) job, as Carol became the full-time case manager, coordinated schedules, and provided direct care. At that time I was taking on teaching new classes at the university, substitute teaching, doing all the cooking, shopping, and most of the housekeeping, while transporting Tally and assisting with much of her care. Our lives were already very full. This was a different and additional routine to what we had known before.

Our time commitments, our daily schedules of getting up and going to bed, were all being altered. It's kind of like having a baby; you don't know what the time commitment is like until you bring that baby home. We are not yet retired and are fully into our work and schedules and Tally's care. In looking back, we hadn't foreseen the ambulance trips to the hospital every other weekend, Friday nights in the emergency room, providers not showing up, or frustration with agencies. We had no respite or time for vacations. We rarely went out of town, even for appointments for Tally in those first years. There was no spontaneity or freedom of our time. We were on call around the clock.

EMOTIONALLY

Emotionally, I was more concerned about how Carol was going to handle the daily decline in her parents' health. Her sanity is sometimes put to the test with all of the schedules and agencies. One of my main reservations at the time was the financial component; the other was Carol's sanity.

COMMUNICATION

Communication with all involved was strained. I feel this process, which should have been an open exchange of ideas, became a conflict of "what's in this for me" among Carol's siblings, and her parents' wishes and choices were being de-humanized.

NOW

Now, over three years later, we have been able to accomplish many things for Carol's mother. Recently, we were able to arrange for her to attend her son's wedding. Communication with some of Carol's siblings is still strained. Time, hopefully, will increase awareness of what we're doing and lessen the strain and anxiety of some family members.

Freedom does not really exist. We are still always on call. It's not quite the demand of emergency room visits, as it used to be when Carol's father was still living. Overall, her mother has stabilized with minor problems.

- The set up of the house and surrounding area:
- Accessible living area
- Accessible decks; 5 decks, 360 degrees around house
- Accessible garden
- Van with lift so she doesn't have to transfer
- Our house is accessible for her to visit (eats dinner with us most evenings)

Contentedness

Was the move worthwhile for them? Yes! I can still picture them out in the sun that first fall, eating their popcorn. It was the most beautiful fall, for the last months of Carol's father's life. They would never have gotten that in a nursing home. The reality hits home when we saw them *both* sitting on the deck; they were home. In the words of Papa Deye, "Mission accomplished."

My mom and dad having popcorn on the deck
on a lovely fall day, September 2005

I am rewarded when I see "Grandma" give me that nod
and smile, that all is okay. The time spent taking her down to
feed the fish at the pond, watching her tend to her deck garden—it's those simple pleasures that make it all worthwhile.
That's what makes it fulfilling for me. Each night when she
leaves our house after dinner, she says, "Good night, Fletcher,"
and I reply, "Have a good night, and see you tomorrow."

Fletch giving Mother one of her favorite things: watermelon!

FUTURE

Life is full of surprises.

As we are seeing, generations are living longer with medical technology and through social program supports (such as home- and community-based programs). To have parents who live into their nineties is becoming more common today, which has not been experienced by generations of the past. I don't think society has done a very good job of preparing us for this or for seeing parents into their nineties, gracefully or financially. Why should they have to be demoralized and live out their final years in a depressing environment, not being together or where they aren't happy?

If we don't make change, we become stagnant or cannot move forward. Thinking back over this whole process, ideas were not flowing, problem-solving was not really occurring from others in the family. We create change to keep ourselves sane!

I hope our children will be there for us, and that we have provided a good role model for them. Some wondered why we would do this. We said, "Why not!"

In response to my oldest brother-in-law, who said, "Come get them, the sooner the better!"—I'm glad we did!

* * * * *

I hope this illustrates, in some small way, what an awesome family I have, and how blessed I am! This process *would not have been possible without them*! I could never have done this alone. We are incredibly blessed with three outstanding young women as our daughters. Fletch, in particular, was the inspiration of the idea. He is a wonderful idea man and has the vision long before I can even get my glasses on!

* * * * *

MY FINAL REFLECTIONS

This entire book project has been a collection of reflections. I want to reiterate what Fletch said—that this did not happen overnight. Our philosophies and priorities have been discussed and developed over our more than thirty-four years together. As I stated at the beginning of this writing, we have had a priority of family, and we chose, as a couple, to invest our time and energy in our children at the expense of being a dual-income family. This has not been easy, but it was our choice. Setting priorities included our giving up many "things" for ourselves and for our children. We believe our time is the greatest gift of all. This philosophy carried over into our approach of the care of our parents. We would offer the same support to Fletch's dad. As his dad's reflection states, he does not expect such an offer or commitment. Still, the offer stands.

Also, in reflection of my own life, I was thinking back to my childhood. I remember that Grandpa (my dad's father) passed away in our home when I was nine years old. I also recall how Grandma (my dad's mother) wanted to die after her husband passed away. I remember thinking how strange a thought it was—to *want to die*—just because your husband died. After that time, I also remember how much time Grandma (my dad's mother) spent time with us, even staying in my room for some time. I had almost forgotten that I had a double and single bed in my bedroom so Grandma could stay there with me. I do remember her staying some with us; then with her daughter in another state. I asked my sisters for some help with the specifics.

In blending their memories with mine, I learned that Grandma (my dad's mother) stayed with us several times. She had started staying six months with each of her two children, and then she stayed longer with her daughter in another state. I seem to remember the six-month stays, but it didn't seem that long.

The first time Grandma (my dad's mother) stayed with us, she slept in my bed. No one remembered where I slept, but it was remembered that she would make our beds in the morning. She said it was a little thing she could do. She would get upset because we would leave drawers half open with things hanging out of the sides. I also remember her straightening out our piles of shoes.

On another stay, my grandma had what was thought might have been a minor stroke, but she never went to the hospital. She got upset with a doctor who asked her when she'd had tuberculosis. Indignantly, she said she never had—that was a disease of the poor and uneducated. Our mother would take her little snacks because grandma did not want to eat anything. One time, I remember a sad look on Mother's face and she said, "I wish I could be taking little snacks to my own mother, too."

Grandma would stay up late during every stay, reading our textbooks. I remember her reading until midnight or 1:00 AM. One day, she came to the kitchen with one of my brother's books, and she was just shaking. She threw *The Grapes of Wrath* down on the table and demanded to know why he was reading this trash, a book with such vulgar language. He said it was for an English class. She was enraged!

My sister recalled how both Grandma and Grandpa (my dad's parents) would get upset about our watching the cowboy shows and seeing someone get shot. I remember not watching the violence, in general, but didn't remember the cowboy shows, maybe because I didn't like them either!

Mother's father passed away before I was born. I never had the privilege of knowing him. Although they had little money, my grandfather (Mother's dad) was known for his kindness and generosity; the person who was the first to help those in need in their community. I remember my grandma (Mother's mother) visiting and crocheting various wonderful creations for us. She never stayed for an extended length of time, but my memories were all fun and special. She lived much farther away, was in a nursing home for about twelve years, and passed away when I was nineteen years old. I do remember visits when we would sing hymns when we visited her, but she didn't know who we were for several years before she passed away. I did wonder how my mom felt about being so far away from her mother, the nonfrequent visits, and how very much she must have missed her.

In thinking back to the experience with Grandma on my father's side, I was her roommate and was used to her visits for months at a time. It seems I have almost come full circle—but then, life does that to us.

In conclusion, I want to clearly state that it is *not* my intent to try to convince all in the baby boomer generation to take their aging parents into their homes and lives, nor to cause guilt for not doing so! I am simply telling our story, sharing various resources and tips and tools that others in similar situations can use—or ignore.

Last, but by no means least ...

MOTHER'S REFLECTIONS

I wanted Mother to have the last word. After all, the creation of the sandwich is a result of our love, care, and commitment to her, her health, her dignity, and her well-being.

Here are the questions and her responses:
THEN:
How did you feel about the plans for you and Papa to move to Kansas? What emotions did you feel?

- I didn't mind doing it.
- I don't know how Papa felt at first. But later, after we moved, he told me four or five times that he was glad we moved here, and that I would be close to one of my children when he died. I would reply, "How do you know you're going to die before me?" and he would say, "Of course I will." I told him he didn't know that.

Did you understand the plan, and how did you feel about it?

- Sort of, but it was more clear once I saw it.

  What reservations/concerns, if any, did you have?

- I worried about how it was all going to work out—moving, flying there.

  How was the process of family communication at that time?

- I didn't think everything was being done right, as far as our whole situation at the assisted living.

  What worked well?

- As long as the money was there, living at our home in Minnesota with twenty-four-hour care worked well.

  What could have been done differently?

- If we had had the money, we would have stayed at our home in Minnesota, with care.

- I remember when I was in the hospital when we were in assisted living, no one would drive him to come see me in the hospital. Papa said he was going to drive up to see me by himself (we still had a car, even though he didn't have a driver's license anymore), and I told him not to; they would put him in jail. I thought I was going to die and never see him again. I even wrote him a letter, thinking I would not see him in this world. But I didn't want him to go to jail for driving without a driver's license.

NOW:

How do you feel about the process now, about where you are? What emotions do you feel?

- I appreciated being with my husband the last months, weeks, days, and hours of his life. I don't think I could have done that in a nursing home. I was able to be with him, next to him, all the time. I can remember when he stopped breathing, and then someone said, "Go get Carol," and then he started breathing again. Carol came and talked to him. She told him, "We'll take good care of Mother." He took one more breath, and then he was gone. If you could call a death beautiful, his was.

How do you feel about your living situation?

- I feel like it's good. Sometimes I think you [Carol] do too much for me, and other times I *know* you do. I like my little place a lot.
- What would we do without Fletcher?
- What reservations/concerns, if any, do you currently have?
- No, I don't have any. It worries me how much you [Carol] do for me.

How was the process of family communication at this time?

- I think some do and some don't believe I should be living here. Some call me, some don't so much; one not at all.
- I got a computer for my ninetieth birthday. I have help e-mailing my children and I get e-mails and pictures from them.

What works well?

- Everything is okay. I like my place. It's a nice place.

What do you think should be done differently?

- It would be nice to have all my children visit me at the same time.

How do you feel about your own plans, communication with your children, etc., regarding where you might live, as you grow older? What do you remember about how your family dealt with your aging grandparents?

- My two grandmothers lived with us in the same house, and they slept in the same bed. Sometimes they got along, but when Grandma B. was tearing the paper off the back of the quilt top, the other one said she should come help her, since she wasn't doing anything. She said she needed scissors, the other said why; she said to cut off the threads. I remember rushing around the house and collecting five pairs of scissors and putting them under my pillow (I was home sick with malaria, in my early teens), so they wouldn't argue about the scissors. I remember my one grandma saying, "Well, I don't think I can help you 'cause I can't find any scissors. Where do you think those kids take all those scissors? There are none to be found!"
  My poor mother, I think she went through an awful lot. She settled quarrels in between them often. Daddy was outside working at the time. I never wanted my children to have the burden that my mother had with both my grandmothers living with us.

ABOUT COMMUNICATION

- As I said, I got a computer for my ninetieth birthday. I have help e-mailing my children and I get e-mails and pictures from them. Carol and her daughters help me with e-mails and notes, even if my children don't write me back. Here is an e-mail, three months before Papa died, to one of my children:

Sept. 23, 2005

Dear _____,

Is there any possibility of you coming down to visit us? You and your wife are welcome to stay overnight. Carol says you're both welcome to stay with them, or she'd be happy to help you find a place to stay.

Papa's not doing so good. It's up and down. It's up and down for me, too. Today I'm pretty good, but tired. Papa didn't think he would like it here, but he really loves it. We've seen a lot of beautiful sunsets and moon rises. Our house faces the west so we have a good view of the sunsets. Some nights it looks like a big ball of fire. We watch the guineas every day, and I make noises, like them to call them. Sometimes they answer back.

Please call or write us sometime to let us know how you are. Here is our new address and phone number:

We miss you and love you very much.
Love & kisses,
Mother

* * * * *

I do believe my mother has lived more years than she ever would have, had she moved into a nursing home. It's going on four years now, and we just celebrated her ninety-third birthday. She served people all her life, she nurtured, and she lived for others. I see myself in my mother, but I have also emerged with more self-advocacy and speaking out on behalf of others, another way of caring. I'm the one who writes down the number of a truck driver who cuts us off on the road. I see something unfair and will advocate for it, particularly on behalf of those who cannot do it for themselves. Advocacy is a part of my everyday life, advocacy that stems from love. It is with love and advocacy that I conclude this project. It is completed with the hope that others will learn from our successes, our challenges, and our mistakes.

I applaud those of you who are working to balance your lives in the midst of "your sandwich." I celebrate those of you who advocate for those who cannot advocate for themselves. I deeply admire you for caring for your loved ones. Love them and celebrate their lives while you are blessed to have them in your life. Remember to take care of yourselves!

What We've Learned

- Rather than asking "if," we ask "how"; instead of asking, "Can we?" we ask, "How can we?" Every problem can be solved; you just have to step back, try another angle, squint your eyes, and breathe. A solution will come.

Quotes

"How you think about a problem is more important than the problem itself, so always think positively."
—Norman Vincent Peale

"Hot heads and cold hearts never solved anything."
—Billy Graham

"It's not that I'm so smart; it's just that I stay with problems longer."
—Albert Einstein

Tips and Tools

Elder Care Checklists
This wonderful source provides well-designed checklists; very helpful for new caregivers or when conditions are changing. This includes excellent Web sites with the best checklists, including:

Elder Care—First Steps
Seniors and Driving Checklist
Getting Started—What kind of help does your loved one need?
Home Alone—Are They Okay?
Home Safety Checklist
Care Interpreter
Living Arrangements—What is recommended for your loved one?
Prescription Drug Reference Checklist
Alzheimer's Living Facility Checklist
Assisted Living Facility Checklist
Nursing Home Checklist

http://www.aging-parents-and-elder-care.com/Pages/Elder_
Care_Checklists.html

AARP offers a wonderful comprehensive resource, with
checklists, tips, talking points, etc. Be sure to check it out
early. It is probably not too early to look at the list for yourself.
Talk with your children. This resource if very well organized,
and the content includes:

- Planning Ahead
- Providing Care At Home
- Preparing Your Home
- Housing Options
- Legal and Insurance
- End of Life

http://assets.aarp.org/external_sites/caregiving/homeCare/

Carol L. Russell, Ed.D.

THE MANY FACES OF GLADYS

I love taking photos of my mom! Here are some great images that I call "The Many Faces of Gladys":

One Cool Mama!

Two Beauties!

Grandma & Easter Hat

The Daisies we picked for Mother by Papa's grave.

New Red Sunglasses!

Mother loved these beautiful deep purple iris each year.

Mother with her painting at the "Art is Ageless" art show.

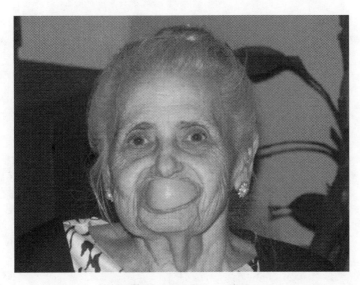

Still Having Fun at 91!

References

15 Ways to Take Care of Your Elderly Parents. (2007). *U.S. News &World Report.* http://health.usnews.com/articles/health/2007

A Window into the Lives of Sandwich Generation Women, An On-line Journaling Project (March 2008). www.social-workleadership.org/nsw/news/press/SandwichGeneration-Study-ExecutiveSummary.doc

Abramson, A. (2004). *The Caregiver's Survival Handbook.* The Berkley Publishing Group.

Aging Parent and Senior Finances http://www.agingcare.com/Finance/?gclid=CJLay4y205ICFQurPAod6ksrnA

Americans with Disabilities Act www.eeoc.gov/types/ada.html

American's with Disabilities Act 2008 Amendments www.2keller.com/blog/americans-with-disabilities-act-ada-amendments-act-of-2008.cfm

Ask the Dr. Checklist, Web MD http://www.webmd.com/default.htm

Assistive Technology for Kansans Project http://www.independenceinc.org/at.html

Association of Assistive Technology Act Programs http://www.ataporg.org/atap/

Baldauf, Sarah (2007). "15 Ways to Take Care of Your Elderly

Parents." *U.S. News & World Report* http://health.usnews.
com/articles/health/2007/11/02/15-things-you-can-do-to-
keep-mom-and-dad-at-home.html (Posted November 2,
2007)

Care Management Techniques You Can Use www.nfcacares.
org/pdfs/CareManagmt.pdf

Caregiver Quiz. http://www.aaaphx.org/node/37

Caring For Elderly Loved Ones http://moneyfitness.com/mc6/
topic.php?b=24544978-0&c=463&h=506,3,2

Caregiver Stress. National Women's Health Information Center
US DHHS, Office on Women's Health http://www.men-
tal-health-matters.com/articles/article.php?artID=725

Choosing an Agency for In-Home Care http://assets.aarp.org/
external_sites/caregiving/homeCare/choosing_in_home_
care.html

End of Life Services

- The Hospice Foundation of America, www.hospice-
  foundation.org

- The Centers for Medicare & Medicaid Services www.
  cms.hhs.gov

- National Association for Home Care and Hospice
  www.nahc.org

- The National Hospice and Palliative Care Organization www.nhpco.org

*EXECUTIVE SUMMARY: Not Ready for Prime Time: The
Needs of Sandwich Generation Women, A National Survey
of Social Workers* (March 2008). www.socialworkleader-
ship.org/nsw/news/press/SandwichGenerationStudy-Exec-
utiveSummary.doc

Family Caregiving 101. NFCA http://www.familycaregiv-
ing101.org/

Family Caregiving and Public Policy: Principles for Change. (2008). *TAKE CARE: National Family Caregivers Association* (vol. 16: no.4).

Fisher, R. & Ury, W. (1983).*Getting to Yes: Negotiating Agreement Without Giving In.* New York: Penguin Books.

Gillman, Steven. *Ten Relaxation Techniques* http://ezinearticles.com/?Ten-Relaxation-Techniques&id=182965

Help I Need; Help I Can Offer National Family Caregivers Association's (NFCA) brochure www.thefamilycaregiver.org/pdfs/326503_SharetheCaring_broch.pdf

Help Wanted: Tips for Hiring a Home-Care Worker http://assets.aarp.org/external_sites/caregiving/homeCare/hiring_home_care_help.html

Henry, Nancy. *People Who Take Care.* http://writersalmanac.publicradio.org/index.php?date=2006/02/11

Informal Caregiving: Compassion in Action. Washington, DC: 1998, and National Family Caregivers Association, Random Sample Survey of Family Caregivers, Summer 2000, Unpublished.)

Jayson, S. (2007). *Caregivers Cope with Stress, Mixed Emotions about Aging Parents.* USA Today June 26, 2007 http://www.usatoday.com/money/perfi/eldercare/2007-06-25-elder-care-emotional-support_N.htm

Mack, Katherine and Thompson (2001). *Caregiving Statistics: Statistics on Family Caregivers and Family Caregiving. http://www.thefamilycaregiver.org/who_are_family_caregivers/care_giving_statstics.cfm*

Mack, Katherine and Thompson, Lee with Robert Friedland. (2001). *Data Profiles, Family Caregivers of Older Persons: Adult Children.* The Center on an Aging Society, Georgetown University.

Meri-K Appy of the Home Safety Council www.youtube. com/watch?v=t5Q5GZGWqzc

Meyer, Don. *SIBSHOPS Web site:* http://www.siblingsupport. org/

Mintz, S. (2002). *Love, Honor & Value: A Family Caregiver Speaks Out about the Choices & Challenges of Caregiving.* Herndon, VA: Capital Books, Inc.

Mulligan, S. A. (2003). *Assistive Technology: Supporting the Participation of Children with Disabilities.* Young Children on the Web.

National Association of Professional Geriatric Care Managers http://www.caremanager.org/

National Family Caregivers Association www.thefamilycare- giver.org

New Study Reveals the High Financial Cost of Caring for an Older Loved

One. National Family Caregivers Association's *Take Care: Self-Care for the Family Caregiver* (Winter, 2008).

Russell, C. L. (1997). We're here too: Brothers and sister of children with special needs. Disability Solutions, Sept./ Oct.

Russell, C. L. (2008). *How are your Person First Skills: A Self- Assessment Tool.* May 2008 issue of *Teaching Exceptional Children Shouldering the Burden of Elder Care,* 2008 *ABC News* Internet Ventures http://abcnews.go.com/WN/ WorldNews/story?id=3888689

Silverstein, S. (1974).*Where the Sidewalk Ends: Poems and Drawings by Shel Silverstein.* Harpercollins Children's Books.

Strength for Caring. Johnson & Johnson articles http://www. strengthforcaring.com/

Stress Management for Healthy Living Quick Mini-Relaxation

Strategies http://www.csupomona.edu/~jvgrizzell/kin370/extras/quickrelaxers.html

Survey of Social Workers Finds Families Ill-Prepared for Time, Expenses, and Emotional Toll of Caring for Aging Parents, New York Academy of Medicine, 2008http://www.nyam.org/news/

Talking to Health Pros: Issues to Consider http://assets.aarp.org/external_sites/caregiving/homeCare/talk_to_health_pros.html

The American Health Information Management Association (AHIMA) sponsors a Web site where you can search for paper-based, software-based, and Internet-based personal health records. See: www.myphr.com/resources/phr_search.asp.

The Older Americans Act in The Aging Network http://www.enoa.org/network/oaa.html

The Ombudsman Program http://www.acombuds.org/About_Us/about_us.shtml

Top 10 Tips for Caregivers. The National Family Caregivers Association http://www.americanheart.org/presenter.jhtml?identifier=3039889

Pain scale: http://www.anes.ucla.edu/pain/FacesScale.jpg

Preserving Family Videos http://genealogy.about.com/library/authors/ucmishkin4a.htm

Quick Relaxation Techniques http://www.law.uidaho.edu/quickrelax

Quiet Care Products http://www.quietcaresystems.com/index_fl.htm

Respite Care Programs http://www.aaaphx.org/CAREGIVER+RESPITE.

U.S. Census Bureau *http://www.census.gov/Press-Release/www/releases/archives/income_wealth/012528.html*

Your Circle of Friends http://www.ecac-parentcenter.org/packets/friends/yourcircle.shtml

Your Parent and You: New Roles http://www.asktransitions.com/infobase/infobase.html

What is a Circle of Friends, A Circle of Support? http://www.ecacparentcenter.org/packets/friends/circles.shtml

Who are Family Caregivers? NFCA (National Family Caregivers Association) (2007).http://www.nfcacares.org/who_are_family_caregivers/

Wright, David. (2007). *Shouldering the Burden of Elder Care,* From: 2008 *ABC News* Internet Ventures http://abcnews.go.com/WN/WorldNews/story?id=3888689

ADDITIONAL RESOURCES

In addition to the references cited, there is a plethora of information about various topics regarding resources, tips, and helpful information to assist you in "your sandwich," as well as an open-faced sandwich (taking care of your elderly parents, without still having dependent children). I have included additional useful, organized resources below.

BOOKS:

Cunningham, Susan. (2005). *Unwrapping the Sandwich Generation: Life Vignettes About Seniors and Their Adult Boomer Children.* Morgan James Publishing

"This collection of vignettes addresses senior concerns and how their adult children address those concerns. Read stories about real people and real events, and how they relate to the aging process."

Kingsmill, Suzanne & Schlesinger, Benjamin. (1998). *The Family Squeeze: Surviving the Sandwich Generation.* University of Toronto Press.

"The Sandwich Generation refers to the growing numbers of middle-aged people who must care for both children and elderly parents while trying to manage the stress of full-time jobs. Advances in technology and medicine are helping us to live longer, but not without extended care from our families. At the same time, the economic climate is making it difficult for young adults to leave home and start their own lives; they, are often 'boomeranged' back to their parents for financial help, emotional support, and accommodation. All those who are or are about to become members of the Sandwich Generation will find this book to be a helpful guide for coping with the multiple pressures they face every day."

Kiplinger's Personal Finance Magazine Editors. (2006). *Kiplinger's Financial Solutions for the Sandwich Generation: Ensuring You Have Enough for You, Your Children, and Your Parents.* Kaplan Publishing.

Kitzman, Patricia Lynn. (2006). *Looking Through the Peephole: The Sandwich Generation.* Dorrance Publishing Company, Inc.

Mintz, S. (2002). *Love, Honor & Value: A Family Caregiver Speaks Out about the Choices & Challenges of Caregiving.* Herndon, VA: Capital Books, Inc.

Smith, Myra F. (2005).*Soul Food for the Sandwich Generation: Meditation Morsels for Caregivers.* Lightning Source Inc.
"Almost half of baby boomers in the age group 45 to 55

have children at home and parents who are still living. These boomers can find their hectic schedules overwhelming. This daily devotional book is written especially for caregivers sandwiched between generations."

Zal, H. Michael. (2001). *The Sandwich Generation: Caught Between Growing Children And Aging Parents.* Perseus Books Group.

More Resources

Free Consumer Referral Service Helps You Find Local Caregivers.
www.ElderCareLink.com

Elder Care Assistance
www.YourSupportNurse.com
Dedicated RN Care Manager to Assist You & Your Elderly Parent.

ElderCare On-line - Information, Education, and Support for Elderly ...
information and support for caregivers to the elderly with Alzheimer's
disease.
www.ec-online.net/

Aging Parents and Elder Care: Solutions for Family Caregivers
Comprehensive elder-care guide. Find information easily and quickly. Covers all stages of elder care. Articles, advice, checklists, support group and more.
www.aging-parents-and-elder-care.com/

CareGuide :
The CareGuide Assessment is designed to help you quickly locate the most
relevant resources and information about your elder care situation.
www.eldercare.com/

Elder-Care Services, Elderly Care, Aging Parents, Seniors
ElderCare Advocates is a team of geriatric care managers and other social
work and health-care professionals dedicated to keeping seniors healthy.
www.eldercareadvocates.com/

Transitions, Inc. Elder Care Consulting
On-line guide to elder caregiving, opinion column written by an older adult,
caregiver's support forum, assessment tools, tips about working with older
www.asktransitions.com/

Tips and Tools from:
Traveling for the Young at Heart
http://www.asktransitions.com/infobase/infobase.html
Travel among seniors has grown in popularity in recent years. In fact, travel by those over the age of sixty-five accounts for the fastest growing segment of the industry.

How Do I Know When to Intervene?
http://www.asktransitions.com/infobase/infobase.html

These are common symptoms that indicate your parents may no longer be able to care for themselves by themselves.

Personal Profile
http://www.asktransitions.com/infobase/infobase.html
This form documents the ways/preferences of an aging adult. It is written from his/her perspective, including everything from favorite music and food to sleep patterns to location of key documents.

Nursing Home Tour Form
http://www.asktransitions.com/infobase/infobase.html
Please don't forget to bring this checklist when you tour a prospective nursing home.

Elder Care Glossary
http://www.asktransitions.com/infobase/infobase.html
This is one of the most popular pieces on our site because it's unique. We've got enough to think about, so why stuff our heads with words when we can easily look them up in the glossary?

Effective Communication
http://www.asktransitions.com/infobase/infobase.html
Communication strategies for dealing with new roles and the ever-changing physical condition of the elderly.

Mapping a Safe Course
http://www.asktransitions.com/infobase/infobase.html
While those of all ages can enjoy traveling, the itinerary should take into account a senior's physical and cognitive abilities and other special needs.

Take Our Parents to Work Day
http://www.asktransitions.com/infobase/infobase.html
Work places come alive in April as young people accompany their parents to "Take Our Daughters to Work Day." We propose a new tradition called "Take Our Parents to Work Day." This article was written in 1997, and since then, the idea has been implemented in many companies.

Everything I Needed to Know about Caregiving I Learned in Kindergarten
http://www.asktransitions.com/infobase/infobase.html
Common-sense lessons that can be applied to caregiving. Play Nice; Share Your Toys. Don't Run With Scissors. Never Skip Recess.

Coping with Alzheimer's
http://www.asktransitions.com/infobase/infobase.html
A personal story about the spirit to go forward.

Caregiving Statistics and Cost Savings
http://www.asktransitions.com/infobase/infobase.html
Who provides most of long-term care? How much money is spent by caregivers? How much money can a company save by educating their employees? Arm yourself with facts about aging and caregiving.

Alzheimer's Pamphlet
http://www.asktransitions.com/infobase/infobase.html
This is a wonderful pamphlet on the four disease stages from the Minnesota Lakes chapter of the Alzheimer's Association. This material is the property of the Alzheimer's Association;

we are making it available to a wider audience who might not otherwise have access to the hard copy.

A Guide to Alzheimer's Information
http://www.youcanbetheone.com/home/index.html

Dollars and Sense
http://www.asktransitions.com/infobase/infobase.html
Learn to bridge the gap between generations in terms of dealing with finances.

Treasures in the Attic
http://www.asktransitions.com/infobase/infobase.html
As caregivers, we often get so wrapped up with the everyday needs of our older relatives that we forget about their thoughts and feelings. Join the author in discovering a most valuable treasure: her grandma.

Stories about Friendship (American Library Assoc.)
http://www.asktransitions.com/infobase/infobase.html
This pamphlet contains suggested readings about relationships between kids and elders.

Health Checkups: Schedule Yours Today
http://www.asktransitions.com/infobase/infobase.html
A handy table showing what needs to be checked and when.

Share Family History in a Fun Way
http://www.asktransitions.com/infobase/infobase.html
How do we impart to the younger generation an appreciation for experiences of those before? Can we engage children and

adults in conversations about the differences and similarities of their lives? Life Story Books are one way to do this.

Preventing Drug Misuse in Seniors
http://www.asktransitions.com/infobase/infobase.html
Preventing drug misuse in seniors is of critical concern to health-care professionals, caregivers, and seniors themselves. In order for any prevention program to be effective, it must be a team effort.

Aerobic Exercise Boosts Mental Abilities in Elderly
http://www.asktransitions.com/infobase/infobase.html
An article about the importance of proper exercise.

Resources adapted from:
Caring for the Elderly by Jane Gross
ttp://www.nytimes.com/ref/health/noa_resources.html

Government Sites

- Medicare.gov. An all-purpose site with interactive tools for planning and paying for long-term care and choosing among drug plans. Includes searchable inspection results, good and bad, for the all the nation's skilled nursing facilities.
  http://www.medicare.gov/

- NIHSeniorHealth.gov. A collaboration of the National Institutes of Health and the National Library of Medicine that provides authoritative information on all diseases and disorders of old age. Each section is available in both large-type and audio versions.

http://nihseniorhealth.gov/

- National Institute on Aging. Describes ongoing research on aging and lists clinical trials seeking participants.
  http://www.nia.nih.gov/

- Eldercare Locator. Links to state and local ombudsmen and agencies serving the elderly.
  http://www.eldercare.gov/Eldercare/Public/Home.asp

- U.S. Administration on Aging. Brief fact sheets on aging and links to outside resources for an assortment of caregiving issues, including financial planning, residential options, in-home services, case management and the law.
  http://www.aoa.gov/

- CarePlanner. Free worksheets help users to create a care plan, keep track of medications and expenses, and plan home modifications.
  http://redirect1.clinicaltools.com/

- Govbenefits.gov. A tool to help determine benefit eligibility for a variety of government programs.
  http://www.govbenefits.gov/govbenefits_en.portal
  Housing and Services

- American Association of Home and Services for the Aging. Consumer information on senior housing from an association of nonprofit nursing homes, assisted living centers, continuing care retirement communities, adult day care centers and the like.
  http://www2.aahsa.org

- Assisted Living Federation of America. Among other resources, offers a database of assisted living facilities searchable by location or parent company.
  http://www.alfa.org/i4a/pages/index.cfm?pageid=3278

- National Center for Assisted Living. Provides a more elaborate "facility finder" that factors in cost, method of payment, mobility, dietary needs, activities and amenities.
  http://www.ncal.org/

- SNAPforSeniors. Offers a searchable housing locator with 60,000 listings, including facilities for assisted living, residential care, nursing care and rehabilitation, continuing care retirement and independent living. (Disclosure: A New Old Age partner.)
  http://www.snapforseniors.com/default.aspx?affiliateid=107954

- National Association of Professional Geriatric Care Managers. Search for a geriatric care manager by location.
  http://www.caremanager.org/

- Visiting Nurse Associations of America. Search for home-health services nationwide. Includes suggested questions to ask service providers.
  http://www.vnaa.org/vnaa/gen/html-home.aspx

- Homemods.org. Advice on home renovation from the University of Southern California.
  http://www.homemods.org/

- HealthGrades. Comparisons and one-to-five-star ranking of nursing homes, for $9.95 for the first report and $2.95 for each additional one.
  http://www.homemods.org/

- UCompareHealthCare. Free search by location for nursing homes, plus data on quality, staffing and outcomes from government sources. (Disclosure: Owned by the *New York Times* Co.)
  http://www.ucomparehealthcare.com/

- Getcare.com. A sleek, three-step process to assess long-term care options, learn about each type, and then search by location for a variety of services, including Alzheimer's day care, grief support, or respite for a caregiver.
  http://www.getcare.com/

- TheSeniorGuide.com. Search by state and region for all types of senior housing, case managers, lawyers and more. Includes a glossary of industry jargon.
  http://www.seniorlivingguide.com/

- National Association of Senior Move Managers (NASMM). A not-for-profit, professional association dedicated to assisting older adults with the physical and emotional demands of downsizing, relocating, or modifying their homes.
  http://www.nasmm.org/

- CareScout. Charges $499 to help users select housing options and services for the elderly who can pay their own way and are not reliant on Medicare or Medicaid.
  http://web.carescout.com/carescoutsite/

CAREGIVING

Elder Care—First Steps
Beginning Your Journey through Elder Care
http://www.aging-parents-and-elder-care.com/Pages/Elder_Care_First_Steps.html

Elder Care Checklists
This wonderful source provides well-designed checklists, very helpful for new caregivers or when conditions are changing. This includes excellent Web sites with the best checklists, including:
Elder Care—First Steps
Seniors and Driving Checklist

Getting Started—What kind of help does your loved one need?
Home Alone—Are They Okay?
Home Safety Checklist
Care Interpreter
Living Arrangements—What is recommended for your loved one?
Prescription Drug Reference Checklist
Alzheimer's Living Facility Checklist
Assisted Living Facility Checklist
Nursing Home Checklist
http://www.aging-parents-and-elder-care.com/Pages/Elder_Care_Checklists.html

- Family Caregiver Alliance. Offers tips on a wide range of topics, including how to hire help, hold a family meeting, balance work and caregiving, find important papers, and decide whether parents should move in with an adult child.

National Alliance for Caregiving. Reviews of more than 1,000 books, videos, Web sites and links.
http://www.caregiving.org/
http://www.caregiving.org/

National Family Caregivers Association. Provides statistics, research and policy reports, tip sheets, first-person accounts, a newsletter and an exhaustive resource list.
http://www.nfcacares.org/

Family Caregiving 101. A separate "how-to" site by the NFCA with advice on time management, asking for help, navigat-

ing the health-care maze and communicating with insurance companies and hospitals.
http://www.familycaregiving101.org/

MetLife Mature Market Institute. Reports from a research arm of the insurance company on the price of assisted living, the strains of long-distance caregiving, and the cost to employers of baby boomer employees involved in elder care.
http://www.metlife.com/Applications/Corporate/WPS/CDA/PageGenerator/0,2752,P2801,00.html

Strength for Caring. A site for family caregivers from Johnson & Johnson with original articles written by experts and how-to materials.
http://www.strengthforcaring.com/

The Alzheimer's Association.
http://www.alz.org/index.asp

LEGAL AND FINANCIAL

BenefitsCheckUp. A search tool developed by the National Council on Aging to determine eligibility for 1,300 benefit programs that help pay for medications, health care, utilities and so forth.
http://www.benefitscheckup.org/

National Academy of Elder Law Attorneys. Search by location for members of the association. Provides questions to ask lawyers about qualifications and areas of expertise, and a wide-ranging resource list for the elderly.
http://www.naela.com/

National Association of Insurance Commissioners. Free fact sheets and shoppers' guides for long-term care insurance, annuities and Medigap policies.
http://www.naic.org/

New Study Reveals the High Financial Cost of Caring for an Older Loved One from National Family Caregivers Association's *Take Care: Self-Care for the Family Caregiver* (Winter, 2008).

Insurance Information Institute.
http://www.iii.org/

Reverse.org. A consumer's guide to reverse mortgages from a nonprofit with no ties to the industry. Links to the AARP's calculator for choosing such policies.
http://www.reverse.org/

ReverseMortgage.org. Similar calculator and search tool to find local lenders, with links to their Web sites.
http://www.reversemortgage.org/

Nolo. Do-it-yourself legal advice. Wills, powers of attorney and other documents.
http://www.nolo.com/

Senior Law Home Page. Advice from a New York law firm on the legal and financial issues facing the elderly. State forms for powers of attorney, health care proxies and living wills.
http://www.seniorlaw.com/

U.S. Living Will Registry. Free state-by-state forms.
http://www.uslivingwillregistry.com/

American Bar Association Aging Tool Kit. This site offers a ten-step process for making end-of-life decisions with worksheets, suggestions and links. This is an excellent, helpful source for some difficult issues.

There Are Ten "Tools" in This Tool Kit:

Tool #1   How to Select Your Health Care Agent or Proxy

Tool #2   Are Some Conditions Worse than Death?

Tool #3   How Do You Weigh Odds of Survival?

Tool #4   Personal Priorities and Spiritual Values Important Your Medical Decisions

Tool #5   After Death Decisions to Think about Now

Tool #6   Conversation Scripts: Getting Past the Resistance

Tool #7   The Proxy Quiz for Family & Physician

Tool #8   What to Do After Signing Your Health Care Advance Directive

Tool #9   Guide for Health Care Proxies

Tool #10 Resources: Advance Planning for Health Care

http://www.abanet.org/aging/toolkit/

END OF LIFE

The National Hospice and Palliative Care Organization. An excellent search tool for finding a hospice, as well as guides on issues related to palliative care, including Medicare coverage and techniques for communicating end-of-life wishes.

http://www.nhpco.org/templates/1/homepage.cfm

Caring Connections. Contains of the consumer information from NHPCO and has state-by-state advance directive forms.
http://www.caringinfo.org/

Hospice Foundation of America. Information on end-of-life issues, such as pain management. One section called "Caregivers Corner" has links, reading lists and a self-assessment tool for caregivers to analyze their own strengths and weaknesses.
http://www.hospicefoundation.org/

MISCELLANEOUS

Elderweb. An eccentric site that includes the history of long-term care policy in America, census maps that show the concentration of people aged sixty and over, book reviews, updates on state laws affecting the elderly, and a dictionary of elder-care jargon.
http://www.elderweb.com/home/

Eldercare On-line. This site has a homemade look and is difficult to navigate but includes a wealth of original and imported information.
http://www.ec-online.net/

Caring.com. An all-in-one site with advice on caregiving, long-term care, talking with elders and insurance issues.
http://www.caring.com/

National Care Planning Council. A work in progress from a couple who "didn't have a life for five years" while caring for four elderly parents. Now a membership organization advo-

cating for long-term care. This site offers great articles on a variety of caregiving topics.
http://www.longtermcarelink.net/

Third Age. Articles, expert interviews, quizzes and discussion boards for caregivers.
http://www.thirdage.com/caregiving

Elder Issues. Some interesting articles on caregiving. Primarily the site for a company marketing on-line medical records for elderly persons.
http://www.elderissues.com/

Aging Parents and Eldercare. A commercial site with free access to same checklists, worksheets and on-line assessment tools found elsewhere. For sale are products like wheelchairs and incontinence supplies.
http://www.aging-parents-and-elder-care.com/

KaiserEdu. An educational site from the Kaiser Family Foundation. Includes a variety of slide tutorials and podcasts on financial and policy issues related to long-term care.
http://www.kaiseredu.org/

ADVOCACY

AARP. Political position papers, member discounts, demographic research, on-line versions of its bulletin, and magazine and consumer advice.
http://www.aarp.org/

Center for Medicare Advocacy. Detailed information about

what Medicare covers, and how to enroll and, if necessary, appeal denial of claims.
http://www.medicareadvocacy.org/

Medicare Rights Center. A similar tutorial on how this government health-care program for the elderly works. A link to the Kaiser Family Foundation's "Medicare 101" and a hotline for questions and complaints.
http://www.medicarerights.org/

National Association of Area Agencies on Aging. Articles on caregiving, policy reports, and links to eldercare service agencies.
http://www.n4a.org/

Emotional Support
Children of Aging Parents. Support groups, both on-line and face-to-face. Newsletter focuses on interpersonal matters like stress among siblings, caregiver depression, and getting through the holidays.
http://www.caps4caregivers.org/

MAGAZINES

Today's Caregiver Magazine
http://www.caregiver.com/

Caring Today
http://www.caringtoday.com/

Blogs
Caring Today's blogs
http://www.caringtoday.com/blogs

KnowItAlz
http://www.knowitalz.com/

Minding Our Elders
http://www.mindingoureldersblogs.com/

Our Alzheimer's
http://www.healthcentral.com/alzheimers/

Aging Care
http://www.agingcare.com/

A Place for Mom
http://www.aplaceformom.com/

Aging Parents Insights
http://www.dsolie.com/blog/

Time Goes By
http://www.timegoesby.net/weblog/

MLBerg's Caregiver's Blog
http://mlberg.spaces.live.com/

3GenFamily Blog
http://www.3genfamily.com/

My Elder Advocate
http://www.myelderadvocate.com/

Alzheimer's Reading Room

http://alzheimersreadingroom.blogspot.com/

Aging Patent's Authority
http://agingparentsauthority.com/

ADS BY GOOGLE

Caregiving
Find Support and Advice through a Community That Cares.
http://www.MyCareCommunity.org

Care for Seniors at Home
Our free caregiver referral service helps you find good care quickly.
http://www.ElderCareLink.com

Long-Term Care Insurance
Read our expert buying guide. Get a free insurance quote today.
http://www.caring.com

Empowering Caregivers
Hundreds of links to on-line resources
http://www.care-givers.com/pages/resources/online/care-sites.html